Collected Essays on Philosophy and on Judaism

MARVIN FOX

COLLECTED ESSAYS ON PHILOSOPHY AND ON JUDAISM

EDITED BY JACOB NEUSNER

VOLUME THREE

ETHICS, REFLECTIONS

Academic Studies in the History of Judaism
Global Publications, Binghamton University
Binghamton, New York
2001

Cover artwork entitled "Torah Mantle" by Suzanne R. Neusner.

Library of Congress Cataloging-in-Publication Data:

Fox, Marvin.
Collected essays on philosophy and on Judaism / Marvin Fox ; edited by Jacob Neusner.
p. cm. -- (Academic studies in the history of Judaism)
Includes bibliographical references.
ISBN 1-58684-144-0 (v. 1 : pbk. : alk. paper) -- ISBN 1-58684-145-9 (v. 2 : pbk. : alk. paper) -- ISBN 1-58684-146-7 (v. 3 : pbk. : alk. paper)
1. Philosophy, Jewish. 2. Judaism. 3. Maimonides, Moses, 1135-1204. I. Neusner, Jacob, 1932- II. Title. III. Series.
B5800 .F69 2001
181'.06--dc21

2001004123

Published and Distributed by:
Academic Studies in the History of Judaism
Global Publications, Binghamton University
State University of New York at Binghamton
LNG 99, Binghamton University
Binghamton, New York, USA 13902-6000
Phone: (607) 777-4495 or 777-6104; Fax: (607) 777-6132
E-mail: pmorewed@binghamton.edu
http://ssips.binghamton.edu

Dedication

This volumeof Marvin Fox's Essays is dedicated to our dear children, Avrom and Debra; Daniel and Barbara, Sherry and Laurence; and our beloved grandchildren, Jeremy, Aliza, Roniel, Emunah, Eytan, Amy, Naomi, Aaron, David, Joshua, Michael and Jonathon.

All of them join me in expressing our profound gratitude to Marvin's esteemed colleague and devoted friend, Professor Jacob Neusner, whose remarkable efforts have brought about the publication of this work.

June Fox

ACADEMIC STUDIES IN THE HISTORY OF JUDAISM

Publisher: Global Publications, State University of New York at Binghamton
Address: LNG 99, SUNY-Binghamton, Binghamton, New York 13902-6000

Table of contents

Volume III

Volume One

Greek Philosophy, Maimonides

I

Greek Philosophy

II

Maimonides

Volume Two

III

Some Philosophers

Preface

Professor Marvin Fox was born October 17, 1922 in Chicago, Illinois and died in Newton, Massachusetts, on February 8, 1996. Professor Marvin Fox received his B. A. in philosophy in 1942 from Northwestern University, the M. A. in the same field in 1946, and the Ph. D. at the University of Chicago in 1950 in that field as well. His education in Judaic texts was certified by rabbinical ordination as Rabbi by the Hebrew Theological College of Chicago in 1942. He served as a Jewish Chaplain in the U.S. Army Air Force during World War II in 1942-1946. He taught at Ohio State University from 1948 through 1974, rising from Instructor to Professor of Philosophy. During those years he served also as Visiting Professor of Philosophy at the Hebrew Theological College of Chicago (1955) and also at the Hebrew University of Jerusalem and Bar Ilan University (1970-1971). In 1974 he came to Brandeis University as Appleman Professor of Jewish Thought, and from 1976 onward he has held the Lown Professorship. In 1975-1982 and from 1984-1987 he was Chairman of the Department of Near Eastern and Judaic Studies at Brandeis, and from 1976 he has also served as Director of the Lown School of Near Eastern and Judaic Studies. In 1980-1981 he was Visiting Scholar in Jewish Philosophy at the Center for Jewish Studies of nearby Harvard University.

He has received numerous academic awards, a selected list of which includes the following: 1956-1957: Elizabeth Clay Howald Post-Doctoral Scholarship; 1962-1963, Fellow of the American Council of Learned Societies; 1975-1978, Director of the Association for Jewish Studies regional conferences, funded by the National Endowment for the Humanities; 1977-1980, Director of the project, "For the Strengthening of Judaic Studies at Brandeis and their Links to the General Humanities," also funded by the National Endowment for the Humanities. From 1979 he has been Fellow of the Academy of Jewish Philosophy; 1980-1981, Senior Faculty Fellow, National Endowment for the Humanities. He has served on the editorial boards of *the AJS Review, Daat, Judaism, Tradition, Journal for the History of Philosophy*, and other journals. He has lectured widely at universities and at national and international academic conferences and served as

Member of the National Endowment for the Humanities National Board of Consultants for new programs at colleges and universities. Over the years he has counseled various universities and academic publishers as well.

His ties to institutions of Jewish learning under Jewish sponsorship are strong. He has served on the Advisory Committee of the Jewish Studies Adaptation Program of the International Center for University Teaching of Jewish Civilization (Israel), since 1982; International Planning Committee of the Institute for Contemporary Jewry of the Hebrew University since that same year; member of the governing council of the World Union of Jewish Studies since 1975; secretary, 1971-1972, vice president, from 1973-1975, and then president, from 1975-1978, of the Association for Jewish Studies; and he has been on the board of directors of that organization since 1970. From 1964 through 1968 he served on the Executive Committee of the Conference on Jewish Philosophy; from 1970 until his death on the Executive Committee of the Institute of Judaism and Contemporary Thought of Bar Ilan University; from 1972 as Member of the Academic Board of the Melton Research Center of the Jewish Theological Seminary of America; Member of the board of directors of the Institute for Jewish Life from 1972 through 1975; member of the board of directors of the Library of Living Philosophers, Inc., from 1948; Associate of the Columbia University Seminar on Israel and Jewish Studies from 1968 through 1974; and many other organizations.

His committee service at Brandeis University has covered these committees: Graduate School Council; Philosophy Department Advisory Committee and Reappointment and Promotions Committee; University Tenure Panels; Academic Planning Committee (Chairman, 1982-1984); Faculty Committee for the Hiatt Institute; Tauber Institute Faculty Advisory Committee and its academic policy sub-committee; Committee on University Studies in the Humanities; Faculty representative on the Brandeis University Board of Trustees (1978-1980). His professional memberships include the American Philosophical Association, the Metaphysical Society of America, the Medieval Academy of America, as well as the Association for Jewish Studies, Conference on Jewish Philosophy, and American Academy for Jewish Research.

When I taught at Brown, I called upon Professor Fox for counsel in the fifteen years after Professor Fox came to Brandeis University. And he responded, always giving his best judgment and his wisest counsel.

Professor Fox was a good neighbor, a constant counselor, and valued friend. In the sequence of eight academic conferences that I presented annually at Brown Universixty in the 1970s, Professor Fox played a leading role in the planning of the programs and in scholarly interchange. At that time, also, Brown and Brandeis Universities held a conference at which graduate students in the respective graduate programs met and engaged in shared discussion of common interests. Professor Fox moreover has taken a position on numerous dissertation committees in Brown's graduate program in the History of Judaism. His conscientious and careful reading of these dissertations give to the students the benefit not only of his learning but also of his distinct and rich perspective upon the problem of the dissertation.

I organized and edited the *festschrift* published in his honor in my series at Scholars Press, as follows:

From Ancient Israel to Modern Judaism. Intellect in Quest of Understanding. Essays in Honor of Marvin Fox. Atlanta, 1989: Scholars Press for Brown Judaic Studies. I-IV.

I. *What Is at Stake in the Judaic Quest for Understanding? Judaic Learning and the Locus of Education. Ancient Israel. Formative Christianity. Judaism in the Formative Age: Religion.*

II. *Judaism in the Formative Age: Theology and Literature. Judaism in the Middle Ages: The Encounter with Christianity. The Encounter with Scripture. Philosophy and Theology.*

III. *Judaism in the Middle Ages: Philosophers. Hasidism. Messianism in Modern Times. The Modern Age: Philosophy.*

IV. *The Modern Age: Theology, Literature, History.*

I also organized the celebration in Professor Fox's honor held by President Evelyn Handler of Brandeis University in connection with the publication of the festschrift.

This volume of his essays offers to a new generation of scholars of Jewish thought and philosophy a selection of his more important writings. Their original publication is indicated in the bibliography of Marvin Fox that follows..

The essays collected and presented here represent the selections of Dr. June Fox in consultation with the editor.

Jacob Neusner

Research Professor of Religion and Theology
Program in Religion and Institute of Advanced Theology
Bard College
Annandale-on-Hudson, New York 12504

neusner@webjogger.net

Marvin Fox - A Memoir

Memoirs have a tendency to be less than faithful to the truth. The writer may romanticize, or rely on anecdotes, or fill in spaces when she was not present at times being recollected in the life of the memorialized. This memoir is different from most, I believe. I knew Marvin all my life—when he was a child, a teenager, a young man, and as my husband of fifty-two years, until his death. I believe that the words, which follow, faithfully describe him, the events of his life, and the goals, and aspirations which animated him, since I was privileged to observe and share them with him for so many decades.

Marvin's parents and his older brother emigrated to the United States from Russia, to escape the persecution of Jews and the turmoil of the Russian Revolution. They came to Chicago (where a number of relatives resided) in October of 1922. Marvin was born within a few days after their arrival. The early years in America were a time of great poverty for his family, which, in truth, was not alleviated for two decades. But his parents knew that a better life for their children depended upon education and study, and they inspired him to read and learn, both the culture of their new society and Jewish texts and sources, which they revered and he came to revere as well.

At a very early age, in the late 1930's, while studying at the Hebrew Theological College, he became a student at Northwestern University, and became fascinated by philosophy. I recall, vividly, listening to him formulate his dream for our future. He wanted to become a professor of philosophy, in a major secular university, and a Jewish scholar as well. It was a hopeless dream, as we well knew, at least the professor part. There were virtually no universities which employed Jews as academics, and few which welcomed them even as students. Although he was extraordinarily gifted, a kind professor in the Philosophy Department spoke to him, and told that such an aspiration for a young Jewish man was virtually impossible, and that he needed to face reality.

It took World War II to create a new reality. Marvin joined the United States Army Air Force, after his graduation from Northwestern and the end of his rabbinical studies at the Yeshiva. He served as a Jewish Chaplain for almost four years, which provided extraordinarily important insights into the many facets of America, which he had never experienced. We were married in the middle of the war. When we returned to Chicago, hundreds of thousands of young men who had served their country were descending upon the universities, subsidized by the G.I. Bill. This influx of ordinary Americans into higher education did more to undermine elitism in American society than, perhaps, any legislative action before or since in the history of our country.

The universities needed professors to teach their students, and though it may not have been their preference, they were obliged to hire as faculty, anyone qualified to teach. During the late 40's, and forward to this day, Jewish men and later women entered academia in large numbers. Marvin started and completed his Ph.D. at the University of Chicago, and in 1948 was appointed to the faculty of Philosophy at the Ohio State University, in Columbus. Here he spent twenty-six years, teaching with great distinction, writing, assuming a leadership role in faculty affairs, engaging actively as a community leader, both locally and nationally, raising our family, and achieving the first part of his dream for his future.

The second part—becoming a Jewish scholar—became a "private" occupation. Marvin wrote, published, and lectured extensively in the field of Jewish thought, at the same time as he studied and published in general philosophy. His good friends and colleagues in philosophy and the humanities at Ohio State good-naturedly referred to the "Jewish thing" as his "hobby." Judaic studies were not considered, by scholars, as worthy of inclusion in the academic curricula of the universities in America. With the exception of Harvard and Columbia, which had a few scholars of Judaica on their faculties, serious Jewish study was confined to the Seminaries, Dropsie College, and Brandeis University, which was founded in 1948.

By the 1960's, this landscape also began to change. Marvin played a significant role in bringing about the change. In the early 60's, a wonderful philanthropic member of the Columbus Jewish community, Samuel Melton, who was very interested in promoting Jewish study at Ohio State, came to Marvin to discuss the possibility of endowing a chair in Judaic studies. Marvin served as negotiator with the University administration, which was receptive to the idea. It was determined that it would be a chair in Jewish History. It was necessary to convince the members of the History Department that Jewish history was a legitimate area of study—the history of the Jews at most merited one chapter or one part of a lecture in a World History class. Marvin found an ideal candidate for the chair: a professor from the Hebrew University who had studied and taught with Salo Baron at Columbia. He was a noted scholar and a charismatic teacher. Upon meeting him, the history department was convinced that Jewish history was indeed a worthy subject for study, and Jewish Studies was instituted at Ohio State. The administration, at Marvin's urging, brought in a professor of Hebrew, acquired a Judaic library collection, employed a Judaic librarian, and a new discipline found its way in to the University in the heartland of our country.

At the same time, a small group of faculty of Judaica at seminaries, at an occasional university, and men and women who were interested in developing Jewish studies in higher education gathered at Brandeis University and founded the Association of Jewish Studies. Marvin was among the group, which grew larger with each passing year, until its membership has surpassed one thousand. More and more universities introduced Jewish Studies, following the Ohio State model or creating alternative models. Marvin served as president of the Association, helped launch its academic journal, and acted as consultant to numerous university administrations as they planned and adopted Judaic Studies in their institutions.

In 1974, Marvin was invited to join the Department of Near Eastern and Judaic Studies at Brandeis University, as a Professor of Jewish Philosophy. He had never taught a course in Jewish studies in his entire career as a professor of philosophy in America. (He had done so only as a visiting professor at the Hebrew University of Jerusalem in 1970.) The second part of his dream then became a reality. He joined a faculty of scholars distinguished in every aspect of Jewish study. He became and served as Chairman of the Department for many years. He was appointed Director of the Lown School of Jewish Studies, which included contemporary as well as classical Jewish Studies. He had, for the first time in his life, many doctoral students in Jewish Studies, whom he guided to degrees and saw them placed in teaching positions in universities all over the world. No longer pursuing a "hobby", he devoted his writing primarily to topics related to Jewish thought. He remained at Brandeis until his retirement in 1994, having experienced the most rewarding professional years of his life.

A final culminating experience came his way after he left Brandeis. Boston University, which occasionally appointed distinguished emeritus professors to its faculty, invited him to join the departments of Religion and Philosophy in that capacity. He enjoyed a wonderfully satisfying year with interesting new colleagues and new students, a pattern which he hoped would continue on into the future. Alas, he became mortally ill at that point and died in a matter of months.

Marvin Fox was a very large, imposing man, with a deep and sonorous voice which he could project in an auditorium filled with one thousand students, using no microphone. He had an infectious laugh and an extraordinary wit. He was more than a teacher—he was constantly involved in solving problems, which he did with consummate skill. He found jobs for students and supported them in obtaining tenure. He raised money for countless needy scholars, and helped them publish their books. He was an advocate for academic freedom and freedom to speak out for professors and students. He mediated disputes, and promoted academic harmony. He lived as an observant Jew among colleagues and friends who had never known an observant Jew and gained their respect. He knew well some of the greatest scholars of his day. He saw the creation of the State of Israel and had the great satisfaction of teaching there. He was the father of three dearly loved children, of whom, together with their spouses, he was inordinately proud. And he lived to see and know his eleven grandchildren, who were perhaps, the greatest joy of his life.

Shortly before he became ill with his last illness, he told me, one day, "I have lived the most richly rewarding life any man could have hoped for. How many of us can say that all the dreams of their youth have come true? I can—and I have been truly blessed."

His life was a blessing for us, as is his memory.

June T. Fox, PhD
Chicago, Illinois
March, 2001

22

ON THE DIVERSITY OF METHODS IN DEWEY'S ETHICAL THEORY

There is a famous passage in *Experience* and Nature which strikes most readers as being strangely out of harmony with the rest of Dewey's moral philosophy. It reads as follows:

> Values are values; things immediately having certain intrinsic qualities. Of them as values there is accordingly nothing to be said; they are what they are. All that can be said of them concerns their generative conditions and the consequences to which they give rise. The notion that things as direct values lend themselves to thought and discourse rests upon a confusion of causal categories with immediate qualities... Values as such, even things having value, cannot in their immediate existence be reflected upon; they either are or are not; are or are not enjoyed.[1]

Dewey concludes this discussion by suggesting that, "In themselves values may just be pointed at."[2] This passage is paralleled by a similar statement in an article which was published in 1925, the same period during which *Experience and* Nature appeared. There, too, Dewey speaks of value as being definable only by pointing.[3] How unusual it appears, at first glance, for Dewey to speak of values in this way! We are accustomed to thinking of values in Dewey's philosophy as dependent on reflective intelligence, as known only through the experimental or scientific method, as fitting perfectly into the same pattern of being and being known that is the framework of the entire instrumentalist metaphysics and epistemology. Dewey believes in the methodological unity of science, and has asserted innumerable times that the knowledge of value is in no methodological respect different from any other kind of knowledge, and that the scientific method is the only proper method by which reflective men can attain this knowledge.

How, in the light of this, can we explain the passages which have been quoted above? There are some who might suggest that these passages are merely an aberration from an otherwise consistently held position. Surely such an aberration could be condoned in a philosopher who has written as prolifically as Dewey. In contrast with this explanation the present paper purposes to show that the views referred to are not an aberration at all, but that they are rather a necessary result and a logical consequence of the position that Dewey takes with regard to values.

There is, if the argument of this paper is sound, a serious sense in which Dewey's commitment to the unity of science is incomplete. He supposedly holds the view that knowledge of whatever subject matter can be acquired by the scientific method and only by the scientific method. There is for him no methodological difference between the way in which we settle problems in the natural sciences and the way in which we solve moral difficulties. In spite of his very regular espousal of these views I think it can, nevertheless, be shown that Dewey does not remain faithful to them. The passages which have been quoted will serve as evidence in support of this contention.

In the first place it must be noted briefly that Dewey's faith in the experimental method is itself not arrived at experimentally. It is, rather, the result of careful dialectical reasoning. Through the use of a scheme of dialectic Dewey concludes that we ought properly to employ the experimental method in order to find intelligent solutions to our moral questions. This observation is sufficiently commonplace to require no documentation in a brief paper. We mention it for the sole purpose of showing that there is at least one well-known instance in which Dewey does not himself employ the experimental method. There is a second, and more crucial, instance, as we hope to show.

If one accepts a rigidly positivistic view in the natural sciences the experimental method is perfectly adequate to its purposes. So long as we are willing to restrict ourselves to an examination of that which is publicly observable and to refrain from inquiring into the metaphysical superstructure which that observed world implies, then we can employ the experimental method successfully. That is to say, that the experimental method is a magnificent instrument by the use of which I can learn much about the modes of functioning of observable phenomena. However, it cannot answer ultimate questions about the ontological status of such phenomena, and working scientists do not expect it to do so. In fact, they have tended deliberately to limit the proper area of scientific inquiry to those questions which the experimental method is in principle capable of dealing with. We ordinarily recognize that there are many other important questions whose answers cannot be found experimentally. There are some who would insist that such questions are meaningless and who, therefore, exclude them from consideration by intelligent men. It cannot be denied, however, that such questions often occupy the attention of serious thinkers, and that if they are to be dealt with at all they must be dealt with by some method other than the experimental. Value questions appear to be of this sort, and it is our contention that Dewey recognized this, at least momentarily, when he wrote *Experience and Nature.*

It is clearly possible to construct a positivistic natural science. It is difficult to see how one can be successful in the construction of a positivistic value theory. For in the case of value judgments we presume to have the answer to an ultimate question, namely what value really is, or-in more specific terms-what the good, the right, or the beautiful really are. When a physicist tells me that bodies fall at a certain rate, I can agree with him if there is experimental evidence to convince me, or if I can perform by myself the experiments which led him to his conclusions. We might disagree about the ultimate nature of physical reality; we might disagree about the structure of the universe in which the events are occurring; we might even disagree about the nature of truth; but in spite of these disagreements we could still maintain our agreement concerning the rate of falling bodies. For we are there dealing with publicly observable phenomena, and we apparently see very similar things no matter how profoundly we differ in our theories concerning what lies behind these things.

The case is quite different with regard to value theory. For here the observable phenomena can provide the answers to many important secondary questions, but we cannot get from them any insight into the basic problem concerning the nature of value. Yet without an answer to this question any value theory is hopelessly incomplete. All that the experimental method can do is to instruct us concerning the consequences of our choices and concerning the means by which we may arrive at those consequences. But unless I know what value is, unless I know what it is that makes a thing good, I cannot possibly arrive at an intelligent solution of my moral problems. When I employ the experimental method in dealing with my moral perplexities then I must already know the nature of value, else the experimental method is useless.

A single illustration will perhaps serve to make this point clear. Imagine a man trying to decide whether he should embezzle funds belonging to his employer in order to pay for the medical care that his wife must have if her life is to be saved. Now, if he is thoroughly unreflective he will in all probability act on the impulse of the moment. Or else he may act in terms of the injunctions or prohibitions of some authoritarian absolutist moral code. But the usual supposition of Dewey's followers is that by using the experimental method our perplexed moral agent can, if he is reflective and unimpulsive, discover an intelligent and reasonable solution to his problem. He is to proceed by inquiring into the consequences that will flow from the various alternative lines of action that are available to him. He must also give careful consideration to the means by which his ends are achievable, since, unless he deliberately deceives himself, his interest in the ends cannot be separated from a readiness to accept the means which they require. Furthermore, he must consider these lines of action in relation to the larger pattern of the ends and purposes of his life, and in relation to the possibilities and requirednesses of his own society. If he does all of this with skill then, says Dewey, he will find the line of action which is right for him in this particular moral situation. It will be the line of action which resolves the battle between his conflicting purposes most successfully, while at the same time resolving whatever conflict may be present between his private ends and those of his society.

In all of this, however, there is one crucial and unjustified assumption, namely that he already knows what constitutes the good. If he does, then the experimental method is extremely useful. By following its procedures he can avoid elementary errors of judgment. The danger of failing to see what it is that he is really doing when he makes a choice is minimized when he engages in the kind of careful analysis of consequences, means, and relationships that Dewey *recommends*. But once all of this has been done, is it not relevant to ask, "Which of these various possibilities is really good, and which evil?" Must not a moral agent know what good is before he can decide on which choice to make from among his possible alternatives? Yet the experimental method does not, and in its very nature cannot, give the answer to this most fundamental of all value questions. It can merely serve as an extremely useful instrument in the achievement of a morally good life if the moral agent already knows what good consists in.

It seems to me that Dewey realizes this clearly when he makes his well known distinction between value and valuation. He emphasizes repeatedly that he is usually, in his writings on ethics, talking about valuation; that is to say, he is concerned with discriminating the processes and methods by the use of which he can make intelligent and defensible judgments of value. He wants to show that when I say of a thing or an act, "this is good," I cannot properly make such a judgment unless I subject it to the experimental test in order to see whether it really is what I think it is, unless, that is, I evaluate it intelligently. But this implies that there is some standard or criterion in terms of which I carry on this valuational process. Our perplexed friend, in the example we gave, must already know the standard, otherwise his experimental efforts are futile.

Dewey has such a standard, but it is not one which he gets through the use of the experimental method. In the article to which reference was made at the beginning of this paper he suggests that "discussion may be abbreviated by setting out from the widely held belief that wherever value is found there something called bias, liking, interest is also found, while conversely, wherever these acts, attitudes, or feelings are found, there also and only there is value found."[4] This is expressed in a more generalized form elsewhere when Dewey asserts that, "There is no value except where there is satisfaction."[5] Dewey is quite sure that such direct satisfactions are not open to question until for some reason they become problematic. Then they become the subjects of value-judgments, and it is at that point that we must apply the experimental method. "Immediacy of the quality in the abstract," he writes, "means nothing except that valueness is valueness; it is what it is. The assertion that a particular thing *which has* been *taken to* be a value *is* a value is, on the other hand, an additive and instructive statement; 'synthetic' in the Kantian sense."[6] It is statements of this latter sort that the experimental method is expected to examine and give adequate grounding to.

This does not change the fact, which Dewey clearly recognizes, that value itself is totally dependent, in his theory, on the qualitative immediacy of the feelings to which he refers. Ultimately, and in the last analysis, it is the inevitable conclusion of his doctrine that such feelings, and only such feelings, are the determinants of the presence of value in any object or act. Granted that these feelings are not reliable in their bare immediacy. Granted that they must be subjected to reflective judgment if they are to serve as guides to intelligent action. This does not, and cannot, change the basic fact that value is constituted, according to Dewey, by feelings of satisfaction, liking, enjoyment, and the like.

This raises two questions: "How do I know when such feelings are present?" and, "How does Dewey know that such feelings are the ultimate determinants of value?" The latter question we can only answer by saying that there is never any real defense of the position anywhere in Dewey's writings. He seems to think that the doctrine is so generally recognized as not to be in need of any defense. He refers to it, for example, as "a widely held belief," and is ordinarily satisfied to leave the matter there.

The former question leads us back to the quotations with which this paper began. We can now see that they are not an aberration at all, but that the views presented there are a necessary consequence of Dewey's belief that values consist of feelings of liking or satisfaction. If we accept this position then what more can we say other than that we know values immediately, intuitively, directly? It is certainly the case that if values are ultimate qualities then Dewey cannot possibly say anything more with regard to them than that they are what they are, and that they do not "lend themselves to thought and discourse." They cannot be dealt with by the experimental method. How do I know, then, that value is present in an object or an act? The answer is merely that I know it as a fact in my immediate experience. "In themselves values may just be pointed at." This does not mean that they exist necessarily as independent entities in the external world. Dewey never espouses such a notion of objectivity. It does mean that the value experience is not discursive, and that nothing can be said in definition or explication of it. Such a view may seem strange when attributed to Dewey, but it is perfectly consistent with all that he has said about value. If you conceive of value as a kind of satisfaction then there is no choice but to describe the method by which it may be known in terms similar to those which Dewey employs. When Dewey speaks of the experimental method as the procedure for arriving at reasonable value judgments, he is speaking not of the direct experience of values on which such judgments are based, but rather (as he says) of "their generative conditions and the consequences to which they give rise."

This is evident in his more recent writings as well. If we examine, for example, an exchange between Dewey and Professor Rice that took place just a few years ago we find there the same basic approach to the problem. One of the issues is that concerning the subjectivity of value. Professor Rice claims that there is some serious sense in which the immediate value experience is ultimate and private. Dewey denies this vigorously. But when we examine his argument we discover that he is denying the subjectivity of the value judgment. He touches only briefly on the status of the immediate value experience on which all such judgments ultimately depend. Instead he adopts his usual method of discussing the conditions under which judgments of value are arrived at. In fact, he admits that

> ...The occurrence of events in the way of prizing, cherishing, admiring, relishing, enjoying, is not in question. Nor is their primary importance for human life in any way depreciated, the events are what make life worth having. Nor is it held that they must be taken out of their qualitative immediacy and be subjected to judgment. On the contrary, my thesis, as respects valuation, is that only when conditions arise that cause doubt to arise as to their value... are they judged.[6]

However, such judgments cannot be made without some reference to the immediate value experience, and this experience, in turn, is qualitatively final, beyond discussion and beyond question. This is the inevitable result of Dewey's position. His usual attempt to make the perception and even the realization of value immanent in the judgmental process does not change this fact. For whenever we press the basic question concerning the true source of the knowledge of value we are forced back to feelings, and, therefore, to *immediate* intuitive knowledge.

That Dewey ordinarily resists recognition of the implications of his position is readily understandable. Believing as he does in unified science and in the experimental method as the instrument of all knowledge it is embarrassing to admit that there is one realm which stubbornly refuses to be included in this unity. Nor can he resign himself to a total skepticism concerning those values which he regards as basically important in man's life. Instead he, for the most part, conveniently ignores basic value questions and deals only with those aspects of the value problem which are susceptible of handling by scientific method. The passage in *Experience and Nature* with which this paper began is not an aberration. It is, on the contrary, one of the rare occasions when Dewey sees with complete clarity the implications of his own position. In one of his most recent articles there is another such occasion. Writing about the need to deal adequately with the crucial moral issues posed by the terrifying uses to which scientific knowledge is currently being put, Dewey says, "What is needed is not the carrying over of procedures that have approved themselves in physical science, but new methods as adapted to human issues and problems, as methods already in scientific use have shown themselves to be in physical subject matter."[7] There is apparently more than one crack in the armor of Dewey's presumed methodological unity.

MARVIN FOX
Ohio State University

NOTES

[1] John Dewey, Experience and Nature (Chicago, 1926), pp. 396-398.
[2] *Ibid.,* p. 398.
[3] Cf., "Value, Objective Reference, and Criticism," *The Philosophical Review,* Vol. XXXIV, No. 4 (July, 1925), p. 314.
[4] *Ibid.*, pp. 314-315.
[5] *Quest for Certainty*, p. 268.
[6] In the Journal *of Philosophy,* Vol. XII (1943).
[7] "Philosophy's Future in Our Scientific Age," Commentary, Vol. 8, No. 4 (October, 1949), p. 393.

23

MORAL FACTS AND MORAL THEORY

I

The following statement, which occurs very early in *Human Nature and Conduct*, is a clear expression of Dewey's belief that a moral theory cannot be formulated adequately without a knowledge of the relevant facts.

Dewey asserts that:

> It is impossible to say how much of the unnecessary slavery of the world is due to the conception that moral issues can be settled within conscience or human sentiment apart from consistent study of facts and application of specific knowledge in industry, law and politics.- It is not pretended that a moral theory based upon realities of human nature and a study of the specific connections of these realities with those of physical science would do away with moral struggle and defeat... But morals based upon concern with facts and deriving guidance from knowledge of them would at least locate the points of effective endeavor and would focus available resources upon them.[1]

This insistence that a moral philosophy is both mistaken and useless unless it is based on a knowledge of the facts of man's nature and of the dynamics of society is characteristic of many current naturalistic and empirical theories.

But even the non-naturalistic and the non-empirical moralists feel called upon to pay homage to the importance of facts. This is hardly surprising when we remember that there is some sense in which every moralist wants his principles to be able to serve as a guide to practice. Even those philosophers who classify ethics as a theoretical science, whose proper end is knowledge and not practice, recognize that what they are aiming at is a theoretical knowledge of practical principles. But if this is the case then it seems reasonable to suppose that such principles cannot be developed in ignorance of the fundamental facts about the beings whose practice they are intended to control. Typical of this position is the attitude of a philosopher like F. H. Bradley who would not normally be thought of as a naturalist or an empiricist. Discussing one of the central problems in his *Ethical Studies* Bradley observes that:

> —what we most want, more especially those of us who talk most about facts, is to stand by all the facts. It is our duty to take them without picking and choosing them to suit our views, to explain them, if we can, but not to explain them away; and to reason on them, and find the reason of them, but never to think ourselves rational when, by the shortest cut to reason we have reasoned ourselves out of them.[2]

For Bradley, as well as for the empiricists, facts are indispensable to a formulation of an acceptable and defensible ethical theory.

II

It is surprising, in the light of such statements, to find that in Dewey's and Bradley's ethical writings facts are not dealt with in the way that we might expect. Surely, if philosophers consider facts to be basically important in establishing moral principles, then they should employ the best possible techniques for determining what the facts are. One would tend to presume that such philosophers would use the most reliable scientific data, that they would be cautious and tentative where the evidence is incomplete, and that their factual statements would be rigorously consistent. Moreover, it would be reasonable to expect that there would be among such philosophers fairly general agreement as to what the facts are. These are expectations which are taken for granted in the factual statements of scientists. Ideally, philosophers who claim central importance for factual knowledge should meet these same minimal scientific standards in dealing with facts.

Yet if we read Dewey's and Bradley's ethical writings we find that their factual statements frequently lack all scientific character. Instead of the rigorous care of the scientists we are offered vague assurances, dogmatic statements, and simple appeals to common opinion. Inadequate as these would appear to be as evidence for presumed facts, the weakness of the factual statements of these philosophers is increased by internal contradictions as well as by the marked disagreements concerning matters of fact which obtain between different thinkers. It is not at all uncommon (as we shall show subsequently) to find that a particular ethical work presents us with factual statements that are internally contradictory. It is even more common to find striking differences and disagreements in the factual statements of different moral philosophers. I shall attempt to show, in what follows, that both Dewey and Bradley deal with facts in the manner which we have discussed, that one can find in their moral philosophies factual statements which are either self-contradictory or mutually contradictory. My main purpose is to offer an analysis and possible explanation for the curious fashion in which these philosophers deal with matters of fact.

Dewey and Bradley have been chosen as prototypical instances for several reasons. First, they are contemporaries, and as such might certainly be expected to agree about matters of fact. A common body of information, common sources, and certain common and well established methods have been available to them. Perhaps we can countenance disagreements about facts between thinkers who are widely separated in time, but it is certainly reasonable to expect that contemporaries will agree. Factual disagreements, then, between two such contemporaries as Bradley and Dewey point up the seriousness of the issues which we are raising. For their very contemporaneity strengthens the likelihood that the differences between these philosophers are genuine and significant, and that they are not merely the result of differences in the information that was available at widely separated times.

Secondly, Dewey and Bradley hold very different philosophic positions. If the thesis which is proposed here can be shown to be true of two such diverse thinkers' then we are, at least, immune from the criticism that what we are pointing out is merely the peculiarity of a certain kind of moral philosophy. Instead it becomes clear that we are examining a phenomenon which may well be characteristic of moral philosophy generally. (If space would permit it could be shown that Dewey and Bradley are in no sense unique, and that the way in which they handle matters of fact is common to many ethical theorists.) Thirdly, in spite of their differences, Dewey, in a number of places, acknowledges a very heavy debt to Bradley.[3] This means that there is enough of a relationship to make comparisons both reasonable and fruitful. Finally, as was pointed out at the beginning of this essay, both Dewey and Bradley take facts seriously. As a result we cannot discuss internal contradictions or mutual disagreements about matters of fact as mere carelessness or unconcern. We rightfully expect deliberate and conscious care in judgments about what the facts are of any writer who emphasizes as strongly as do these two the inescapable importance of facts for moral theory. Thus, the ethical works of Bradley and Dewey seem to offer us an excellent opportunity to study the way in which facts are dealt with by moral philosophers.

The central thesis of this paper is that even philosophers like Dewey and Bradley, who acknowledge the importance of facts for their theories, do not establish their facts scientifically. Instead, it can be shown that they see the facts primarily in the light of the requirements of their theories. As a result, their conceptions of what the facts are tend to change as the requirements of their theories change. We can explain their internal contradictions, as well as their mutual disagreements, in this fashion. For it turns out that, in spite of their open espousal of the need for accurate knowledge of the facts, their own statements of facts are sometimes inconsistent, and this is a result of the varying needs of their theories. It is a commonplace that sound theories must be based on accurate facts. We are proposing a consideration of the view that the facts, at least of moral philosophers, tend to be derived from their theories. Given any moral doctrine the facts must be conceived in a way that will be consistent with it. This means that frequently theory dictates what the facts must be.

IV

One of the questions regarding matters of fact which occupies the attention of both Bradley and Dewey is the following: "Are moral judgments universally the same, or do they differ greatly from one society to another? Do people everywhere have identical opinions concerning what constitutes the good and the evil, or is there a great diversity of opinion on this fundamental question?" This question involves the kind of facts which most contemporary scholars would hold to be readily ascertainable. The social sciences, and especially anthropology, should, presumably, be able to give us this kind of information. Yet neither Bradley nor Dewey, though they both wrote within the decades which have marked the ascendancy of the social sciences, attempt to substantiate their factual judgments by appeal to these authorities. Instead their views on such matters of fact as the uniformity or diversity of moral judgments are supported by nothing more than their own pronouncements, occasionally tempered by an appeal to common sense observation. It is our contention that it can be shown clearly that their particular views on these questions are, at least, a necessary corollary, if not the direct result of the positions they hold with regard to certain theoretical matters. As the most economical way of dealing with our general problem, we shall devote ourselves to an analysis of the way in which Dewey and Bradley deal with this one area of factual knowledge.

In his *Ethical Studies* Bradley offers two kinds of answers to the question of the uniformity of moral judgments. In some regards he assures us that there is complete uniformity, that all men are agreed about moral questions, while in other connections he claims that there is a great diversity of moral judgments and that different men and different societies have radically differing moral rules. The area of uniformity in moral matters arises in connection with what Bradley calls "the voice of the moral consciousness".[4] He speaks of it as a "common consciousness",[5] and it is clear that he believes that all men possess this common moral consciousness. It is a sort of intuitive moral sense that Bradley believes every man has, merely by virtue of the fact that he is a man. It follows that such a moral sense will, within the scope of its operation, lead all men to identical judgments. Bradley conceives this moral sense as concerned only with some very general principles of morality, and with regard to these he assures us that there is universal agreement.

We must remember that for Bradley the facts are supposedly given. It is the business of theory merely to explain and account for the facts. However, it appears that he has in actuality reversed this procedure. He tells us that it is a matter of fact that the common moral consciousness affirms certain things. Consequently, men everywhere, irrespective of the particular elements of their moral situation, can be expected to acknowledge these affirmations of the moral consciousness. Yet it is clear enough that there are many who have denied and still deny what Bradley tells us that the moral consciousness affirms. He himself mentions, as one instance, the hedonists. Yet in the face of this he continues to talk as if it were a fact that these are matters on which all men are agreed. It is my contention, in the light of this, that Bradley is not explaining facts that are given, but that he is instead affirming as facts items which his theory requires of him.

Before we can demonstrate this we must first examine some of the dictates of the common moral consciousness as Bradley describes them. According to him our moral sense informs us (presumably all of us) that virtue is its own end, and consequently that the only reason that I ought to be moral is because I ought to be moral. For he considers it an obvious and unquestionable fact that "to take virtue as a mere means to an ulterior end is in direct antagonism to the voice of the moral consciousness."[6] It is that same moral consciousness that informs us that "to do good for its own sake is virtue, to do it for some ulterior end or object, not itself good, is never virtue."[7] In line with this view Bradley goes on to point out that morality must be accepted as a present reality, but cannot be justified by any external justification. The title of the chapter in which these reflections occur is "Why Should I be Moral?" Bradley concludes without any hesitation at all that "The question has no sense at all; it is simply unmeaning."[8]

How can we explain Bradley's insistence that these are matters of universal agreement? Bradley conceives of both knowledge and being as dialectical in character. That is to say, dialectic is not merely a method by which we acquire knowledge, but reality itself is a dialectical structure. Within that dialectical conception of reality Bradley describes the various sub-phenomena as dialectical also. Thus, morality is conceived as the process of self-realization, and this is understood by Bradley as a developmental movement in which contradictory aspects of the individual personality are brought together in a higher unity. In each case this synthesis is a movement toward the fulfillment of the true nature of the self, that is, of self-realization. This is not merely a process in which man engages casually, if and when the inclination strikes him. It is bound up with his very nature as man and with the metaphysical structure of the world which he inhabits.

> Morality is an endless process, and therefore a self-contradiction; and, being such, it does not remain standing in itself, but feeds the impulse to transcend its existing reality... Neither in me, nor in the world, is what ought to be what is, and what is what ought to be...[9]

It is, in some sense, an inevitable and inexorable process, and it is for this very reason that the question, "Why should I be moral?", is in Bradley's eyes, totally meaningless. Both metaphysical and moral reality make the process an absolutely necessary one. To ask why I should be moral is equivalent to asking why I should be a man living in this kind of world. Neither question is answerable.

> if I am asked why I am to be moral, I can say no more than this, that what I can not doubt is my own being now, and that, since in that being is involved a self, which is to be here and now, and yet in this here and now is not, I therefore cannot doubt that there is an end which I am to make real; and morality, if not equivalent to, is at all events included in this making real of myself... The only rational question here is not why? but what? What is the self that I know and will?'[10]

To ask why I should want to realize that self is, from this point of view a total absurdity.

We can now see, why Bradley must hold that virtue is an end in itself, and that this is recognized by the moral consciousness. If the very meaning of morality is the process by which we realize the whole as a synthesis of its various parts, then it is necessarily the case that virtue is its own end. For nothing stands beyond the consummation of the striving for virtue. In the dialectical movement the realization of the whole is a finality. It makes no sense to say that one does this for still another purpose. It is self-sufficient and nothing can be postulated beyond it.

We must point out in passing that Bradley is fully aware that the realization of the individual self is by his own principles not enough. It, too, is merely a partial realization. He goes on to require as a moral duty the social realization of the individual self. Every man must see himself as a member of society, and, as such, can find his genuine fulfillment. Self-realization is only a step on the way toward social realization. Social realization, furthermore, is also a stage in the process of realizing the absolute whole which is the ultimate reality.

We may still ask, in spite of all that has been said, why Bradley thinks that the common moral consciousness affirms that virtue is its own end. It is certainly possible for him to recognize that while his metaphysics requires this another metaphysical position may not. The answer lies in the fact that Bradley felt certain that his metaphysics was correct, and that every reasonable man must see the truth of his doctrine. In so doing one cannot help but recognize its consequences for morality. The common moral consciousness is merely an extension of the rational faculties which all men may be presumed to possess in common. Thus, we see that his statement of supposed fact is really a necessary consequence and extension of his prior theoretical commitments.

We may now return to the problem which we posed earlier, namely how Bradley, in the face of his belief in a common moral consciousness, is able to explain the existence of hedonists and others who believe that virtue is a means to another end. One would have expected that a common moral consciousness would express itself through a series of universally held judgments. As a matter of fact, Bradley suggests that this very situation obtains. For he assures us, among other things, that "never, except on a misunderstanding, has the moral consciousness in any case acquiesced in Hedonism."[11] How, then do we explain the presence of hedonists in the world? For Bradley the answer is quite simple. Hedonists are men with a theory. They have an ax to grind. As a result their perceptions and understanding are distorted in the effort to make the facts fit their theory. They are guilty of a basic misunderstanding resulting from the effort to justify their own position.

Bradley does not seem at all disturbed by the two most obvious objections that might be raised. In the first place, he, too, has a theory, but this does not seem to impede his feeling of assurance in the correctness of his own moral insights. Furthermore, if there is a common moral consciousness then the hedonists, being human, ought to share in it. But Bradley ignores these objections completely. He merely insists that when "moral persons without a theory on the matter" are told that the end of virtue is pleasure, "there is no gainsaying that they repudiate such a result." [12] The hedonists, having a theory, are thus incapable of seeing what all men of unbiased insight are immediately able to grasp.

Bradley's conception of virtue as self-realization leads him to several other supposedly factual statements. He tells us, for example, that "if we turn to life, we see that no man has disconnected particular ends." [13] According to this view men plan their lives in a kind of hierarchical pattern. They conceive their immediate choices as means leading to the realization of certain ends, and of those ends as means to still further ends, and of the whole structure as controlled by some single final purpose. This purpose is, of course, the realization of the whole. "If the life of the normal man be inspected, and the ends he has in view (as exhibited in his acts) be considered, they will, roughly speaking, be embraced in one main end or whole of ends." [14] Here, again, we see the effect of Bradley's scheme of dialectic on his description of the facts. If it is true that both knowledge and being are dialectical in character then it seems to follow, at least in Bradley's judgment, that the processes of the individual human life must also be structured dialectically. What is true of the macrocosm ought, according to such a theory, to be true of the microcosm, What is true of the world as a whole is equally true of each individual man who embodies the entire cosmic process within the limits of his being. Bradley's theory seems to require that the facts be as he describes them to us.

This same theme is further carried out in his initial comments on happiness where we can again see the dialectical pattern at work. Bradley denies that "every man has a different notion of happiness." On the contrary, here, too, there is a kind of uniformity of judgment. There may be some variations in the particular details of how happiness is conceived by various individuals, but the basic pattern is the same for all men.

> ...if you take (not of course anyone, but) the normal decent and serious man, when he has been long enough in the world to know what he wants, you will find that his notion of perfect happiness, or ideal life, is not something straggling, as it were, and discontinuous, but is brought before the mind as a unity, and, if imagined more in detail, is a system where particulars subserve one whole.[15]

One can see here, also, the same conception and the same dialectical pattern that has already been described. Happiness, according to Bradley, must be a "unity... where particulars subserve one whole," because both man and the universe are, in his view, similarly constructed according to this pattern.

Furthermore, every man must acknowledge that this is what he means by happiness. If he denies it then he is irrational, and, consequently, we need not reckon seriously with his opinions. Bradley, himself, admits that what he means by "every man" is "not of course anyone, but the normal decent and serious man", i.e., the man whose opinions coincide with his own. This may seem to be a somewhat strained way to achieve uniformity of judgment in moral matters, but it seems undeniable that this is Bradley's way. We need only recall that he employed an essentially similar device when he rejected the opinion of the hedonists as unimportant since it came from men with a theory to defend. In neither instance does he abide by his own statement of purpose, namely to account for acknowledged facts. On the contrary, where his theory requires it he appears to be quite ready to explain away facts that even he admits as true.

It is a matter of considerable interest, in the light of our discussion, to note that there is also an area in which Bradley acknowledges the existence of an extensive moral diversity. When we examine the practices of particular societies we find that they differ extensively and in many fundamental regards.

> It is abundantly clear that the morality of one time is not that of another time, that the men considered good in one age might in another age not be thought good, and what would be right for us here might be mean and base in another country, and what would be wrong for us here might there be our bounden duty.[16]

He goes on to assure us that, "Different men, who have lived in different times and countries, judge or would judge a case in morals differently."[17] This is a curious statement from one who believes in the existence of a common moral consciousness. But these apparently contradictory factual statements can be explained in the terms of the position which we are seeking to defend here, namely that Bradley's facts are derived in many instances from the requirements of his theory, rather than from an examination of the world. Our discussion and analysis will now move on two levels. First we shall try to analyze the opposing instances of the uniformity and diversity of moral judgments as necessary functions of the theoretical distinction which Bradley draws between moral science and moral art. Then we shall go on to show that at a deeper level the assertion of some uniformity and some diversity is an inevitable result of the dialectical scheme which Bradley employs to explain the nature of things.

Bradley distinguishes between what he calls moral science and moral art. Moral science is what we more usually call moral philosophy, and its end according to Bradley is knowledge. Its purpose is to "understand morals which exist." Moral art has as its end successful moral practice. It is not concerned with understanding morality, but rather with developing the techniques which are required for moral action.

When Bradley develops his theory of the common moral consciousness and its universal moral dictates, he does so in the context of his discussion of moral science. It is that part of the structure of his moral philosophy in which he is seeking to understand the nature of morality. For this purpose it is necessary to conceive moral phenomena as characterized by certain basic uniformities. He thinks that no knowledge is possible unless we can discover in a mass of apparently diverse phenomena some general patterns and structures in terms of which we can describe and organize our subject matter. Unless there is some uniformity we have utter chaos, and under these circumstances the end of moral philosophy or moral science is incapable of achievement. So long as his goal is theoretical knowledge Bradley is forced to assert that there are some basic similarities in morality, wherever and whenever it occurs. The belief in the existence of a common moral consciousness and its supposedly uniform prescriptions serves this purpose.

When, on the other hand, Bradley freely admits the existence of considerable moral diversity he is no longer concerned with moral science, but only with moral art. He is not interested in understanding moral phenomena, but rather in helping his reader decide what he, as a moral agent, must do. The passage which was quoted as an example of Bradley's belief in the diversity of moral judgments is preceded by a caution "against the common error that there is something 'right in itself' for me to do."[18]

Insofar as his concern is practical rather than theoretical Bradley can allow for a great measure of diversity. In fact, when he is establishing the procedures of moral art he is almost forced to acknowledge moral diversity, since morality as an art necessarily deals with the particularities and specificities of each individual moral situation. Here the common moral consciousness can serve no good purpose, for in this situation the facts must be presented so as to emphasize the diversities, rather than the uniformities, of the moral life.

There is, however, a more deeply rooted explanation than the one we have given for the presence of elements both of uniformity and diversity in Bradley's description of the facts of the moral life. We showed earlier that there is a clear sense in which Bradley's dialectic requires the conclusion that there is a common moral consciousness with certain universal moral judgments. But there is another sense in which this very same dialectic requires the belief in a diversity of moral patterns. For Bradley believes that apart from the absolute whole which represents the ultimate fulfillment and the highest synthesis of every developing tendency—apart from this absolute whole whatever exists implies the existence of its contradictory. If there is moral uniformity then there must, in the very nature of things, be moral diversity as well. Bradley expresses this by making reference to the Kantian principles of homogeneity and specification.[19] Whatever exists must have certain universal characteristics, certain features that it shares with all other existing things, or, in a more limited respect, features that it shares with all other things of the same genus. But at the same time it must also have those qualities and characteristics that specify it as uniquely what it is. Human societies, conceived as moral entities, must share certain features. These are the features ascribed by Bradley to the common moral consciousness and its prescriptions. But at the same time each of these societies is a unique and special entity, and insofar as this is the case it must have its own special characteristics. These mark it out as a morally diverse unit.

We can see the workings of this pattern in the case both of individuals and societies. For all individuals there are, according to Bradley, certain common moral rules, as we have already shown. But one of these rules is that the good for me as for every other individual is determined by "my station and its duties." This means that each individual recognizes his moral obligations as specifically determined by the particular society in which he lives and by the particular place which he occupies in that society. The general rule is one which in its very uniformity implies endless diversity.

What is true of each individual person is also true of human societies. Bradley's doctrine is such that he is forced to represent each individual society as a separate and distinct moral unit. For in the moral process, as it has already been described, each individual strives for self-realization and each society strives for its own realization. Furthermore, the totality of social realization is a moment in the realization of the absolute unity which is the end goal of the entire cosmic process. Now unless societies were morally different, and even, in some regards, antithetical, the developmental movement would be stopped. Each society must first unify the diverse tendencies within itself in order to fulfill its own special destiny. But having done so it must then merge with the stream of history in order that humanity may arrive at a higher state of development. In connection with this Bradley develops his belief that there is a process of social evolution in which each historical period is an advance over its predecessors. History is not merely blind change. It is teleological in character. It is a purposive movement of human societies from lower to higher stages.[20] And the development of these societies is measured by the degree to which they are an advance in the realization of the absolute whole toward which history inexorably is directed. All of this-the view of social evolution, as well as the moral diversity which it necessarily implies—is expressed clearly and succinctly by Bradley when he says that:

> ...if evolution is more than a tortured phrase, and progress to a goal no mere idea but an actual fact, then history is the working out of the true human nature through various incomplete stages toward completion, and 'my station' is the one satisfactory view of morals. Here... all morality is and must be 'relative', because the essence of realization is evolution through stages, and hence existence in some one stage which is not final; here, on the other hand, all morality is 'absolute', because in every stage the essence of man is realized, however imperfectly.[21]

This, then, is the explanation of Bradley's position. The very same dialectic requires him at one pole to assert that the same moral insights are possessed by all men, and at the other pole to assert that every society, and even every individual, is a unique moral entity with its own special set of moral prescriptions. In both cases the facts seem to be dependent on his theory rather than the reverse. He appears to have been guilty of the very thing against which he cautions us. For he, too, like those whom he condemns, does not merely account for the facts that are given. He relies on his theories to help decide what those facts must be.

Like Bradley Dewey also has more than one position with regard to the question of the uniformity and diversity of moral judgment and practice in various human societies. In some areas and concerning some matters he believes that there is very extensive diversity. In these particular regards morality, as he pictures it, is conditioned by the specific character of the moral situation in which it occurs. On the other hand, there are some aspects of the moral life which he assures us are universally the same irrespective of when or where they occur.

Particular codes and particular patterns of practice differ, according to Dewey, from culture to culture and from age to age. The ancient and the modern, the rural and the urban, the savage and the civilized, all have their own ways of doing things. "The notion of the intuitional theory that all persons possess a uniform and equal stock of moral judgments is contrary to fact."[22] Instead of this kind of uniformity as the actual pattern of moral practice Dewey informs us that, "At some place on the globe, at some time, every kind of practice seems to have been tolerated or even praised." He goes on to ask with considerable wonder, "How is this tremendous diversity of institutions (including moral codes) to be accounted for?"[23] This belief in the extensive diversity of moral codes and practices is one to which Dewey has held consistently. In the earliest of his writings on moral philosophy he already comments on the fact that, "The savage and the civilized man may vary greatly in their estimate of what particular acts are right or wrong."[24] It is in similar spirit that, writing in a more recent book, he says:

> The conception which looks for the end of action within the circumstances of the actual situation will not have the same measure of judgment for all cases... The absurdity of applying the same standards of moral judgment to savage peoples that is used with civilized will be apparent.[25]

Thus we see that Dewey is clearly committed to the view that in matters of moral practice and judgment men differ very considerably. These are, presumably, facts which would be born out by observation. We must remember that Dewey places great emphasis on the necessity of knowing the facts before we can theorize about them adequately. He describes himself as within the empiricist-naturalist tradition and he is very respectful of scientific procedures. So far as is possible he urges that these procedures be transferred to moral and social studies. He conceives his own ethical theory as scientific in method, and we, therefore, have every reason to expect that the facts which he offers will satisfy the requirements of scientific criticism and scrutiny.

It is, therefore, a source of considerable wonder to us when we discover that, in spite of his belief in the diversity of moral practice, Dewey occasionally insists on a rather total uniformity. We find, for example, in one of his discussions of utilitarianism the following statement:

> A man who trusted simply to details of external consequences might readily convince himself that the removal of a certain person by murder would contribute to general happiness. One cannot imagine an honest person convincing himself that a disposition of disregard for human life would have beneficial consequences.[26]

In a very similar spirit he asserts that, "A normal person will not witness an act of wanton cruelty without an immediate response of disfavor; resentment and indignation immediately follow."[27] These are views which seem totally out of harmony with the statements which were quoted above. If it is the case, as Dewey says, that somewhere on this earth at some time just about every conceivable practice has been approved, then with what ground and justification are we told that no honest man can ever believe that murder might have beneficial consequences? Clearly Dewey is involved in some sort of internal contradiction.

His belief that murder is universally disapproved, or more precisely that "a disposition of disregard for human life" is by honest men always considered evil is especially puzzling in the light of contemporary anthropological studies. We can presume that Dewey would almost certainly pay attention to such inquiries, and it is common knowledge that these studies consistently represent the facts in an opposite fashion. Of course, there is the possible alternative that Dewey considers all people living in cultures which approve homicide to be dishonest, but this hardly seems likely. Yet, if they are honest, then there is considerable evidence that there are honest men who do have little regard for human life. One example of what anthropologists have to say on this point will suffice for our purposes. In her well known book, *Patterns of Culture*, Ruth Benedict is very clear and forthright in her assertion that, "The diversity of cultures can be endlessly documented." As an illustration of this point she makes the following set of observations:

> We might suppose that in the matter of taking life all peoples would agree in condemnation. On the contrary in a matter of homicide, it may be held that one is blameless if diplomatic relations have been severed between neighboring countries, or that one kills by custom his first two children, or that a husband has the right of life and death over his wife, or that it is the duty of the child to kill his parents before they are old. It may be that those are killed who steal a fowl, or who cut their upper teeth first, or who are born on a Wednesday.[28]

In the face of presumably factual reports of this sort-and they can be paralleled by many more-it is somewhat puzzling to find Dewey taking an opposite stand. It is even more puzzling when we recall that in other places he expressly recognizes the existence of the kind of diversity which Miss Benedict describes. This seems to be another instance in which our thesis can be shown to be correct. For it seems clear that, like Bradley, Dewey is forced to relate fact to theory. In any given instance his conception of the facts must be related to the particular theoretical requirements of the discussion. We shall attempt to show that this is the case in the analysis which follows.

Dewey's more usual view is that there is almost total diversity of moral judgment and practice, and this is a view which we might properly expect him to hold. Common observation, historical research, and the inquiries of contemporary social scientists all seem to lead to this conclusion. Moreover this is the view that Dewey's general theoretical position would seem to require. Unlike Bradley he does not distinguish between ethical theory whose sole end is knowledge and moral practice which is concerned only with appropriate action. For Dewey the end of all theory, including moral theory, is action. Even at the highest level of theoretical abstraction our theory is significant and meaningful only if it leads to successful practice and it can be verified only by such practice. If this is the case, then Dewey must estimate the adequacy of any aspect of his moral philosophy in terms of its practical aims. But while theories and principles may be general all activity is particularized. Each act is done by a particular individual, at some specific time and place, and under a given set of conditions. Action, to be successful, must be cognizant of the uniquely individual character of the situation in which it occurs. A moral philosophy whose end is action cannot help but take note of the peculiarities and particularities of each individual moral agent and of his situation. Within this kind of framework it is almost inevitable that Dewey (like Bradley when he deals with moral art) should be extremely sensitive to the diversity of moral fashions that occur in human society. The various passages which we quoted as examples of his belief that there is such diversity are taken from different books and from different periods of his writing. However, they are all in agreement because all are derived from a theory whose consistently avowed aim is to make successful action possible. Given this goal Dewey's emphasis on moral differences is both necessary and understandable.

However, like Bradley, Dewey cannot let the matter rest there. Any systematic structure has to base itself on some uniformities and regularities. Without at least a minimum of uniformity and regularity there is not a systematic structure, but mere chaos. Dewey yields to this general need, just as Bradley does, and the passages which were quoted as apparent contradictions of his general position are clear cut instances of this yielding. When he tells us that no honest man could really believe that disregard for human life could have beneficial consequences, Dewey is in the midst of a discussion of hedonism. In typical fashion he is searching for those elements of hedonism that he can retain in his own theory, and has already concluded that approval and disapproval are original facts. Every morality must recognize, says Dewey, that approval and disapproval are among the most elementary moral attitudes and that they are always present in moral judgment. In such judgment, accordingly, the character and disposition of the judger enters very strongly into the picture, for these determine to a considerable degree what he will approve and disapprove. And it is at this point that a certain amount of uniformity must be postulated. For, if we are dependent on individual judges and each of these differs from his fellows there can only be moral chaos. In such a situation no moral principles would be possible and whatever anybody approved would be good at least for the approver himself. To avoid this Dewey is forced to assert that there are certain uniform attitudes possessed by honest men. If we grant this then our difficulties are considerably lessened. If we know that all honest men have a given disposition and attitude with regard to certain matters then we also know that they will, so long as they are honest, necessarily approve or disapprove of certain kinds of acts. Given this knowledge it is then inevitable that we should conclude that in all societies there are certain areas of moral and social practice which are the same. Dewey's examples involved murder and cruelty, hence it was with regard to these that he felt compelled to assert a uniform disposition. Presumably had he chosen other illustrations he might still, within the context of his discussion, have found it necessary to believe that all men had uniform dispositions and attitudes concerning these matters. His statement that somewhere and sometime "every kind of practice seems to have been tolerated or praised" must be narrowed and restricted. For if praise is a basic element of moral judgment then it seems necessary to insist that there are some things from which men always withhold praise and some which they are always inclined to praise. Otherwise we would have total moral chaos.

There is a second kind of uniformity which Dewey conceives to be present, which is even more important than this specific uniformity of particular moral attitudes. I refer to his belief that the framework of morality is everywhere the same. No matter how particular practices may differ the general framework from which they are derived is everywhere the same. This is again significant as a device by which systematic order is brought into a subject matter which would otherwise be chaotic. The technique by which Dewey achieves this is quite simple, and it is appropriate within the context of his system. He believes in a total unity of science. Moral theory is for him an extension of biology and psychology and thus must share certain of the characteristics of these disciplines. Like them it must be rooted in human nature, and must presume that human nature is everywhere the same. If this is the case, then it is inevitable that the phenomena of morals should be characterized by certain uniform attributes which are understood as rooted in the essential nature of man. It is precisely this which Dewey has in mind when he says:

> Special phenomena of morals change from time to time with change of social conditions and the level of culture. The facts of desiring, purpose, social demand and law, sympathetic approval and hostile disapproval are constant. We cannot imagine them disappearing so long as human nature remains human nature, and lives in association with others. The fundamental conceptions of morals are, therefore, neither arbitrary nor artificial. They are not imposed upon human nature from without but develop out of its own operations and needs. Particular aspects of morals are transient... But the framework of moral conceptions is as permanent as human life itself.[29]

We see here how far the process of selectivity is operative in determining what the facts are and which facts are relevant. Because Dewey conceives morality as natural the only facts which concern him arc natural facts. The artificial has no place in the framework of morality. Moreover, because these facts are natural they must be everywhere the same. This introduces the uniform framework which his theory requires. Furthermore, out of the vast array of available natural facts he chooses as relevant primarily psychological and social facts. This is perfectly consistent with Dewey's conception of the subject matter of ethics, since according to him ethics is concerned with deliberate conduct which affects the self and society. If this is the subject matter of ethics then it follows necessarily that the facts which interest us will be psychological and social facts, and that insofar as these are conceived as natural they will be described as everywhere the same.

Thus, he is certain that on the one side all morality must involve some kind of pleasure, for he believes that one of the most basic elements in man's nature is desire. "Desire belongs to the intrinsic nature of man; we cannot conceive a human being who does not have wants, needs, nor one to whom fulfillment of desire does not afford satisfaction." [30] The satisfaction of desire is a natural striving, therefore, of all human activity, and morals must everywhere be judged within this general framework. For this reason Dewey is able to assert that, "There is nothing good to us which does not contain an element of enjoyment and nothing bad which does not contain an element of the disagreeable and repulsive." [31] The facts must be so if this aspect of morals is rooted in man's nature and Dewey asserts clearly and unequivocally that it is so rooted.

On the other side Dewey can equally hold it to be a fact that morality everywhere is social. Again this is derived from man's nature as a social animal and thus must be thought of as part of the general framework of morality. Man is a social animal, according to Dewey, and his conduct is affected by, and affects, his society. There is no non-social conduct, and since morals deals with conduct its framework must be social.

> These two facts, that moral judgment and moral responsibility are the work wrought in us by the social environment, signify that all morality is social... Our conduct is socially conditioned whether we perceive the fact or not." [32]

Again this fact is relevant because the subject matter of ethics is defined by Dewey as involving the social situation, and it is universally the case because it is presumably rooted in human nature.

We may note the difference between Dewey's uniformities and those which Bradley claims to have found. Their conception of the facts is considerably different. Dewey derives his uniform aspects of the moral life from what he conceives to be human nature, from the biological, psychological and social disciplines. Bradley, on the other hand, derives his uniformities from the requirements of the metaphysical framework on which his ethical theory depends. Thus Bradley has no need to assert that any particular moral dispositions, such as the disapproval of murder, are universal. For he is in no way dependent for his uniformities on such simple psychological issues. He is not concerned with desire and approbation as crucial elements in the moral life. Instead he is forced by his metaphysical position to assert that virtue is always recognized as its own end. This, in turn, is a formulation which Dewey is forced to deny, since it comes into conflict with his emphasis on practice and his concern with the ongoing process. In this process there are no final ends, only ends-in-view which are destined to become means to still further ends. We see here again the way in which different theories are required, first to select different sets of facts as relevant to their purposes, and then to describe their facts differently even when they concern the same matters.

Perhaps we can best summarize the position which this paper has sought to defend and explicate by quoting another very revealing statement of Bradley's. At the beginning of his *Ethical Studies* he announces that his first task is "to enter on a question of fact." However, he goes on to caution us, "that asking is reflection, and that we reflect in general not to find the facts, but to prove our theories at the expense of them. The ready-made doctrines we bring to the work color whatever we touch with them."[33]

NOTES

[1] John Dewey, *Human Nature and Conduct* (New York: The Modern Library. 1930), pp. 11-12.
[2] F. H. Bradley, *Ethical Studies* (Oxford: The Clarendon Press, 1927), P. 251.
[3] Cf. John Dewey, *Outlines of a Critical Theory of Ethics* (Ann Arbor: Register Publishing Co., 1891), p. vi.
[4] Bradley, *op. cit.,* p. 61.
[5] *Ibid.,* p. 63.
[6] *Ibid.,* p. 61.
[7] *Ibid.,* p. 62.
[8] *Ibid.,* p. 64.
[9] *Ibid.,* p. 313.
[10] *Ibid.,* p. 84.
[11] *Ibid.,* p. 89.
[12] *Ibid.,* p. 88.
[13] *Ibid.,* p. 69
[14] *Ibid.,* p. 70.
[15] *Ibid.*
[16] *Ibid.,* p. 189.
[17] *Ibid.,* p. 195.
[18] *Ibid.,* p. 189.
[19] Cf. *Ibid.,* pp. 74 ff.
[20] Cf. *Ibid.,* pp. 190-192.
[21] *Ibid.,* p. 192.
[22] John Dewey and James H. Tufts, *Ethics, Revised Edition,* (New York, 1932), p. 311.
[23] John Dewey, *Human Nature and Conduct,* (New York, 1930), p. 91.
[24] John Dewey, *Outlines of a Critical Theory of Ethics,* (Ann Arbor, 1891), p. 183.
[25] *John Dewey, Reconstruction in Philosophy,* (New York, 1920), p. 176.
[26] *Ethics,* (revised edition), op. cit., p. 265.
[27] *Ibid.,* p. 292.
[28] Ruth Benedict, *Patterns of Culture,* (New York, 1946), p. 41.
[29] *Ethics,* (revised edition), op. cit., pp. 343-4.
[30] *Ibid.,* p. 343.
[31] *Ibid.,* p. 210.
[32] *Human Nature and Conduct, op. cit.,* p. 316.
[33] Bradley, *op. cit.,* p. 2.

24

Judaism, Secularism and Textual Interpretation

In this introductory essay I shall not deal directly with questions of Jewish ethics. My purpose is rather to set forth what I understand to be the basic methodological principles that underlie the common efforts of the participants in this volume to understand and interpret important aspects of Judaism. The Institute of Judaism and Contemporary Thought, under whose auspices these papers were originally presented, was established by a group of people who share the conviction that "Judaism" and "contemporary thought" are not mutually exclusive. On the contrary, we are convinced that one of the great strengths of Judaism is the fact that it has a method for remaining true to itself while absorbing, or, at least, fruitfully confronting, various aspects of non-Jewish thought. In every age, including our own, Jewish thinkers have had a vital need to come to terms with the insights of the science, philosophy, and morality of their time. They have been forced to accept or reject, absorb or shun, ideas and doctrines whose initial source is not within the Jewish tradition. Judaism itself provides a method for carrying on this intellectual-spiritual confrontation. It is a method by which the boundaries between the Jewish and non-Jewish worlds are sometimes erased, and are at other times drawn sharply. Some outside teachings are accepted, naturalized, and given a home within the Jewish fold. Others are rejected and excluded from any claim to Jewish legitimacy.

This method, an instrument of intellectual honesty and spiritual survival, is necessary because Judaism, as it has sometimes been described, is a "book-religion," that is, a religion that bases itself on texts that are considered sacred and that are canonized. These texts include the Bible, the Talmud, the later rabbinic writings, the codes, and similar works. It is well known that these works have been, almost from their first appearance, the subject of continuous exegesis, for Jews were hardly ever satisfied with a bare text without commentaries. The process of exegesis did not come to an end at some specified time, but continues down to the present. When the text of the Bible was fixed, the activities of biblical interpretation were centered in the Talmud and the Midrashim. When the Talmud was closed and its text set, the processes of interpretation were carried forth in the Geonic literature and in the commentaries. In fact, the commentaries are normally treated by students as if they were a part of the text itself. The textual commentaries generated super-commentaries, and the process of interpretation went on. If, as Jewish tradition teaches, the oral law was given at Sinai together with the written text, it would appear that the practice of treating the text as always requiring interpretation began at Sinai and has continued down to the present. Inside the Jewish tradition, an uninterpreted text is practically an unknown phenomenon.

What I shall argue in this paper is that this process of exegesis and interpretation is the most important device that Jewish tradition used in order to be able to stand simultaneously in the classical tradition of Judaism and in the contemporary world. Each age, living in its particular cultural and intellectual milieu, had fashioned its way of being faithful to the teachings of Judaism while accommodating itself to the best of contemporary scientific and philosophic doctrine. The integrity of the texts on which Judaism rests is respected, while, by the process of exegesis, their openness to the contemporary world of ideas is assured.

One of the greatest dangers to Jewish faith and Jewish thought is the fundamentalist tendency that occasionally manifests itself (in our own time, as in others) and that seeks to freeze doctrine at a particular point. Such fundamentalism, which often claims to rest on a literal reading of the texts, is alien to the dominant tendencies of Jewish intellectual history. It ignores the obvious fact that we have no literal uninterpreted texts, and seeks to arrogate to a position of authoritative permanence particular views that are themselves only one more interpretation of Jewish doctrine. In denying to Judaism the flexibility to retain its essential nature while at the same time using the freedom of interpretation to come to terms with the world of contemporary ideas, this fundamentalism is not only unfaithful to the whole tenor of Jewish thought but also poses a serious threat to the ability of Judaism to survive.

Religious fundamentalism has as its counterpart a kind of secularist fundamentalism that is equally insensitive to the fact that we are always dependent on and involved in processes of interpretation. This secularist fundamentalism sometimes masquerades under the guise of being purely scientific in character. It is, in fact, a caricature of science, just as Jewish fundamentalism is a caricature of historic Judaism. It stems from a desire for the perfect security that it hopes will come to us if we are able to reduce all human knowledge to a single plane and to restrict ourselves to a single authorized method for pursuing and establishing all claims to knowledge. This goal was brilliantly expounded and defended in the seventeenth century by the great philosopher-mathematician Gottfried Wilhelm Leibniz. In a youthful essay, one of many that he wrote on the subject, Leibniz set forth his general plan for a universal system of notation in which all subject matters could be adequately expressed. This system was to be mathematical in character, so that all differences of opinion about any matter whatsoever would be subject to resolution by mathematical means. Leibniz assures us that when the universal characteristic has been invented, and when we learn to apply it with proper skill, there will no longer be room or occasion for the interminable disputes to which we are accustomed among thinkers in the various fields of human inquiry. A dispute between philosophers, he says, will become simply a dispute between bookkeepers, or, to read him more literally and with admiration at his prophetic foresight, a dispute between computers. The parties who have a complex issue about which they differ "will only have to take pens in hand, seat themselves at their counting-boards, and say to each other, 'Let us calculate.'"[1] Although Leibniz himself was extremely interested in the advancement of religion, metaphysics, and ethics as well as logic, mathematics, and the natural sciences, he nevertheless left us a heritage that set monistic reductionism as its intellectual ideal. At its worst, that reductionism has taken the form of a scientistic fundamentalism that claims to know the world with certainty. This kind of science ignores the extent to which it engages in more than pure observation and forgets that there are no uninterpreted data. It denies all exegesis, or what amounts to the same, recognizes only one official authorized interpretation of the data available to us. As such, it claims, in effect, to be in exclusive possession of the truth, or, at least, of the only way to truth, and denies the possibility or legitimacy of alternate ways.

All responsible scientific thought is aware that, in fact, there is no more possibility of dispensing with exegesis in the sciences than there is in the treatment of religious texts. For the true scientist the world is a text that needs both to be discovered and interpreted, and often the discovery is the interpretation. Like his counterparts in the world of religious thought, he works with a combination of tradition and freedom. Were he to cut himself off totally from the established ways of scientific thought and understanding, he would lack an operating framework. Were he to insist on a fundamentalist literalism that makes the framework of his time permanently fixed, he would prevent his science from developing and from speaking meaningfully to its own age. As one of the most distinguished contemporary historians of science expresses it:

> Observation and experience can and must drastically restrict the range of admissible scientific belief, else there would be no science. But they cannot alone determine a particular body of such belief. An apparently arbitrary element, compounded of personal and historical accident, is always a formative ingredient of the beliefs espoused by a given scientific community at a given time.[2]

He goes on to argue that all scientific research is affected by the professional education of the scientist in question. That education has provided him with certain modes of thought and understanding that Thomas Kuhn calls "normal research activity." He describes this as a strenuous and devoted attempt to force nature into the conceptual boxes supplied by professional education. We shall wonder whether research could proceed without such boxes, whatever the element of arbitrariness in their historic origins, and, occasionally, in their subsequent development. Normal science, for example, often suppresses fundamental novelties because they are necessarily subversive of its basic commitments. Nevertheless, so long as those commitments retain an element of the arbitrary, the very nature of normal research ensures that novelty shall not be suppressed for very long.[3]

A slavishly conservative adherence to the currently established ways of viewing things would end all scientific progress. A total rejection of all that is currently held to be known would paralyze all efforts at understanding. Science, as we know it today, moves from the established to the novel, using its own techniques of interpretation and discovery. Judaism, I shall argue, does precisely the same with its materials, and it is by the use of the various modes of textual interpretation that Judaism retains its power to be faithful to its past while, at the same time, coming to terms with the secular world in which it lives. It is in this way that it becomes possible for Jewish faith and secular science to live together in harmony. Each rests, in part, on the legitimacy and inescapable necessity of exegesis and in interpretation.

As a first step we must see whether Jewish teaching recognizes as legitimate and proper an independent secular realm. In particular, we must ask what status and authority Judaism gives to knowledge that we gain through reason alone or through scientific inquiry. We must, however, begin with a caveat. The richness and diversity of views that have emerged over many centuries of Jewish tradition are so great that it is irresponsible to speak of what Judaism teaches. All we claim to do is to establish that within the official literature some of the most respected and recognized rabbinic teachers of various periods of Jewish history have affirmed the propriety of accepting as true what we learn through the natural sciences. Though other opposed views could be cited, my contention is that those which I shall present are widely held and are a thoroughly legitimate version of Jewish doctrine.

There were some eminent talmudic sages who did not hesitate to affirm the truth of scientific claims although they contradicted the then accepted Jewish views. Their position seems to have been that in such matters the best evidence must be accepted, whatever its source. The Talmud records, for example, a discussion concerning an astronomical question on which the Jewish authorities held a different view from that current among the non-Jewish astronomers. Our printed texts record that Rabbi Judah the Prince sought to defend the standard Jewish view but that he failed. In a reading that we no longer have, but that was available to Maimonides, the text says explicitly, "The gentile sages vanquished the sages of Israel." In another reading, that of Rabbi Isaac Arama in his *Akedat Yizhak,* the passage says, "The sages of Israel admitted their error." Later in that same talmudic passage there is a second discussion of a similar question, now concerning the course of the sun, and this time all the texts carry the statement that Rabbi Judah the Prince said, "Their view is preferable to ours." It would appear that they did not consider such matters open to purely internal Jewish resolution, but rather held that the best evidence and the most persuasive arguments must prevail.

This openness to scientific knowledge, whatever its source, has not been the universal Jewish attitude. At a later time there were Jewish authorities who simply could not accept the idea that there could be non-Jewish doctrines even on such scientific matters that were true while the teachings of the sages of Israel were in error. Rabbenu Tam (c. I 100- 1 17 1), the grandson of Rashi, is reported to have explained the talmudic passage that we cited above in the following way. "Though, at the time, the gentile scholars prevailed over the sages of Israel, this was only a rhetorical victory which stemmed from the fact that they offered superior arguments [which the Jewish scholars did not know how to refute]. However, the truth of the matter is still that which was taught by the sages of Israel."[5]

In contrast with this strong feeling that even on scientific matters Jews must seek their own internal truth, Maimonides sees in the talmudic passage in question a model case for the principle that we should be controlled only by the best arguments and the best evidence, not by any respect for eminent Jewish figures and their revered traditions. "For everyone who argues in speculative matters," he says, "does this according to the conclusions to which he was led by his speculation. Hence the conclusion whose demonstration is correct is believed."[6] In a later passage he affirms even more explicitly that in astronomy we have no obligation to accept any traditional Jewish teachings. The sages of Israel, we now know, were mistaken in some of their views about astronomy. This is due, Maimonides believes, to the fact that the general development of mathematics was in a fairly primitive state in talmudic times, hence, they lacked an essential tool for achieving sound astronomical knowledge. We should not be troubled or ill at ease when we are forced to reject talmudic teaching concerning scientific issues, since when the Rabbis dealt with such questions, "they did not speak about this as transmitters of dicta of the prophets, but rather because in those times they were men of knowledge in these fields or because they had heard these dicta from the men of knowledge who lived in those times."[7] For Maimonides, there is no authoritative prophetic teaching about the natural world that we must view as binding on faithful Jews. On the contrary, when the sages of Israel made scientific judgments it was not in their role as the official transmitters of prophetic teaching but only as men of science or the pupils of men of science. As such, their only claim to authority is the evidence they can marshal in behalf of their doctrines. If at any time their evidence is superseded by superior evidence and argument, we are, of course, bound to accept that view for which the best evidence is offered, no matter who its author. As Maimonides puts it in an early work, "One should accept the truth from whatever source it proceeds."[8]

The extent to which Maimonides succeeded in establishing his principle is eloquently clear when we see that a nineteenth century orthodox Bible commentator approached Maimonides' science with exactly the same critical attitude that Maimonides evinced toward the science of the ancient Jewish sages. Rabbi Meir Loeb Malbim opens his commentary on the Book of Ezekiel with a brief introduction in which he explains that we can no longer accept Maimonides' interpretation of the Chariot Vision because it is based on a natural science and philosophy that are outdated. Maimonides bases his conclusions, says Malbim, on principles that "have all been undermined by developments in scientific research in recent times. This research has given us an astronomy and other natural sciences which rest on foundations which are both stronger and more reliable." Here we have an instance of a recent exegetical work, fully accepted in the most orthodox Jewish circles, which acknowledges that even in the case of so sensitive a text we must adjust our religious understanding to the best scientific information we have, rather than the reverse.

Although trust in the independence of rational inquiry and scientific research experienced varying fortunes in Jewish intellectual history, its strongest support came from the philosophers. In the philosophic literature we consistently find reason defended and praised as a sound independent source of human knowledge. Though this defense is often coupled with the assurance that religious teaching is in accord with the dictates of reason, it still lays great stress on the duty to pursue rational inquiry. A typical statement is that of Saadia Gaon, who assures us that "the Bible is not the sole basis of our religion, for in addition to it we have two other bases. One of these is anterior to it; namely, the fountain of reason. The second is posterior to it; namely, the source of tradition. Whatever, therefore, we may not find in the Bible, we can find in the two other sources."[9] Saadia's belief in the primacy of reason is cited with approval by Bahya ibn Paquda in the introduction to his *Hovot Ha-Levavot* and is echoed also in the *Kuzari* of Judah Halevi.[10] It is surely reasonable to suppose that these thinkers, and others like them, would have the same confidence in natural science, if they were living today, that they had in the powers of reason in their own time. It is equally reasonable to suppose that they would be sensitive, as well, to the limitations of science, and would recognize the extent to which the sciences themselves depend on interpretation.

The accepted methods for accommodating the Torah to a diversity of doctrinal positions are exegesis and interpretation. The range of interpretation often seems virtually unlimited, especially when we are dealing with narrative or aggadic passages, with matters of doctrine rather than with questions of practical law. A Midrash compares the interpretation of Torah texts to the interpretation of dreams. "Behold, it says, 'A dream carries much implication' (Eccles. 5:2). Now by using the method of *kal vahomer* we may reason: If the contents of dreams which have no effect may yield a multitude of interpretations, how much more then should the important contents of the Torah imply many interpretations in every verse."[11] This principle is based on the biblical verse, "Is not my word like as fire, saith the Lord; and like a hammer that breaketh the rock in pieces?" (Jer. 23:29). The Rabbis interpreted this to mean that just as the hammer breaks the rock into many pieces, so is the Torah (God's word) open to a multiplicity of interpretations.[12] Especially in the realm of Aggada, though not exclusively there, Jewish tradition kept the gates of interpretation wide open.

A few specific examples, chosen from the very many that are readily available, will show us to what extent free interpretation is normal Jewish practice. It is widely taken for granted in the tradition that the *locus classicus* that provides us with the ideological and juridical model for conversion to the Jewish faith is the case of Ruth. In the standard interpretation of the events, Ruth, a pagan Moabite woman, was married to the Jew, Mahlon. She remained a pagan until after her husband's death when she chose to accompany her mother-in-law, Naomi, back to the land of Israel. At that time she was formally converted to Judaism. Ruth's declaration of adherence to the faith and people of Naomi was, in the view of the Rabbis, a model of proper religious conversion. Ruth pleads with Naomi to be allowed to accompany her, and declares, "For whither thou goest, I will go; and where thou lodgest, I will lodge; thy people shall be my people, and thy God my God" (Ruth 1: 16). In the Talmud this is interpreted as pointing to the various detailed steps involved in the process of becoming converted to the Jewish faith.[13] That talmudic interpretation is rarely disputed in the traditional literature. Yet, no less a figure than Abraham ibn Ezra categorically rejects this line of interpretation. According to ibn Ezra, despite what the Talmud has to say, Ruth and Orpah were both converted before they married Mahlon and Chilion. For, says ibn Ezra, it is unthinkable that Jews of such distinguished position would have married unconverted gentile women. "It is not possible that Mahlon and Chilion married these women before they were converted."[14] His case rests, initially, on his own understanding of the facts, and he then proceeds to read the verses in the text to conform with his view. Thus, he construes Orpah's leaving as an abandonment of her Jewish faith, and Ruth's moving declaration as a reaffirmation of that Jewish faith which she had accepted prior to her marriage. Ibn Ezra feels no need to apologize for or to justify his rejection of a standard talmudic-midrashic tradition, for the gates of interpretation and exegesis are open.

We find similar diversity in the case of the identity of the Cushite woman whom Moses married.[15] Now the explanation of what took place in this episode is not to be treated lightly. It is of high importance since it has to do with the life story, the personal behavior, and the moral standards of the supreme prophet, Moses. We need to know what seeming impropriety in his behavior evoked both the open criticism by his brother, Aaron, and his sister, Miriam, and God's high praise and fierce defense of him. One might have expected that about so grave a matter there would be a single fixed tradition. Instead, there are at least two lines of interpretation, very different in character and with very different moral implications. One line holds that the reference to the Cushite woman simply is another way of speaking of Zipporah, the wife of Moses, whom we know from the Bible. She is called Cushite, either because she was in fact dark-skinned, or else because she was so beautiful that she was referred to euphemistically by an opposite term, just as Job's wife urges him to "Bless God and die," when she means, "Curse God and die."[16] In this case, Moses is accused of having abandoned his wife, who is both virtuous and beautiful, so that he might devote himself completely to his career as prophet, without being encumbered by family responsibilities. Moreover, there is the suggestion that he is motivated by a desire to emphasize his special holiness and purity, a kind of posing that Miriam and Aaron find offensive. A second line of interpretation bases itself on a legend that Moses served as king of Ethiopia for forty years, during the period after his flight from Egypt and before he appeared in Midian. In Ethiopia he was given a royal wife, who is the "Cushite woman whom he married."[17] Miriam and Aaron speak against him for reasons that are connected with this Ethiopian woman, but we are not told precisely what their complaint is.

Our understanding of the charge against Moses, which is never made explicit in the Bible itself, depends on which of the two versions we accept. Though we are dealing with the life of the supreme prophet, there is no attempt to limit our interpretation to a single authorized version. On the contrary, the two versions literally live side by side in the various editions of *the Mikraot Gedolot.* There are three Targum versions of the text in the standard printed editions. The first, Onkelos, translates "Cushite woman" as "beautiful woman," with no further comment. Targum Yerushalmi I (Pseudo-Jonathan) construes the passage as referring specifically to

Zipporah, but Targum Yerushalmi II construes it as referring to the Ethiopian queen whom Moses is supposed to have married. Ibn Ezra mentions this last view, but rejects it. Rashi interprets the passage as referring to only Zipporah, but his grandson Rashbam insists that only the Ethiopian queen could possibly be intended here and those who hold that the Cushite woman is Zipporah (and his grandfather Rashi is among them) are simply in error. All this can be found on a single page of the standard Pentateuch with commentaries regularly used by pious Jews to this day. What is instructive is the fact that such opposed ways of understanding the text can and do live side by side without generating any tension or uneasiness. This is possible only because of the deeply rooted principle in the Jewish tradition that there is no single fixed way of understanding the text. The gates of interpretation are open and it is fully proper to go through various gates, at different times and for different purposes.

Lest it be thought that the cases we have cited deal with matters of little practical consequence and only for that reason are they open to a variety of interpretations, let us consider another case that is unquestionably of major practical importance in determining the way in which a Jew should live his life. Does Judaism approve, perhaps even require, ascetic self-denial, does it permit it grudgingly, or does it condemn such a life pattern? The model case is that of the Nazirite, whose vows include among other restrictions, abstinence from "wine and strong drink." [18] How does the Jewish tradition regard his abstinence? Because he has voluntarily denied himself that which is permitted is he a man of superior virtue, or is he a sinner? Should we imitate him, or should we shun his ways? Now it should be made clear that so far as the practical laws of the Nazirite are concerned there is no problem. Once he has made his vow the law is clear as to what he may and may not do, what the standard term of his vow is, what offerings he must bring and under what circumstances. Yet, with respect to the wider question of what value we should put on his asceticism there is deep disagreement. In a familiar passage in the Talmud the asceticism of the Nazirite is severely condemned. "R. Elazar ha-Kappar, Berabbi, said: Why does Scripture say, 'And make atonement for him, for that he sinned by reason of the soul' (Num. 6:11). Against what 'soul' did he then sin? It can only be because he denied himself wine. If then this man who denied himself only wine is termed a sinner, how much more does one sin who is an ascetic in all things!"[19] For this reason, it is held, a Nazirite who becomes impure must bring a special sin-offering, since he is now required to extend the term of his abstinence. The Tosafot comment that he is guilty because he "extends the fixed period of his suffering during which he suffers the pain of abstinence from wine."[20] Asceticism is clearly condemned here as undesirable self-denial that is contrary to good Jewish practice. The ascetic is judged guilty of sin, and the more he extends his asceticism the greater his sin. Some contemporary scholars are so certain that this negative attitude toward asceticism is normative that they simply declare without qualification that, "The Nazirite was severely discouraged by the rabbis since asceticism was against the spirit of Judaism".

Yet, in the Talmud itself there is also a quite different view of asceticism. In another passage where the same statement of Rabbi Elazar ha-Kappar is cited, there follows a disagreement. The other view holds that the Nazirite is called "holy" in Scripture because his self-denial is a mark of special piety. Asceticism is represented as an ideal to be imitated and admired, for, "If this man who denied himself only wine is termed holy, how much more so he who denies himself the enjoyment of ever so many things."[22] The one qualification seems to be that he who takes the vows of an ascetic must be confident that he has the capacity successfully to endure his self-affliction, otherwise he might well turn into a violator of his vows or even a bitter denier of God. This praise of ascetic self-denial as a state of superior holiness is taken up by certain medieval authorities. Maimonides, for example, ends his codification of the laws of the Nazirite with high praise for one who makes Nazirite vows with complete sincerity. Such a man rises, in Maimonides' view, to a special level of holiness, and has merit equal to that of a prophet. In his philosophic work Maimonides maintains the same position. He praises the Nazirite for abstaining from wine, "which has caused the ruin of the ancients and the moderns. Whoever avoids it is called holy and is put in the same rank as a High Priest as far as holiness is concerned."[24] Nahmanides, in his commentary on the Pentateuch, explains that the sin offering that the Nazirite is required to bring when he completes the term of his vow is an atonement for the fact that his period of abstinence has come to an end. Directly contradicting Tosafot, Nahmanides says that ideally he should remain in the ascetic state of Nazirite holiness permanently. When at the end of his fixed time as a Nazirite, he reverts to an ordinary nonascetic pattern of life, he is considered a sinner who must offer a sin-offering as atonement. Here we have a case where practical consequences ensue from general attitudes. Yet, even in this case, different patterns of interpretation are permitted, and with them the different practical ideals they imply.

There were important rabbinic authorities who evinced deep opposition to the openness of interpretation that we have described. They directed their attack in particular against the Aggada, because they saw that with respect to the interpretation of aggadic texts only a very low degree of control is possible. Despite the long history of differing decisions and rulings with respect to the practical law, the law does tend to become fixed and crystallized. On the other hand, the Aggada tends to have almost unlimited flexibility, and in the interpretation of any given text it accommodates an astounding variety of doctrines, attitudes, and ideals. There were those who saw in this openness a danger to sound doctrine and the possibility of both intellectual and spiritual corruption. They were fierce in their expressions of opposition to those who occupied themselves with Aggada. In one passage the danger of Aggada is established by showing that by its methods it is possible to interpret a single biblical verse in directly contradictory ways. Rabbi Zeira concludes that the Aggada is unstructured, that it turns true teaching upside down, and that one cannot extract sound doctrine from it. For that reason he strongly advises his son to give up all study of Aggada and devote himself rather to the Halakha, which is alone sound and reliable. In another such passage, we are warned that dire consequences and a divine curse await those who occupy themselves with the Aggada.[26]

Notwithstanding these instances of intense opposition to preoccupation with the Aggada, throughout most of the Jewish tradition the principle of free exegesis, especially of aggadic materials, prevails. Perhaps the tone and mood that dominates Jewish tradition is best expressed in a Midrash on the verse, "The voice of the Lord is according to the strength" (Ps. 29:4). The Midrash stresses the point that the verse reads, "according to *the* strength" and not "according to *His* strength." Had it contained the latter reading, we might conclude that God speaks to all men in a single voice and in a single language. If that were the case, only those who could hear and understand would know Him, whereas those who could not hear or failed to understand would be cut off from Him. The Midrash teaches that, on the contrary, God addresses us in such way that each individual may hear him in accordance with his own particular capacity. Even at Sinai "the divine voice went forth to all Israel and was assimilated by each person in accordance with his particular capacity-the elders in their own way, the youth in their own way, the children in their own way, the sucklings in their own way, the women in their own way, and also Moses in his own way...

For this reason it is written, 'The voice of the Lord is according to *the* strength' and not 'according to *His* strength' to teach us that each one grasps His message according to his own particular power and capacity."[27] This conviction that the one divine truth may be apprehended and expressed in a variety of ways runs very deep in the Jewish tradition. It serves as the ground on which freedom of interpretation rests.

The joining together of respect for secular knowledge and open exegesis leads often to new, sometimes even startling, readings of the biblical text itself. Perhaps most striking is the introduction into Judaism of the doctrine that God is absolutely incorporeal, a doctrine that appears to run directly counter to a simple literal reading of the Bible. It is true that the Bible appears to be ambiguous on the subject of God's corporeality. On the one hand, there is the very strong prohibition against any representation of the divine in a physical form. There is no need to cite the numerous passages, in the Ten Commandments and elsewhere, that express revulsion at the very idea of a statue or picture of God. At the same time, it can hardly be denied that the Bible does speak of God anthropomorphically and anthropopathically. Although some of the biblical writers are engaged in a struggle against actual idolaters or those who attempt to represent the true God by way of a physical form, the later Jewish generations have to come to terms not with actual idolatry, but with the language of the Bible. One can discern a steady movement from earlier periods with their relatively mild attempts to interpret the anthropomorphisms in ways that blunt their offensive uses to the totally unrestrained attack that the medieval philosophers unleashed on any attempt to read the anthropomorphic passages literally.

In the case of the philosophic interpretations, which have since become normative in Jewish religious thought, we see a model of how secular learning and the biblical text were brought together through the devices of textual interpretation. Unlike the earlier Jewish teachers, who objected to literalizing the anthropomorphisms on purely religious grounds, the medieval philosophers based their objections primarily on the grounds of purely secular philosophic knowledge. They held that reason teaches that God is incorporeal, and this secular source of knowledge was decisive for them. Given their conviction that rational argument establishes beyond all question the fact of God's incorporeality, they read the Bible mindful of a secular doctrine that controlled their interpretation. For these Jewish thinkers it was axiomatic that if the Bible is to be accepted as a source of truth, then it must conform to the principles of reason. If it seems to contradict the truths of reason, then we must read it in such way as to make it harmonize, for only by way of such a non-literal reading will we be able to uncover the true teaching of Scripture. Saadia Gaon expressed the point with complete clarity when he said, "For all divine attributes pertaining to either substance or accident that are encountered in the books of the prophets it is necessary to find in the language of Scripture non-anthropomorphic meanings that would be in keeping with the requirements of reason."[28] What should be especially noted is his explicit statement that Scripture must be read in accordance "with the requirements of reason." That is to say, the sacred text and secular knowledge are brought into harmony by interpreting the text so that it will conform to the results of rational reflection. The text is not to be construed as meaning what it literally says, for it simply cannot mean what it appears to say. Non-literal interpretation is not only permitted; it is mandatory. In the most extreme case we have the legal ruling of Maimonides that one who reads such texts literally, and thus attributes to God corporeal qualities, is guilty of heresy. "Five classes are termed heretics [*minim*]... He who says there is one Supreme Being but that He is a body and has a shape."[29] Despite the outcry of Rabad, contained in his gloss on this passage, that those who hold such a view cannot be called heretics because they are simply following a literal reading of Scripture and Aggada, the bulk of opinion would tend to support Maimonides. Even Rabad, while defending them from charges of heresy, explains the views of these people as resulting from their dependence on *dibre ha-aggadot ha-meshabbeshot et ha-de'ot,* "the words of the *aggadot* which confuse (or corrupt) sound beliefs."[30] Though he is reluctant to go to the extreme of excluding such people from the community of the faithful, Rabad recognizes that they are misled into holding a false doctrine because they read the texts literally, rather than interpreting them in accordance with the teachings that are set down by reason. Even he accepts the principle that we must interpret texts in a non-literal way if that is required by sound rational doctrine.

Let us consider a final case that will show how deeply committed Jewish tradition is to the processes of textual interpretation as a way of bringing together the worlds of secular learning and the teachings of religious faith. If we examine briefly the treatments of the problem of creation, that is, whether God created the world *ex nihilo* or out of a prime matter that is eternal, we can see how the secular and the sacred are brought together. The scriptural text is ambiguous on this point. It simply announces that God created the world, but it tells us nothing about the process of creation. We are only informed that it took place by divine fiat. Yet, by rabbinic times the doctrine of creation out of nothing was very deeply rooted in Jewish thought. E. E. Urbach holds that there is no suggestion among the Tannaim of the doctrine that the world was created from an eternal prime matter.[31] Whether the propagation of the doctrine of *creatio ex nihilo* was part of a polemic against gnosticism, whether it had its roots in some other source or motive, is a problem that lies beyond the limits of the present discussion. What is clear, however, is that, with minor exceptions, it became a standard Jewish doctrine, and the biblical texts were interpreted in accordance with this doctrine.

When we turn to the philosophers, and I refer, of course, only to philosophers who are recognized as Jewish authorities, we find a rather different situation. Saadia stays firmly within the rabbinic tradition. He holds that the doctrine of creation out of nothing is fully established by a set of sound philosophic arguments. When the philosophic evidence is added to the force of the tradition that also supports this doctrine, he is left with no doubt that all the scriptural texts teach only this view. In Scripture "our Lord, exalted be He, made it known to us that all things were created and that He had created them out of nothing. Thus Scripture says: In the beginning God created the heaven and the earth (Gen. 1:1)... Besides that, all this was verified for us by Him by means of miracles and marvels, so that we accepted it as true."[31] (We should note that the evidence about miracles is itself derived only from Scripture.) For Saadia, the scriptural verses are to be understood in only one particular way, despite their patent ambiguity, because both the tradition and reason require it. This being the case, we must then interpret any biblical passage that seems to cast doubt on creation out of nothing in such way that it conforms with this doctrine. And that is exactly what Saadia does.

Later philosophers were far less certain than Saadia that the philosophic issue was settled. They were aware that alternate lines of philosophic reasoning were possible, and that it was difficult to provide definitive proof of the doctrine of creation out of nothing. Thus, Judah Halevi held a far less fixed position. He recognized that there were no decisive philosophic arguments that could settle the question as to whether the world was created or eternal. Consequently, though for himself he accepted the traditional view, he did not read out of the faith or accuse of irreparable error those Jews who believed in the eternity of matter. As he puts it:

> The question of eternity and creation is obscure, whilst the arguments are evenly balanced. The theory of creation derives greater weight from the prophetic tradition of Adam, Noah, and Moses, which is more deserving of credence than conclusions reached only by speculation. Nevertheless, if a follower of the Torah finds himself compelled to believe by rational argument that there is an eternal matter and that many worlds preceded our present world, this would not constitute a major defect in his faith, since he could still believe that the present world was created at a particular time and that Adam and Noah were among the first men.[33]

Tradition teaches us one way to understand the scriptural passages concerning creation, and philosophical speculation suggests another possible way. Halevi inclines toward tradition, since the philosophic arguments are not demonstratively certain. At the same time, he accepts the legitimacy of the nontraditional view, and by implication admits that Scripture could be interpreted to conform with it.

The classic statement of this position was set forth by Maimonides. He examined all the arguments for creation and for eternity, and concluded that none was decisive. Since there were no compelling rational grounds for choosing between opposed views, he held that it was legitimate to make a decision on other grounds. Because other aspects of religious faith would be deeply and adversely affected by the acceptance of the eternity of matter, Maimonides opts for the theory of creation out of nothing. However, he makes a strong and explicit point of saying that were there any decisive philosophic-scientific evidence for the eternity of matter, he would accept it without hesitation, and would be able with no difficulty to interpret Scripture accordingly. He assures his readers "that our shunning the affirmation of the eternity of the world is not due to a text figuring in the Torah according to which the world has been produced in time. For the texts indicating that the world has been produced in time are not more numerous than those indicating that the deity is a body. Nor are the gates of figurative interpretation shut in our faces or impossible of access to us regarding the subject of the creation of the world in time. For we could interpret them as figurative, as we have done when denying His corporealty."[34]

Here the point is made openly and without any ambiguity. Secular knowledge, if it is based on sound evidence such as should properly persuade any rational man, must command our assent. Whenever we have such knowledge we must proceed to understand Scripture so as to conform to it, and it is our right, perhaps even our duty, to interpret Scripture in such way that it accords with philosophic understanding and scientific knowledge.

The issue becomes even more pointed when we come to Gersonides in the fourteenth century. He openly affirms the Platonic theory of creation, which asserts that there is an eternal unformed prime matter out of which the world is formed by God. Though he runs counter to the vast bulk of the rabbinic tradition as well as to the Jewish philosophic tradition, Gersonides feels no hesitation about affirming his view. Moreover, he assures us that a correct interpretation of Scripture will support the claim that this is the doctrine of creation that is taught in the Bible. How could it be otherwise, since this theory of creation, Gersonides believes, is shown to be true for science and philosophy, and the Torah neither teaches nor requires us to believe that which is false.[35] It follows, therefore, that having discovered through science and philosophy a doctrine that we are convinced is demonstratively certain, we are justified in our confidence that any sound interpretation of Scripture will construe it so as to show that it accords with such doctrine.

The various essays in this volume exemplify the principle that we have set forth and explicated here. They approach problems of Jewish ethics with full respect for the tradition, and yet with confidence that the tradition is responsive to values and knowledge that come to it from outside its own boundaries. Like Jewish thinkers and teachers of all ages they rely on the devices of exegesis and interpretation to bring together the ideas and values of the contemporary world and the world of classical Judaism. Free exegesis serves as the bridge that connects the fixed tradition with changing ideas, with different times, different places, and different ways of understanding the world.

If we had no regard for Jewish tradition, we would no longer justly claim that our views are authentically Jewish. If we had only a rigidly fixed tradition we could not survive as thinking Jews in a world that grows and changes. It is our aim to remain faithful to our tradition while using its commitment to the openness of interpretation to bring to it the best insights and achievements of the human spirit in our time. Such freedom admittedly involves a serious risk that we may lose our connection with Jewish tradition and fall into a pure secularism to which we wrongly attach the label "Jewish". It is a risk to which we expose ourselves with appropriate concern, but with the conviction that as faithful Jews we have no choice. A Judaism that would demand of us the sacrifice of secular learning or intellectual integrity would betray its own highest principles and could no longer command our loyalty. Whatever the differences of doctrine among the contributors to this volume, all affirm the rabbinic teaching that "The seal of the Holy One, blessed be He, is truth."[36] It is on that ground that we come together to explore from a variety of perspectives the ways in which Judaism and contemporary thought may be joined. Even those of us who are firm in their adherence to Jewish law and consider it to be fixed and binding recognize that there is a very wide range in the ways in which we may legitimately understand Judaism and interpret its fundamental ideas.

NOTES

[1] G. W. Leibnitz, "De Scientia Universali seu Calculo Philosophico," *Opera Philosophica,* ed. J. E. Erdmann (Berlin, 1840), pp. 82 85 (author's translation).
[2] Thomas S. Kuhn, *The Structure of Scientific Revolutions* (Chicago, 1962), p. 4.
[3] *Ibid.*, p. 5.
[4] *Pesahim,* 94b. For the alternate readings see Maimonides, *Guide of the Perplexed,* 11:8 and Isaac Arama, *Akedat Yizhak,* Bo, sec. 37. For a discussion of the problem of the alternate readings and of the rabbinic attitude on this question, see *Moreh Nebuchim* (ed. Yehuda ibn Shemuel), 11:8, p. 129, fn. 4, where additional references are also given.
[5] Cited in *Shila Mekubbezet to Ketubot* 13b.
[6] Maimonides, *Guide of the Perplexed,* II:8.
[7] *Ibid.*, III:14(end).
[8] Maimonides, *Eight Chapters,* ed. Gorfinkle (New York, 1912; repr. 1966), Foreword, p. 36.
[9] Saadia Gaon, *The Book of Beliefs and Opinions,* trans. Samuel Rosenblatt (New Haven, 1948), III: 10, p. 174.
[10] Cf. *Kuzari,* I:67.
[11] *Midrash Haggadol Bereshith* (ed. Schechter), p. xxv; ibid. (ed. Margulies), p. 39. Cited in Saul Lieberman, *Hellenism in Jewish Palestine (New* York, 1950), p. 70.
[12] Cf. Rashi to Gen. 33:20 and *Shabbat* 88b.
[13] *Yebamoth,* 47b. Cf. Targum to Ruth 1:4,5,10, and 16, which explicitly states that they are gentile women and that Ruth was converted after her husband's death.
[14] Abraham ibn Ezra, Commentary to Ruth 1:2.
[15] Num. 12:1.
[16] Job 2:9.
[17] For a detailed discussion see Louis Ginzberg, *The Legends of the Jews* (Philadelphia, 1946), vol. 2, pp. 286-89; vol. 5, note 80, pp. 407- 10; vol. 6, note 488, p. 90.
[18] Num. 6:3.
[19] *Nazir,* 19a (Soncino translation).
[20] *Ibid., Tosafol,* s v., *V'hainu Ta'ama.*
[21] *Encyclopaedia Judaica,* vol. 12, p. 909-
[22] *Ta'anith,* II b.
[23] *M T, Nezirut, 10:14.*
[24] *Guide of the Perplexed,* III:48 (end).
[25] *P. T. Ma'asrot,* III: 10, 5 1a.
[26] *P. T. Shabbat,* XVI: I, 15c. It may be that the stress in this passage is on a prohibition against writing Aggada, as is suggested by the parallel passage in *Soferim,* XVI:2; however, it is clear from the context that beyond a desire to restrict Aggada to an oral form there is also a deep distrust of Aggada in general.
[27] *Shemot Rabbah,* V:9. Cf. *Mekhilta, Bahodesh* 9 (ed. Horovitz-Rabin), p. 235.
[28] Saadia Gaon, *The Book of Beliefs and Opinions,* ed. Rosenblatt (New Haven, 1948), II:8, pp. 111-12; cf. 11:3, p. 100. For Saadia's extended discussion of the conditions under which Scripture should be read nonliterally, cf. VII:2, pp. 265-67.
[29] *M T, Teshubah,* III:7.
[30] *Hassagot ha-Rabad, ad loc.*
[31] E. E. Urbach, *Hazal: Pirke Emunot V'Deot* (Jerusalem, 1969), pp. 168-69.

[32] *The Book of Beliefs and Opinions,* I: 1, p. 40.
[33] Judah Halevi, *Kuzari,* I, 67.
[34] *Guide of the Perplexed,* II:25.
[35] Levi ben Gerson, *Milhamot Ha-Shem,* VI:2, 1.
[36] *Shabbat, 55a; Sanhedrin,* 64a; for a somewhat different, but instructive formulation, cf. *Yoma,* 69b.

25

THE PHILOSOPHICAL FOUNDATIONS OF JEWISH ETHICS: SOME INITIAL REFLECTIONS

The literature of Jewish ethics is, for the most part, not philosophical. We have large numbers of moralistic treatises which are primarily aimed at guiding the reader to living a virtuous life, but relatively few systematic treatments of the theoretical foundations of Jewish ethics. Even the occasional efforts in this direction, such as Maimonides' Eight Chapters, tend to be limited in scope. There are no works which focus on the theoretical foundations of Jewish ethics which are in any way comparable to such major works as Aristotle's *Nicomachean Ethics* or Kant's *Critique of Practical Reason.* While we have studies of the first rank in both quality and comprehensiveness in the field of Jewish law and in the traditional types of *mussar* literature, the basic philosophical work on Jewish ethics still remains to be done. In the present study, I attempt one small and preliminary step in the direction of fulfilling this need. I shall point out some of the problems that face us and some of the tasks that must be done if we are to have a comprehensive philosophical account of Jewish ethics. To illustrate what I believe to be the types of issues which must occupy our attention, I shall discuss some substantive questions of Jewish ethics. These discussions, however, should be seen as little more than a preliminary approach to a subject which requires far more study and far more extended examination than is possible here.

I

Perhaps the most common error in dealing with our subject is the tendency to treat Jewish ethics as if it were a single homogeneous body of doctrine and practical instruction. There is, in fact, not one Jewish ethic, but varieties of Jewish ethics. Important differences can sometimes be found among the teachings of various Jewish moralists who are contemporaries. There are, further, diversities of doctrine and practice as one moves from one era to another and from one part of the world to another. A conservative approach to Jewish legal teaching may have held these differences to severe limits in the sphere of the law itself, but they become strikingly evident when we move from the legal codes and rulings to statements of the moral concerns which underlie these codes. Both with respect to the practical guidance of human behavior and with respect to the theoretical foundations on which the ethical rests, recognized Jewish teachers have differed significantly. Consequently, when we study Jewish ethics we must be aware of the range of doctrine and practice which legitimately falls under the rubric "Jewish."

Evidence of these diverse ethical positions is readily available. To begin with the classic sources, it is arguable that a careful consideration of the written Torah and the oral Torah reveals (at least from an extra-dogmatic perspective), that they often reflect strikingly different value orientations. This is exemplified in a general way in the following statement in the Talmud: "Why were the bazaars of Beth Hini destroyed? Because they based their actions upon Scripture."[1] As Rashi notes, they found support in Scripture to permit that which had been forbidden by rabbinic legislation. Here we have a case where Scripture is seen as more lenient than the decisions of the Rabbis, and the transgression of the people of Beth Hini consisted in their using Scripture to justify their actions. There are, of course, numerous counter-instances in which rabbinic legislation tempered the rigors of the literal sense of pentateuchal law.

Perhaps most instructive for our purpose are those cases in which the same rules of scriptural law are treated in directly opposed ways by the legal authorities, as they seek to achieve what they consider to be desirable ends. Consider how the laws of evidence are interpreted in the case of *agunah*, the deserted wife, on the one hand, and in cases of capital crimes, on the other. Scriptural law is quite explicit in demanding that at least two witnesses are required in order to establish a valid body of testimony. It is also clear that a married woman is free to remarry only if she has a valid divorce from her husband or if there is legally acceptable testimony that her husband is dead. Yet, as is well known, talmudic legislation and all subsequent Jewish law consciously adopted especially lenient rules of evidence in order to save women from becoming *agunot*. The rabbinic authorities could not accept as morally sound a situation in which women would lead lives of permanent solitude only because, based on the rigorous rules of evidence, courts were forced to conclude that there was no legally certain knowledge of the death of their husbands. Rabban Gamaliel the Elder dealt with the problem by tempering the requirements for legal evidence. He established a rule, which is codified in our Mishna, that gives full legal standing to the testimony of only one witness, even of one witness who has only hearsay knowledge, or of a woman, even a bondwoman, or a slave. Although in all normal circumstances these are not legally valid forms of evidence, testimony was accepted from any of them to establish the death of a man so that his wife might be free to marry again.[2] Scriptural rules of evidence were made more lenient in order to protect innocent women from a life of inordinate hardship.

So strong is the commitment to protecting women from the dangers of becoming *agunot* that it persists throughout later Jewish law. The basic orientation of the law is expressed by Maimonides in a responsum concerning a case in which there was only the testimony of a non-Jewish woman that a certain man had been killed. This testimony was brought to the court as hearsay evidence by the witnesses whom she had informed. When asked for an opinion, Maimonides ruled that the evidence is satisfactory and that the wife is free to marry again. In justification of his ruling he laid down a basic principle to the effect that "we do not enter into lengthy and detailed examinations of the testimony which is offered in behalf of an agunah. Moreover, whoever adopts a stringent position in such cases and subjects the evidence which is offered to detailed investigation and examination does not behave properly. Our sages are displeased by his conduct, since it was their specific rule that we are to take the most lenient position in the case of an *agunah*."[3] R. Moses Isserles refers to this responsum of Maimonides as the basis of his own similar ruling some four centuries later.[4]

In contrast, when it came to dealing with capital punishment, the Rabbis invoked the most extreme rigor of the laws of evidence in such ways as to minimize, if not to remove entirely, the likelihood that transgressors would be put to death. The Torah rules that the death penalty is to be imposed for a very large number of different types of wrongdoing, ranging from murder to adultery to violation of the Sabbath and blasphemy. Furthermore, some cases are recorded in the Torah in which the penalty was actually carried out.[5] We cannot discuss here the complex and unsettled question concerning the extent to which Talmudic legislation on capital punishment reflects historical reality. However, even if it should be the case that the recorded legislation, which stems from a later period, does not mirror the practices of Temple times, it does, nevertheless, tell us a great deal about the attitudes of the later Rabbis to capital punishment. The statement is attributed to Rabbi Akiba and Rabbi Tarfon that if they had lived when the Sanhedrin was still functioning (i.e., when the death penalty could be imposed by the Jewish authorities), no one would ever have been put to death.[6] Such a statement, whatever its relation to historical reality, certainly reflects a deep antipathy to capital punishment, and a conviction that the rules of evidence could be enforced in such ways as to effectively ban all capital punishment.

One need only study the Mishnayot which set forth the procedure for cross-examining witnesses in capital cases.[7] Again, we are looking for attitudes and value-orientation, rather than any assurance of a faithful historical picture. The fear of God (literally) was put into the witnesses before they began their testimony. They were to be questioned about every detail, relevant or irrelevant, surrounding the event about which they bore witness. It is recorded that Rabban Yohanan ben-Zakkai once required witnesses in a murder case to give detailed descriptions of the stalks of the figs on the tree near which the murder was alleged to have been committed.[8] In the case of the agunah, the Rabbis made the rules of evidence as lenient as possible, even contrary to the rule of Scripture, in order to save women from needless suffering. In the case of accused wrongdoers, they made the same rules of evidence as stringent as possible in order to prevent the death penalty from being imposed lightly. While in the case of the agunah the rule is that we are not permitted to subject a witness to rigorous cross-examination, exactly the opposite rule is invoked in cases of capital punishment. Here the requirement is that nothing less than the most extensive examination and cross-examination is acceptable.[9]

The text of the Torah, standing alone and read literally, seems to reflect a set of values different from those of the rabbinic authorities whom we have been discussing. Furthermore, these very authorities seemed to adjust the rules and procedures of the law to the values which they were anxious to preserve. In the cases we have considered, humane concern for persons threatened by tragedy apparently dictated how the rules of evidence would be applied. It should be noted that in other cases, where it was thought to be essential for the preservation of religion or even the very security of the community, the death penalty was imposed as an emergency measure in a way contrary to all the normal rules set down in the Torah. As one of the Rabbis of the Talmud expresses the point in a comment on a famous case, "I have heard that the Beth Din may impose flagellation and pronounce capital sentences even where not warranted by the Torah; yet not with the intention of disregarding the Torah, but in order to safeguard it."[10]

In later times it is easy to find similar instances of basic differences of orientation with respect to ethics. Let us consider briefly two examples in which diametrically opposed views concerning the theoretical foundations of Jewish ethics are set forth by respected and authoritative figures. Maimonides denied that there is any cognitive foundation to the rules of morality. Anticipating a well-known modern position, he argued that all claims about good and evil or right and wrong are non-cognitive. He held that statements such as, "X is good," "Y is evil," have no truth-value, and are, of course, in no way capable of being demonstrated. Consequently, in the field of ethics we can only appeal to some authority which determines for us what constitutes the good and the evil. For some peoples that authority is the sovereign. For others it is accepted social convention. And, according to Maimonides, for the Jews it is divine commandment as recorded in the Torah and interpreted by the Rabbis. No demonstrative argument can be offered in favor of these commandments. We accept them because we believe that God is their source, and we rely on His wisdom and benevolence. Of course, we can and should try to understand the reasons for these commandments, but Maimonides never confuses the understanding of reasons with demonstration. They are, for the most part, reasons which set forth the social utility of the commandments, but they never establish an objectively demonstrated right or wrong, good or evil.[11]

In striking contrast with this view concerning the foundations of Jewish ethics, Moses Mendelssohn argued that the principles of ethics are mathematically demonstrable. They are known to be true in the same way as geometric principles are known to be true. Ethics is in no way a product of local convention or of special commandments to a particular people. Ethical principles are universal. They are part of the common heritage of mankind, and are known to all men, or at least can be known to all men, through the independent operation of human reason. Mendelssohn was particularly disturbed by the stance of Maimonides which he considered to be neither a true rational understanding, nor a proper religious understanding of the ethical.[12]

In more recent times a similar debate took place between two well-known interpreters of Jewish ethics. Moritz Lazarus held that the root characteristic of Jewish ethics is moral autonomy as over against heteronomy. The good is known immediately and independently of any external source. Following a Kantian model, he argued that God commanded us to behave in certain ways because they are objectively right, not that they are right because God commanded them. In his attack on Lazarus, David Neumark expressed astonishment that anyone could attempt to propound such a doctrine as legitimately Jewish. As Neumark put it, "When Lazarus speaks of the relationship between divine teaching and the ethical teaching of man, he is using a concept which, so far as Judaism is concerned, is empty. The ethical teaching of man, indeed! From the perspective of Judaism there is no place for any ethical teaching which is not a direct result of divine commandment... Even the rational commandments obligate us only because they were commanded by God; not because their content is ethical, but because God commanded them... Our sages forcefully rejected anyone who sought in any of the commandments a content which could stand independently without being divinely commanded, even in cases where there seemed to be no question of their moral value... They did so because in their opinion the only ground for the obligatory nature of the commandments is the fact that they are God's commandments, and not for any other reason." [13]

We see in both these cases instances in which deep divisions are present among recognized Jewish scholars with respect to the foundations of Jewish ethics. Even if there were no implications for practice (and there certainly are), such theoretical differences are of critical importance. They determine our understanding of all aspects of the ethical within the Jewish tradition. Because such diversity is common from early times to the modern period, we cannot speak simply of a body of teaching which we call "Jewish ethics." Students of this subject must be prepared to deal with the varieties of Jewish ethics. Their work will be most fruitful if they go beyond the description of these differences to consider certain basic issues. First, they must explicate the grounds of these differing views. How did these differences arise? To what extent are they historically and culturally conditioned? To what degree are they purely philosophical in character? Second, they must try to understand how the individual thinkers integrated their ethical teachings into the established body of Judaism. How did they go about the task of justifying their claim that their particular versions of the ethical are authentically Jewish? In what ways and according to what methods did they treat the relationship between their views and the classical Jewish sources? These and similar questions demand study.

II

In order to illustrate the types of problems which must occupy our attention if we are to produce sound philosophical studies of Jewish ethics, I propose to consider two basic questions. The first is the problem of justification, that is, how is the ethical demand justified within any given system. This is a matter to which relatively little study has been given in works on Jewish ethics. Yet, without attention to this question no account of an ethical theory or a moral system can be complete.

The moral life, in almost any version of what constitutes such a life, is not merely behavior in accordance with natural inclinations or even acquired tastes. Moral precepts are either prohibitions or injunctions. They forbid us to behave in certain ways and require us to behave in certain other ways. In either case they tend to run counter to our natural inclinations, as Kant noted when he distinguished sharply between behavior grounded in moral duty and behavior grounded in inclination. If we were free, without restriction, to behave as we liked, it is by no means obvious that we would follow the rules of any conventional western moral system. As Plato notes, the problem of moral justification is to find convincing reasons for following a set of moral rules in the absence of all forms of external coercion. Human beings are subject to an endless variety of temptations. They are often moved to act as a result of deep passion. Lust, anger, jealousy, greed are among the forces which drive us. Is there any reason why we should restrain these forces? Plato imagines a paradigmatic situation in which one would be free to follow his inclinations with no danger of punishment. In such a case, if there is no fear of consequences which are unpleasant, why should one choose to be honest, chaste, kind, unselfish, etc.?[14] This concern with justifying traditional moral values becomes especially urgent in a time, such as the present, which is characterized by moral permissiveness and in which it is widely held that the satisfaction of one's own desires is the only sensible mode of human behavior.

The need for justification of moral rules is intensified by the fact that there seems to be no limit to the diversity of behavior approved or disapproved in various human societies. Ethnological studies by cultural anthropologists have made us aware of the range of diversity in the patterns of human behavior and in the value systems which give form and structure to that behavior. As Ruth Benedict expressed it, "The diversity of cultures can be endlessly documented. A field of human behavior may be ignored in some societies until it barely exists; it may even be in some cases unimagined... It is a corollary of this that standards, no matter in what aspect of behavior, range in different cultures from the positive to the negative pole. We might suppose that in the matter of taking life all peoples would agree in condemnation. On the contrary, in a matter of homicide, it may be held that one is blameless if diplomatic relations have been severed between neighboring countries, or that one kills by custom his first two children, or that a husband has the right of life and death over his wife, or that it is the duty of the child to kill his parents before they are old. It may be that those are killed who steal a fowl, or who cut their upper teeth first, or who are born on a Wednesday."[15] The awareness of such diversity has often led to cultural relativism. This doctrine holds that there are no universal or objective grounds for morality, but only the peculiar values that are internal to a particular culture. Such a view presents an intense challenge to philosophical ethical theories which teach that there is a universal morality, as well as to those religious theories which deny that moral values are in any significant respect culturally bound.

How does one justify a general prohibition against murder in the face of such a variety of patterns of approved and disapproved forms of homicide? What is to be done about other moral rules? It is not enough to proclaim dogmatically that adultery, however defined, is always wrong, or that incest is morally abhorrent. Such prohibitions demand justification, as do other conventional moral rules. A reasonable man may quite properly ask why he should be expected to share his possessions with strangers whose only claim is that they are in need. Why should one's natural acquisitiveness yield to the needs or interests of others? Is truth-telling a virtue? Why so, when to tell the truth is distinctly not to one's advantage? The questions grow more intense when we come to know that our local standards are by no means universal, and that what we consider good is thought by others to be evil or silly, while what we consider evil is elsewhere a mark of true virtue. The justification of a given moral system is thus an inescapable demand set forth by ordinary human intelligence. It is not the exclusive concern of the professional moral philosopher, but rather a need of every thinking person. Any proper understanding of Jewish ethics must seek a full understanding of the ways in which moral teachings have been justified in the Jewish tradition. If we fail to come to terms with this question, we condemn ourselves to a superficial and inadequate account of the various forms of Jewish ethical teaching.

When we turn to the question of modes of justification in Jewish ethics, we learn very quickly that here too there is a wide range of diversity. We referred earlier to one mode of justification, namely, the rational model. Here the argument is that reason establishes for us the rules of moral behavior. According to this view, for a rational man the conclusions of rational reflection on moral questions are as forceful and binding as the conclusions of reflection on mathematical issues. We may be deficient in character and unable or unwilling to follow in practice what our reason dictates with respect to proper behavior. But we can never, according to this view, deceive ourselves into thinking that the right, as reason knows it, is less than binding, or that the wrong is permissible. The most familiar modern philosopher who advanced such a view was Kant, although its source goes back to Plato. As we noted earlier, Moses Mendelssohn and Moritz Lazarus are proponents of the claim that Jewish ethics, like all ethics, rest finally and unequivocally on reason. They would recognize no other mode of moral justification. It has been widely held that Rav Saadia Gaon subscribed to this view many centuries earlier when he introduced into Jewish usage the terms "mizvot sikhliyyot," i.e., rational commandments. We cannot investigate here the correctness of this claim, although I have tried to argue against it elsewhere.[16]

A second model is the Aristotelian. It rests on a view concerning nature and human nature from which there follows a conception of the ultimate end of man which is held to be the highest good. The justification of claims about the highest good in Aristotle's ethics rests on the view that each thing is good specifically insofar as it fulfills its own proper nature. Or to put it differently, the good is in each case the adequate performance of characteristic function. In the case of man it is argued that his characteristic function (i.e., the specific difference which constitutes his distinctive humanity) is his rational capacity. To be truly a man is to be rational in the fullest and most complete sense, and this, in turn, means to use one's reason in the most effective way for the contemplation of the highest and most perfect things. Operationally, this is construed to mean that the highest human good is the rational apprehension and contemplation of God. In response to the challenging question, "Why should I direct all my efforts to the realization of this end?" Aristotle can only answer, "Because this is the only way in which you can become what your nature properly directs you to be, namely, a fully rational being." We should note that when it comes to justifying the moral virtues, as distinct from the intellectual virtues, Aristotle can only argue that they are necessary conditions for the realization of the highest good. Particular patterns of moral behavior, however, depend for their justification on local convention and on the judgment of the man of practical wisdom.[17]

This way of conceiving and justifying the highest good penetrated deeply into Jewish thought. The most familiar of all its advocates is Maimonides. He praises the eminence of Aristotle and follows his lead in designating the true knowledge and contemplation of God as the highest good and the most complete fulfillment of man's nature. While the mode of justification is not spelled out as clearly as in Aristotle, there is little question that, with regard to intellectual virtue, Maimonides is following an Aristotelian line. Where he differs significantly from Aristotle is in his understanding of the moral virtues and in his justification of them. For Maimonides, the standard of moral virtue is not given either by nature or society, nor is the judgment of the man of practical wisdom by itself a source for normative prescriptions. When it comes to moral virtue the teachings of the Torah set the standards, and what justifies their claim on us is the fact that they are God's commandments.[18]

Associated with this mode of justification is another which lays the primary stress on pleasure or happiness. This is already present in Aristotle who equates the highest good for man with true human happiness.[19] The extent to which this notion of happiness in Aristotle is associated with pleasure is not clear. At the very least, it does claim to offer man the way to the highest satisfaction of personal fulfillment in his life. This theme is repeated in Maimonides and other Jewish thinkers who follow this line. There are later Jewish thinkers who explicitly use the language of pleasure. For them the highest justification of the rules which are laid down in the Torah is that they lead us to the most intense and most perfect pleasure open to man.

A prime example of this mode of justification is Luzzatto. He begins his *Mesillat Yesharim* with the assertion that the life of saintliness and true piety requires man to know fully what his duty is in this world. Why is it so important for man to know his duty? Because it is only by fulfilling his obligations, namely, God's commandments, that man can reach the most satisfying of all human goals. "Our Sages have taught us that the purpose of man's having been created is so that he can find true pleasure in God (*lehitaneg al ha-Shem*) and to enjoy the radiance of the divine presence, since this is the true pleasure and the greatest of all possible delights."[20] This is not a crude hedonism which holds that whatever is pleasurable is good, but, however refined, it is still a form of hedonism. Man ought to fulfill divine commandments because only in doing so can he ever experience the greatest and most deeply satisfying of all pleasures. Elements of this same kind of justification can be found in a number of Jewish moralists.

It is only fair to note that Luzzatto, in emphasizing the value of a special kind of pleasure, is by no means unique among hedonists. Most philosophers who argued that the only justification for doing anything is that it brings pleasure or prevents pain also introduced standards for distinguishing higher and lower or better and worse pleasures. One has only to think of John Stuart Mill's struggle to give an account of qualitative distinctions among pleasures which would provide criteria for determining which pleasures are truly worthy of man and thus constitute appropriate ends of human striving. Luzzatto does not sanction all pleasures without exception. On the contrary, there are base pleasures which are in no way permitted because they are unworthy of man and prevent him from reaching his true goal. Yet, he affirms without hesitation that the true end of man is pleasure, more specifically, the highest and purest pleasure which it is possible for a human being to enjoy.

Perhaps the most common mode of justification for observing the commandments is the hope for reward and the fear of punishment. This theory would answer Plato directly by saying that there is in fact no reason why a man should ever behave counter to his own inclinations, except that to do so might either bring him rewards that he prizes or subject him to punishments that he fears. In Scripture this mode of justification occurs repeatedly. The people as a group are warned of the consequences which they will suffer if they reject the way which God has set out for them. Similarly, they are assured of the rewards which will come to them as compensation for being loyal to God and fulfilling His commandments. In a typical instance, we are promised that if we observe God's commandments. the rains will fall abundantly and in their proper season and we shall have ample crops. If, however, we turn away from God, then He will be severely displeased with us and will punish us by withholding the rain so that there will be no food produced in our fields.[21] Similarly, when Joshua addressed the Israelites at the end of his life he reminded them that it was to their advantage to be faithful to God. "For your own sakes, therefore, be most mindful to love the Lord your God." If you reject God's way, then He will no longer support you in your conquest of the land. "But just as every good thing that the Lord your God has promised you has been fulfilled for you, so the Lord can bring upon you every evil thing until He has wiped you off this good land which the Lord your God has given you."[22] A similar approach is taken toward individuals, not only toward the people as a corporate body. One has only to think of the prohibition against eating the forbidden fruit in the Garden of Eden, "for on the day that you eat of it you shall die."[23]

In contrast to this purely prudential mode of justification there is the mode which puts the primary stress on the fact that the commandments come from God, and this alone is sufficient to make them binding on man. This may be the most deeply religious mode of justification, since the concern here is not with reward or punishment, but only with the love of God or with pure submission to His will. In this mode the ideas of love of God and fear of God often coalesce. When Antigonos urges that we serve God as do workers who serve their master with no expectation of reward, he is generally thought to be emphasizing love of God as our main motive.[24] When he adds, "And let the fear of heaven be upon you," he is not contradicting himself or adding a different motive. True love of God is associated with deep reverence before His incomparable majesty. When Abraham submitted to the divine commandment to offer up his son, he did so despite the fact that there was no threat of punishment.[25] His act is an act of faith based on the absolute loyalty which is associated with love of God. He serves his Master with no expectation of reward. On the contrary, he is ready to suffer the greatest of all personal losses. Yet, when the heavenly voice addresses him it says, "For now I know that you fear God." This fear of God was not a fear of punishment, not a prudential decision in favor of his own advantage, but rather that total submission to the divine will which results from perfect love.

This is what Abraham meant when he justified himself to Abimelech by saying, "I thought, surely there is no fear of God in this place, and they will kill me because of my wife."[26] Local law, enforced by the temporal authorities, offered the stranger no protection. If Abimelech and his people had been bound by religion, i.e., by submission to the divine will, even when it carries no threat of punishment with it, then Abraham could have felt secure. However, knowing that this fear of God which stems from love did not exist in Gerar, Abraham had to resort to deception to save himself. We can see that Abraham judged correctly, for when God spoke to Abimelech, He addressed him in the only way that he would understand, that is, by threatening him with death if he did not release Sarah.[27] Abraham's mode of justifying the moral life presupposes that one recognizes love of God as the height of human achievement, and understands that to love God means to follow faithfully in His way.

We have attempted here to set forth in a completely preliminary way some of the various styles for justifying the moral life which are found in the Jewish tradition. A full study would have to investigate each of these with great care. It would work out the various types of argument that are either the explicit or implicit foundation of each mode of justification. It would examine these arguments for their validity, but would also be concerned with an evaluation of the premises on which the arguments rest. The arguments would have to be considered in their own contexts and in their historical backgrounds. The passages in Scripture, the sayings of the Rabbis, the works of philosophy or of moralistic teaching, which are the main texts for the study of this question, would have to be analyzed both historically and contextually. It would also be necessary to work out the connections between a given theory of justification and other aspects of the moral teaching of a particular work or of a given thinker, and, of course, to see the ethical teachings within the wider philosophical, theological or religious context of which they are a part.

III

We now turn to the discussion of a second problem which illustrates the type of theoretical questions which must be taken up in any proper study of Jewish ethics, namely, the question of the relationship between law and morality. The question was phrased pointedly by Aharon Lichtenstein in the title of his essay, "Does Jewish Tradition Recognize an Ethic Independent of the Halakha?"[28] The question arises because there is some tension, if not direct contradiction, between the view that the Halakha is the source of all Jewish teaching concerning right behavior and the fact that the legal texts themselves introduce seemingly non-legal moral considerations into the legal process. Such principles as *lifnim mishurat hadin, middat hasidut*, and similar recommendations (or prescriptions) for proper action seem to have standing within the law even while they go beyond the requirements of the law. Furthermore, there are statements in the Talmud which suggest that without the law, i.e., without divine commandment, we could still have learned from the order of nature many basic principles of right action. There are those who argue on this basis that Judaism teaches that there is a natural moral law which can be known without any divine revelation. In some cases, such as that of Moses Mendelssohn, which we cited earlier, this natural moral law is identified with a rule of reason and is thus held to be universally known (or knowable) and universally binding.

Let us examine some of these claims. Those who argue that the classical Jewish sources recognize a natural ethic often cite as evidence the following passage: "If the Torah had not been given, we could have learned modesty from the cat, not to rob from the ant, chastity from the dove, considerate behavior to our wives from the rooster."[29] Lichtenstein, like many others, asserts that this passage leaves no doubt whatsoever that the rabbinic sources recognized the existence of a natural morality.[30] In fact, it has become a standard source which is regularly cited as decisive evidence in favor of a Jewishly authorized natural morality. Yet, careful reflection will show how unsound such a claim is. In the first place, the very text and context make clear that there is no statement here about a natural morality which is known independently. What it says is that if we did not have the Torah we might have been able to imitate certain forms of animal behavior which are useful for the maintenance of an ordered society and good personal relations. The immediately preceding passage speaks of some other limitations of animal behavior which have nothing at all to do with morality. The fact that we would have before us animal models for imitation is no assurance that we would recognize those models and follow them. Moreover, the imitation of such models would never arise from a sense of obligation or duty. The Torah forbids us to rob and commands us to be chaste. Without the Torah we might decide to imitate the honesty of the ant and the chastity of the dove on prudential or other grounds, but this would not bring us to a knowledge of our duty to behave in this way. Yet, both law and independent morality require some ground of obligation. We may freely choose to observe the law or to follow moral principles, but they can only have standing as law or morality if our free choice is motivated by our awareness of being duty bound. No such awareness of duty could emerge from a prudential decision made by men in a state of nature who chose to imitate some aspects of animal behavior.[31]

There is an additional consideration which seems to have escaped the notice of those scholars who put such great weight on this text. It is all very well, after the fact, to say that if we did not have the Torah, we could have learned virtuous behavior from the cat, the ant, the dove and the rooster. In reality, however, since we have already been taught by the Torah the virtues of modesty, honesty, chastity, and conjugal considerateness, we can now note with admiration that these forms of behavior are normal for certain animals as well. But, if we had not come to our study of the animal kingdom with the standards of the Torah already in hand, that is, if we were in a pure state of nature, what would have moved us to admire and imitate these particular animals and these particular aspects of their behavior? Might we not have decided just as readily to imitate the ferocity of the lion, the murderousness of an aroused pack of wolves, or the sexual behavior of the rabbit? Ants may be meticulous in their respect for the property of others, but this is hardly a characteristic of the entire animal world. It is by no means obvious that, given free choice, we would have found the ant, rather than some other species, an ideal model. In short, we ascribe an unmerited simple-mindedness to Rabbi Yohanan when we read so much more into his statement than it can possibly mean. Such statements are no ground for deciding that we have an unimpeachable Jewish source for natural morality.

A second source that is often cited for natural law in Judaism is the Noahide laws, the seven commandments which are directed to all mankind who are the descendants of Noah.[32] The idea seems to be that since Judaism teaches that every human being is obligated to observe these laws, they must be known through reason or in some other natural way.[33] Proponents of this view conveniently overlook two relevant facts. First, in the classical Jewish sources these Noahide laws are understood as divine commandments and not as the result of independent rational reflection. They are derived by various exegetical methods from a biblical verse which reads, "And the Lord God commanded the man (Adam) saying, 'Of every tree of the garden you are free to eat.'"[34] The stress here is on the fact that God commanded, not that man came to know through his reason or through some other natural force. Second, an examination of the individual commandments casts doubt on any claim that they could be known by unaided reason. Prohibitions against blasphemy, unchastity or eating of a limb torn from a living animal are not readily shown to be rationally demonstrable.[35]

A third source commonly proposed as evidence for an independent morality in Judaism is Nahmanides' commentary to Leviticus 19:2. In this familiar and frequently quoted passage Nahmanides makes the point that one might observe all the rules of the Torah, but do so in a way which would make one a *nabal bireshut ha-Torah*, a crude vulgarian with the permission of the Torah. From this it is inferred that Nahmanides holds that there is an additional and higher standard of behavior which tempers and brings refinement into the law of the Torah itself. This higher standard is expressed. it is supposed, in the requirement that "You shall be holy." It is curious that those who argue this way overlook the fact that the requirement to be holy is presented in Scripture as a divine mandate. "The Lord spoke to Moses, saying: Speak to the whole Israelite community and say to them: You shall be holy, for 1, the Lord your God, am holy." Furthermore, in the very passage which we cited Nahmanides speaks explicitly of the fact that this verse is a commandment of the Torah which requires of us those elements of restraint and refinement which might otherwise be lacking in the law.[36]

None of these sources serves as a sound ground for the view that Judaism recognizes an ethic which is independent of divine commandment. It is not my purpose here to argue against that view as such. It may well be possible to produce convincing evidence in its favor. That question must be left open. My purpose has been to show the kinds of problems we face as we try to deal with such a basic theoretical question in the field of Jewish ethics. We must be sensitive to the dangers of misreading texts, of seeing them in a partial perspective, or reading into the texts doctrines which are not there. This danger is particularly great with respect to Jewish ethics, because this is a field which tempts scholars to engage in apologetics, a field in which investigators often find it difficult to suppress their personal commitments and predilections. One need only remember, as an example, the way in which Moritz Lazarus regularly read rabbinic texts so as to confer on them a moral universalism which may have been to his personal taste, but which is not justified by the texts themselves. One instance out of many will suffice to make the point. A Talmudic passage reads as follows: "God made a condition with the works of creation saying, 'If Israel accept my Law, it will be well, but if not, I shall reduce you to a state of chaos.'"[37] Lazarus renders the first part of this passage as follows: "God made the following condition with His creation: if the children of Israel-and through them all nations-accept the Torah, i.e., the moral law, all will be well."[38] The danger of this kind of tendentious reading, or similarly tendentious interpretation, always confronts us. Our task is to go back to the sources and to study them in as open and critical a fashion as possible, without preconceptions and without having our preferred answers in mind even before we have asked the right questions.

IV

More serious grounds for the claim that Judaism recognizes an independent morality arise from some general principles of Jewish law and from the way in which the legal texts deal with certain concrete cases. These are. in general, cases in which there appear to be conflicts between legal norms and moral considerations. In some of these cases the tensions are easily resolved in ways which do not put any strain on the legal system. These are cases in which conflicts of duties are such that there is no question as to which should take precedence. For example, we are commanded both to revere our parents and to keep the Sabbath. In the case in which a conflict arises because parents command one to violate the Sabbath, the rule is unambiguous. We are to disobey our parents and keep the Sabbath because the Sabbath commandment comes from a higher authority whose rule obligates parents as well as children. Obedience to parents does not supersede obedience to God.[39] There is no question here of introducing some external standard, but only of clarifying in a perfectly reasonable way the relative standing of conflicting claims.

In other instances, however, the matter is not resolved in nearly so simple and clear-cut a fashion, since we confront conflicting views which appear to rest on opposed value principles. A classic case is that posed by the problem as to whether it is permissible, or even meritorious, in disputes involving monetary claims to substitute arbitration or compromise for a full legal court decision. Now, it would seem initially that there should be no problem. The law (which is considered by its framers to be divine, or at least to derive from divine principles) gives authority to the courts to decide in such cases. The law gives clear guidance to judges by which they can decide who owes what to whom. It would seem then that simple justice requires us to invoke the full force of the law to make certain that the disputed property will go to its rightful owner. Anything less deprives the owner of his due and allows another person to retain property which does not belong to him. Reflecting precisely this line of reasoning, Rabbi Eliezer the son of Rabbi Jose the Galilean says, "It is forbidden to arbitrate, and whoever arbitrates is a sinner, and whoever praises such an arbitrator scorns the Lord... Rather, let the law cut through the mountain, as Scripture teaches: 'For judgment is God's.'"[40] O The text goes on to distinguish between Moses and Aaron. Moses who served as a judge could only follow the strict rule of law, while Aaron, the priest, who was concerned with peaceful and harmonious relations within the community placed less emphasis on law and more on whatever compromises would reduce conflict. Something like this latter view is then expressed by Rabbi Joshua ben Korha who speaks in opposition to Rabbi Eliezer. He holds that, "To arbitrate is especially meritorious (or even obligatory), as Scripture says, 'Execute the judgment of truth and peace in your gates.' Surely, where there is strict imposition of law, there is no peace, and where there is peace there is no strict imposition of the law. What kind of justice is it then which brings with it peace? We can only say that this is arbitration."[41]

It would be a mistake. in my judgment, to construe this dispute as a conflict between one who seeks a strict observance of the revealed law and one who asserts that there are moral norms which stand above the law, and which must be invoked to temper it. That is one possible way to read this text, but it seems to me unsatisfactory. R. Joshua is not rejecting the law in favor of some external norm. He does after all base himself on a scriptural verse, and we do have the example of Aaron which has been invoked as well. The concern for peace and for good relations among members of the community is as much a teaching of the Jewish tradition as is the concern for rigorous honesty in the distribution of property to its rightful owner. The question here is not that of a Torah norm opposed by an external moral rule, but rather of the kind of conflict between values within a system which arises inevitably. R. Eliezer considers the value of the rule of law in the assignment of property rights to have a superior claim, no matter what the cost in bruised feelings and bad human relations. R. Joshua considers the maintenance of peace and harmony of greater importance than the possible assignment of some property to other than its legally rightful owner. Both base themselves on thoroughly authoritative internal Jewish sources. Unlike the case of violating the Sabbath at the command of one's parents, what we have here **is** a genuine difference of perspective. So far as I know, no halakhic authority ever ruled that duty to parents took precedence over fulfilling God's commandment to observe the Sabbath. With respect to the status of arbitration over against strict legal proceeding there is a genuine difference of view. It happens that the position of R. Joshua won out in the long run, so that the codifiers tend generally to follow his ruling.[42] However, this in no way eliminates strict legal proceeding as improper or inoperative. We do not have here a conflict between Jewish law and an independent morality, but rather an internal struggle between equally valid norms of Jewish practice which at times come into conflict. As between Moses and Aaron, it is hardly possible to argue that one is legitimately within the Jewish tradition while the other stands outside.

This pattern is not unusual in rabbinic legislation. While one can find that in a conflict between the strict law and a seemingly moral norm the latter often prevails, it is generally the case that the so-called moral norm is itself based on either unimpeachable sources or, at least, sources that legitimately serve as authoritative support. Typical is the case of the marriage contract arrangements which guarantee that if a wife predeceases her husband, her property is protected as an inheritance for her sons. It does not become part of her husband's general estate to be shared by all his heirs, including children from other wives. The reason for this assignment is to encourage fathers to settle property on their daughters so as to make them more attractive in the marriage market. Fathers are more likely to do so if they are assured that this property will remain in their own family as an inheritance for their grandchildren and will not be transferred to strangers. The Talmud asks a troubled question. How can such arrangements be approved and institutionalized when they run counter to the rules of the Torah for inheritance? The answer is that providing husbands for our daughters is also a duty imposed by the Torah and in this case that duty takes precedence over the usual rules for the inheritance of property.[43]

Here the conflict of norms is resolved fully in favor of the obligation to marry off our daughters. The scriptural support which is offered would initially seem of lesser standing than the Torah rules of inheritance since it is a verse from Jeremiah. In fact, the Jeremiah verse is identified in the Talmud as *d'oraita*, i.e., as having pentateuchal authority, but most commentators treat is as *asmakhta*, that is, as offering a kind of scriptural support for a principle whose foundations rest on rabbinic legislation.[44] However that may be, we have here a case in which a sense of obligation toward young women of marriageable age forces a change in property inheritance procedures that are otherwise standard and have clear Torah sanction. The value of marrying off daughters is not purely external to the tradition by any means. Given that value, a decision was made which put normal property rights in a subordinate position to the advancement of the interests of good marriages. Unlike our previous case, there is no serious conflict here in which the opponents line up on opposite sides. The approved practice is codified in the Mishna, defended by a scriptural verse, and adopted by the later authorities. Nevertheless, it is not clear on what theoretical foundations it was determined which value would prevail. It is this question which must be investigated in a serious study of the sources of value decisions in Jewish law.

Even more striking is an extreme case in which it is acknowledged that the law authorizes certain practices, but also considers it thoroughly unacceptable for one to behave in accordance with the legal norms. The basic rule in acquiring title to movable property is that there must be some physical act of drawing the property into the new owner's possession. As a result, no agreement to purchase is binding, even if money has been paid, unless there is the physical act of drawing into one's possession. In accordance with this, the Mishna rules that if an agreement has been made to purchase produce, and the money had been paid to the vendor, but the buyer did not draw the produce into his possession, he can withdraw from the purchase agreement with no penalty. This is the law as explicitly formulated by the legal authorities.[45] However, the Mishna goes on to state that it is considered improper for anyone to take advantage of this legal right, Of one who chooses to nullify his agreement because he has the legal right, the Mishna says, "But the Sages said: He who punished the generation of the flood and the generation of the dispersion, He will take vengeance of him who does not stand by his word." Although one has the full right to cancel his agreement to purchase or to sell, a terrifying curse is invoked against the person who takes advantage of his rights.[46]

The discussions in the literature raise various questions about this curse, such as whether it is just a warning or an actual curse. There are views that go so far as to hold that the courts may enforce the agreement, despite the lack of the act of drawing into one's possession. These are matters which lie beyond the scope of our present concerns. What matters for the development of an understanding of Jewish ethics is the fact that we have here a case in which the law (whose force and soundness is not questioned) comes into conflict with the value of keeping one's word. Although the cancellation of the transaction is perfectly legal, it is considered to be improper for a Jew to behave in a way which makes his word less than binding. The language of Maimonides reflects his reading of the Talmudic discussion and reveals his specific perception of the matter, "If one paid money but did not draw the produce into his possession, even though the movable property had not become his, nevertheless, whoever changes his mind, whether it be the seller or the buyer, has not behaved in a way which is proper for a Jew (*lo asah maoseh Yisrael*) and he is required to submit to the curse of *mi shepara*."[47] Some authorities dispense with the curse and simply proclaim that this person is behaving in a way which is displeasing to the sages.

In this case, as in the others, the opposed values are both well-founded in the tradition. The laws of property acquisition have deep roots in the legal system deriving from the scriptural sources. The obligation to keep one's word is no less well-established. Yet, in this case where the law specifically authorizes one not to keep his word in a situation in which rights to property are at stake, we are confronted with a complex decision which seems to retain both values. If the party who wants to cancel his agreement is determined, then he is permitted to do so as his legal right. At the same time, the value of keeping one's word is so strongly endorsed that he is anathematized for violating his agreement, even though to have done so was fully legal. We do not have here a moral norm which comes from outside the tradition as a critique of the law. However, even though it is from within the tradition, it nevertheless must be seen as a criticism of the law whose technicalities make it permissible to break one's word. Careful analysis is required in order to understand the relationship between the legal norm and the moral value which opposes it. We have yet to learn just what are the methods and principles which determine when one value dominates over another, when both have equal standing, and when, as in this case, the legal option remains open, but only at the price of public humiliation joined with the threat of severe divine punishment. We confront similar questions in all those cases in which the Talmud rules that a man is judged to be innocent in the eyes of the human authorities, but guilty in the eyes of God.

V

It has not been our intention to suggest that we have offered a definitive analysis of any of the cases that have been cited. That work still remains to be done. It has only been our intention to illustrate the types of problems that arise as we deal with the area of Jewish ethics in rabbinic literature. The suggested solutions are, in every case, a first tentative attempt and will stand only if they are sustained by detailed analysis of all the relevant evidence. There are additional types of problems with which we have not dealt at all. The question of the status of such norms as *lifnim mishurat hadin, darkhei noam*, middat *hasidut,* and similar appeals to a seemingly higher morality require extensive study. Some work has, of course, been done on this subject, including some recent studies which are eminently worthy of attention.[48]

While it is my view that our most urgent scholarly need is for a study of the philosophical foundations of the varieties of rabbinic ethics, it is obvious that this is by no means all that needs to be done. Similar studies are required of the later rabbinic writers, of the Jewish philosophers, and the *mussar* literature, in fact of every type of Jewish literature in which ethical doctrines are contained explicitly or implicitly. The problems posed by these different types of literature will not be identical with those that were discussed in this brief study. Careful method will identify the issues that are appropriate to each type of literature and will deal with them in the context of their particular setting. What should emerge from such studies is an understanding of the intellectual foundations on which various types of Jewish ethical doctrines rest and of the interpretation of Jewish teaching and practice which flows from them. We should imitate those scholars who have moved beyond the stage of self-serving apologetics in this field. Here, as in all other areas, "God's seal is truth."

NOTES

[1] *Baba Mezia,* 88a.
[2] *M. Yebamot,* 16:7.
[3] *Teshubot ha-Rambam*, ed. A. Freimann, (Jerusalem, 1934), No. 159, p. 157.
[4] *Eben ha-Ezer,* 17:21.
[5] Lev. 24:23, Num. 15:32 ff.
[6] *M. Makkot,* 1: 10.
[7] M. Sanhedrin, 4:5-5:5.
[8] *M. Sanhedrin,* 5:2.
[9] *Ibid.* The text praises the procedure of extending the examination as much as possible.
[10] *Sanhedrin* 46a and parallels. We do not want to suggest that the opposition to capital punishment was absolute. As we see from these latter cases, there were circumstances under which capital punishment was freely imposed even without paying attention to the most elementary procedural safeguards that the Torah sets forth. When public welfare was at stake, whether religious or physical welfare, the rabbis exercised their power to suspend all the usual rules. See for example the episode which the Mishna records concerning R. Simeon ben Shetah, M. Sanhedrin 6:4. Even in later times, we have records of informers being put to death by the order of rabbinic courts at a time when by all standard rabbinic law the authority to issue the death penalty was no longer in force. Nevertheless, it is clear enough that for the cases to which we referred in which the laws of evidence were made unusually stringent we have clear indications of an effort to restrict the death penalty.
[11] For a discussion of Maimonides' views see, M. Fox, "Maimonides and Aquinas on Natural Law." *Diné Israel*, III (1972) v-xxxvi.
[12] For a discussion of Mendelssohn see. Alexander Altmann, Moses *Mendelssohn's Frühschriften zur Metaphysik* (Tübingen, 1969), 341-391: Alexander Altmann, Moses Mendelssohn, a *Biographical Study* (Philadelphia, 1973). 125-130@ M. Fox, "Law and Ethics in Modern Jewish Philosophy: The Case of Moses Mendelssohn," PAAJR. XLIII (1976).
[13] Moritz Lazarus, *The Ethics of Judaism* (Philadelphia, 1900), Vol. 1, 111-112; D. Neumark, "Mussar ha-Yahadut," Ha-Shiloah, VI (1899), 71-72. Some time later Julius Guttman argued that there are other respects in which Jewish ethics closely resembles Kantian ethics. He held that Kant's conception of moral duty is a perfect typification of Jewish ethics. See his essay on "Kant and Judaism," in *Dat U'Madda* (Jerusalem, 1955), 225-227.
[14] *Republic,* 11, 359a-361C.
[15] Ruth Benedict, *Patterns of Culture* (New York, 1946), 41.
[16] See M. Fox, "On the Rational Commandments in Saadia's Philosophy: A Reexamination," Modern *Jewish Ethics:* Theory and *Practice,* ed. M. Fox, (Ohio State University Press, 1975), 174-187.
[17] For an extensive discussion see, M. Fox, "The Doctrine of the Mean in Aristotle and Aquinas: A Comparative Study," in *Studies in Jewish Religious and Intellectual* History, Presented to Alexander Altmann, (University of Alabama Press, 1979), 43-70.
[18] *Ibid.*, 56-67.
[19] The problem of a precise English translation of *eudaimonia*, as Aristotle uses the term, is not easily resolved, but for our present purposes the usual equation with "happiness" seems acceptable.
[20] *Mesillat* Yesharim, opening of Ch. 1.

[21] Deut. 11:13-17.
[22] Josh. 24:11-16.
[23] Gen. 2:17.
[24] *M. Abot,* 1:3.
[25] Gen. 22:1-19.
[26] Gen. 20:1-11.
[27] Gen. 20:3. I am indebted to my colleague, Professor Nahum M. Sarna, for the interpretation of Yirat Elohim which I have followed here.
[28] In M. Fox, ed., Modern *Jewish Ethics: Theory and Practice,* 62-88.
[29] *Erubin*, 100b.
[30] Basing himself on this Talmudic passage, Lichtenstein asserts that, "If the issue be reduced to natural morality in general, it need hardly be in doubt." *Op. cit.,* 62.
[31] For further discussion of this point see E. E. Urbach, Hazal: *Pirke Emunot ve-Deot* (Jerusalem, 1969), 285-287; M. Fox, "Natural Law in Maimonides and Aquinas," viii-ix.
[32] Sanhedrin, 56ab.
[33] While many later thinkers seized on the Noahide laws as natural moral law, Maimonides rejected this view categorically. The classic source is *M. T. Melakhim,* 8:11, where Maimonides requires that all men recognize the revelation at Sinai as the source of these laws. Moses Mendelssohn was deeply disturbed by this and sought clarification in an exchange of letters with R. Jacob Emden; cf. Mendelssohn, *Gesammelte Schriften,* Jubiläumsausgabe, v. 16, 178f. For a general discussion see S. S. Schwarzschild, "Do Noachites Have to Believe in Revelation?", *JQR* 57,4 (April, 1962); M. Fox, "Law and Ethics in Modern Jewish Philosophy," PAAJR, XLIII (1976); M. Fox, "Natural Law in Maimonides and Aquinas," xii-xix.
[34] Gen. 2:16.
[35] Cf. sources cited in n.33 above for discussions of this point.
[36] For a sound interpretation of Nahmanides on this point, cf. Lichtenstein, *op. cit.,* 69.
[37] *Abodah Zarah*, 3a.
[38] M. Lazarus, *Ethik des Judenthums* (Frankfurt a.M., 1899), Vol. 1, 256.
[39] Lev. 19:3 and Rashi ad loc,; Yebamot 5b; *Baba Mezia* 32a.
[40] *Sanhedrin*, 6b.
[41] *Ibid.*
[42] Cf., e.g., *M. T. Sanhedrin*, 22:4; *Hoshen Mishpat, 12:2.*
[43] *Ketubot,* 52b.
[44] *M,T. Ishut 12:2.* For a discussion of the use of d'oraita for non-pentateuchal texts see *Encyclopaedia Talmudit, s.v. Dibrei Kabbalah* and *Dibrei* Torah, v.8, 106b-114b; 134b-135a.
[45] *M. Baba Mezia,* 4:2; cf. *M. Shebiit,* 10:9.
[46] *M. Baba Mezia, 4:2.*
[47] *M. T. Mekhirah* 7:1.
[48] See, among others, Saul Berman, "Lifnim Mishurat Hadin," Journal of *Jewish Studies* 26 (1975), 86-104: 28 (1977), 181-193; Shmuel Shilo, "On One Aspect of Law and Morals in Jewish Law: Lifnim *Mishurat* Hadin," *Israel Law Review* 13 (1978), 359-390.

26

THE MISHNA AS A SOURCE FOR JEWISH ETHICS

In recent decades there has been ongoing debate about the nature and foundations of Jewish ethics. Questions have been raised about the relationship between ethics and *halakhah,* about the recognition of an ethic independent of the law, and similar issues. These concerns have a history which goes back at least to the eighteenth century, if not earlier. Nineteenth-century Jewish thinkers, particularly in western Europe, wrote a number of treatises on Jewish ethics. The revival of interest in this subject in our own time has also generated a considerable literature.

Hardly anyone has raised the most fundamental question of all, namely, whether the very concept "Jewish ethics" has legitimate standing. It is worth noting that neither biblical nor rabbinic Hebrew has a term for "ethics." Such currently familiar terms as *mussar* or *middot,* when used in the sense of "ethics," are from a later period. There is a trivial sense in which we can speak of Jewish ethics as referring to the modes of behavior commanded or prohibited by the Torah. More specifically, we have discussions of Jewish medical ethics or Jewish business ethics, but these are generally no more than an exposition of the *halakhah* of these particular areas of concern.

Neither the Torah nor rabbinic literature provides us with a fully developed philosophical theory of the nature and ground of morality. The later literature is also singularly poor in such theoretical concerns. Beginning with Saadia's introduction of the notion of *mitzvot sikhliyyot,* through the non-cognitivism of the Rambam, to the natural law theory of Moses Mendelssohn, our literature contains some important efforts to address the philosophical problem of the foundations of Jewish ethics. Such theoretical concern has not been dominant, however, and has not resulted in major studies comparable to Aristotle's *Nicomachean Ethics* or Kant's *Critique of Practical Reason.* This is by no means surprising once we remember that we are dealing with a system where the norms of behavior and their axiological foundations rest on divine commandment. This is not a hospitable atmosphere for the generation of ethical theory. In fact, some of the contemporary literature which seeks to develop a theory of Jewish ethics begins by seeking evidence of a source of morality in Judaism independent of divine commandment. Such an independent morality is then often turned into a criterion of the moral validity of the divine commandments.

I do not propose in this essay to try to resolve the large problem of the theoretical foundations of Jewish ethics. My aim is limited to considering one question alone. I want to see what results the study of the Mishna will yield for our understanding of Jewish ethics. What does this first post-biblical code of Jewish law and lore teach us about how to approach the problem of Jewish ethics? Does the Mishna offer us any theoretical approach to our subject? Does it even recognize moral and ethical norms that are distinct from the rest of the law? Does it provide us with a set of values which can be validly generalized? These are. some of the questions which I propose to address.

We should keep in mind that our questions are embedded in a larger context. The one clear theoretical commitment of the Mishna is to the proposition that the law is divine in origin and contains God's commandments to the Jewish people. This is explicitly stated in the opening to M. Avot, and is implicit in all of mishnaic law. The actual law, as we have it in the Mishna, should be understood as positive law which results from the application of the principles of the divine commandments to concrete cases and circumstances. The authority of the positive law in Judaism is established by way of the concept of the oral law which is the principle validating all of the positive law. There may be debates about the soundness of any particular ruling in the positive law, as is the case in every legal system, but there is no debate about the foundations on which that law rests. If we want to consider whether the Mishna contains or rests on principles of morality which guide or govern the system, we can only begin with the positive law. It is of this law that we shall ask our questions about so-called ethical foundations of the Mishna.

Let us begin by laying down a rule of method. We shall treat the Mishna as a single unified work which is capable of speaking for itself. Although, in traditional Jewish learning, we are accustomed to seeing the

Mishna only through the eyes of the large body of later literature, we must remember that when it was redacted and published (whatever publication meant in Jewish antiquity) it certainly served initially as an integrated and coherent source of instruction. Like every code, it quickly generated its own body of commentary and exegesis, but it is still possible (and desirable) to look at the Mishna itself, and to ask what we can learn from it. Moreover, we are not concerned here with the complicated questions of the history of the Mishna text and the process of its final redaction. For our purposes, we can deal with the received text without addressing these important scholarly problems which are of only marginal interest for our philosophic inquiry. Certain of our conclusions can be summarized in advance. Except for the recognition of the divine source, we find no formal ethical theory in the Mishna. Neither do we find any systematic account of the right and the good as peculiarly moral ideas. There is no setting forth of the grounds on which moral judgments are based, nor is there (with rare exceptions) any effort to justify particular judgments. In fact, there is little evidence, if any, that the Mishna recognized morality as a category of act and value different from the law. For this reason, it is important to note that when we speak of moral or ethical concerns in the Mishna, we are using these terms in the modern sense, not as internal categories of the Mishna. We do not mean to graft these concepts onto the Mishna, but only to confront the kinds of questions that are being debated today about the moral foundations of Jewish law.

A general survey of the materials shows us that there is no single set of moral generalizations which we can extract from the Mishna or validly impose on it. The Mishna text which, for halakhic purposes, is treated as a unified structure in which all inconsistencies must be resolved, does not lead us to any comparable unity or consistency with respect to moral issues. Moral rules and values, as we understand these ideas today, are, of course, present in the Mishna, but there is very little evidence to support the claim that they form a coherent system.

Let us consider a small but typical sampling of cases that illustrate various aspects of the problem of formulating a moral theory from the Mishna. To begin with, in a well-formed moral system we expect uniform rules that apply to everyone within the system without exception. When the Torah forbids adultery or murder, it makes no exceptions for particular individuals or circumstances. This is underscored in the later rabbinic rule that one must never violate these prohibitions, even if it is at the cost of one's own life (יהרג ואל יעבר) Yet, we frequently find in the Mishna a pattern in which individual judgment or individual idiosyncrasy is substituted for a fixed rule. In M. Kelim 17:6 this point is clearly illustrated within a single discussion. It has been established earlier with respect to required amounts of foods to be consumed for certain ritual purposes that the official legal measure is the size of an egg. Our Mishna rules that the measure in question should be a medium-sized egg. In the discussion that follows, the question is then raised how do we determine what is a medium-sized egg. R. Judah sets forth a technical procedure which should produce a uniform measure for everyone. R. Yose rules, however, that no uniform measure is possible or necessary. Each individual will have his own perception הכל לפי דעתו של רואה. We see here the tension between the demand for a uniform rule and the assertion of the validity of individual judgment. There is a similar tension in M. Sheviit 2: 1, where the discussion raises the question as to the date when one must stop ploughing in grain fields in the year that precedes the Sabbatical year. Initially, a standard is proposed which would vary with individual practice. To this R. Simeon replies with a severe complaint that allowing such individual judgment undermines the requisite universality of the law – נתת תורת כל אחד ואחד בידו.

A final case makes the point in a striking way. There is a rule in M. Berakhot 2:5 that a bridegroom is exempt from reciting the *Shema* on the night of his wedding. Although the Mishna gives no reason, one may assume, as do the later sources, that this exemption is due to the fact that the bridegroom is seriously distracted by other matters and will not be able to recite the *Shema* with proper thought and intent. The text then records an exceptional case, in which it is reported that Rabban Gamliel did recite the *Shema* on his wedding night. When challenged by his disciples that he is going against the rule which he himself had taught them, the Sage replied with the assertion that the general rule is valid, but it does not apply to him personally – איני שומע לכם לבטל ממני מלכות שמים אפילו שעה אחת. His superior piety requires him to act in accordance with a different rule. A few lines further on, another text underscores this tension between general rules and particular exceptions. In 2:8 the exemption for reciting *Shema* on the wedding night is made voluntary, so that anyone who wishes may follow the practice of Rabban Gamliel. At this point his son, Rabban Simeon, responds with a sharp and restrictive remark that condemns those who presume to arrogate to themselves the piety of the great sage –

לא כל הרוצה ליטול את השם יטול. Unlike the case with the norms of conventional morality, the mishnaic law maintains a tension between universal applicability and individual exceptions.

In ethical theory it is generally taken for granted that intention is a critical factor in determining the moral status of an action. Unintended acts do not generally have standing as morally relevant. The same is widely true in mishnaic law, where intention is required if an act is to have legal standing as the responsibility of a particular individual. Thus, we are taught in M. Baba Kama 8:1 that a person who injures another owes him compensation for five types of damages that he has caused. The last of these is compensation for the shame or indignity that the victim suffers. With regard to the actual injury, the perpetrator must make restitution even if his act was unintentional. The Mishna rules, however, that shame or indignity can only be caused intentionally. Therefore, if the perpetrator was asleep when he caused the injury, or it came about when he fell off a roof, he must pay for the injury, but he is exempt from payment for the shame or indignity. This is then made into a general rule—אינו חייב על הבושת עד שיהא מתכוין. In this case it appears that intention is a necessary condition for responsibility. This is in striking contrast to a case where one might have thought that intention would be essential on moral grounds, but the opposite turns out to be true. In M. Yevamot 6:1 we learn that if the levir *(yavam)* has sexual relations with his childless brother's widow *(yevamah)* she becomes his levirate wife, no matter what the circumstances under which the act was performed. It matters not if it was deliberate or accidental, coerced or freely performed, the act serves as acquisition in marriage בין בשוגג בין במזיד בין ברצון בין באונס – קנה ולא חלק בין ביאה לביאה. In this case, where so much that is humanly important is at stake, the ruling openly sets aside all questions of intention. The act is effective, even if totally unintended.

A curious combination of free action and coercion joined together is seen in M. Arakhin 5:6. Certain sacrificial offerings which are due the Temple from individuals may be taken from them forcibly. The text points out that the Torah rules explicitly that such offerings are not effective instruments of atonement unless presented voluntarily. Yet, the Mishna rules that they compel him until he says, "I do this of my own free will." The text adds that the same applies to the giving of a divorce which must also be voluntary act on the part of the husband – כופין אותו עד שיאמר רוצה אני. Here we have the paradox of forced freedom of choice, a strange conception from any purely moral perspective. In these various cases we see that even with respect to so fundamental an issue in moral theory as the status of intention, the Mishna does not present us with a single unified view.

One can easily enough find cases of mishnaic legislation in which it is evident that value considerations are a determinative force. Yet here, too, we shall see that it is difficult to establish a single consistent pattern. An instance of such open axiological concern is to be found in the debate concerning the carrying of weapons on the Sabbath. The controlling principle of law is that one may carry such items only if they are in the category of ornaments or adornments. In M. Shabbat 6:4, the sages rule that a man may not go out on the Sabbath carrying a sword or other weapons. To this, R. Eliezer responds with a value judgment when he proclaims that these weapons are adornments –תכשיטן הן לו. He perceives weapons as adding an attractive, perhaps manly, dimension to the dress of a man as he walks the streets on the Sabbath. The Sages, however, object vigorously, saying that weapons are a disgrace and a reproach to the one who wears them –אינן אלא לגנאי, and they support their judgment by citing Isaiah 2:4, which gives voice to the hope for an era in which all weapons will be converted to peaceful use and war will no longer be known. It seems that R. Eliezer is able to maintain a value position even contrary to the seemingly unambiguous teachings of a biblical verse.

In a somewhat parallel case, M. Middot 3:4 codifies the biblical prohibition against using iron implements to prepare the stones with which the altar in the sanctuary is built. What is of interest here is that the biblical text gives no clear reason for this prohibition. The first biblical statement on the subject prohibits building an altar of hewn stones, "for by wielding your tool upon them you have profaned them" (Ex. 20:22). No explanation is given as to why the cutting of the stones with an iron tool profanes them. The second statement, in Deut. 27:5, 6, is even more cryptic. It prohibits the use of an iron tool in preparing the stones for the altar, but omits the earlier statement that iron profanes the altar. Our Mishna, however, introduces an explicit value explanation for the apodictic biblical rule. First, it sets forth the rules which prohibit the use of any iron implements in building the altar, even to the extent that an iron trowel may not be used to plaster it. Then the Mishna adds the following explanation: "For iron was created to shorten man's days, while the altar was created to lengthen man's days; it is not right that that which shortens [life] should be used in preparation of that which lengthens [life]." Unlike the debate concerning the value status of weapons in M. Shabbat, here there is no dissenting voice. Although the law against using iron to build the altar would stand without the value explanation, the Sages added a moral dimension to their account of the rules. They have given a moral justification which is absent in the Torah itself.

Human dignity is widely, and correctly, thought to be a central value in Judaism, and this value is reflected in various places in the Mishna. There is legislation which is explicitly motivated by the concern to prevent people from suffering embarrassment, especially in public. When Jews brought their first fruits to the Temple, they were required, as part of the ritual, to recite a certain passage from the Bible. M. Bikkurim 3:7 records that the original practice was, for those who were able, to read the passage by themselves, while for those who were not able, the priest read the passage and they recited the words after him. When it became clear that people were refusing to bring the first fruits because they were ashamed to display their ignorance in public, the Sages altered the procedure so that the priest read the words for everybody. In M. Taanit 4:8 there is recorded a celebration in which the unmarried girls of Jerusalem came out in their finery to be seen by young men who were looking for wives. The Mishna reports that every girl was required to wear clothes borrowed from someone else, so as not to embarrass those who did not own elegant dresses, שלא לבייש את מי שאין לו. Such explicit concern with protecting human dignity is common enough in the Mishna.

The Mishna moves to an even more comprehensive value position when it addresses directly the question of the unique and irreplaceable worth of every human being. M. Sanhedrin 4:5 tells us that witnesses who were about to testify in a case carrying the death penalty were carefully instructed by the court as to the gravity of their duty. To have a hand in ending a human life, even when required and justified by the law, is a responsibility which must fill the witnesses with awe. The judges pointed out that when a man is put to death it is not only his own life which is ended, but that of all the generations which might have been born from him. That is why one who destroys a single human [or Israelite, according to most readings] life is considered as if he had destroyed an entire world, and one who saves such a life is as if he had saved an entire world. Moreover, each human being is unique, so that every person must affirm that "for my sake the world was created." It seems, then, that human worth and human dignity are central value concepts in the thought of the Mishna.

Even with respect to these values, however, we find contrary instances. Let us consider just two such counter-instances. If all human beings have an intrinsic worth and dignity, then it follows that we must always treat them in such a way as to respect their worth and protect their dignity. There are special human relationships in which we are particularly enjoined to behave toward the other with respect. The case of parents comes to mind immediately, since the Torah commands us explicitly about honoring parents. The value system of the Sages, as seen in certain post-mishnaic statements, also puts great stress on the obligation of a man to honor his wife. According to one formulation, he should love her as much as he does himself and honor her more than himself (b. Yevamot, 62b). Yet, despite the general mishnaic teaching about respect for all persons, and the specific later teaching about special respect for one's wife, we find laws which do not accord with this attitude.

In M. Ketubot 9:4, we find the following ruling. If a man puts his wife in charge of his shop or appoints her to manage his property, he may, whenever he chooses, force her to take an oath that she has not been dishonest in her dealings. According to a second opinion, he may even demand such an oath with respect to work that she does at home. In the very relationship in which we would expect the highest level of respect and the deepest trust, the law authorizes a practice which can only arise from disrespect and mistrust. We see here that one cannot easily make sound generalizations about moral values in the Mishna.

An even more striking instance of apparent utter disregard for human dignity is found in M. Kilayim 8:6. There is a biblical prohibition against ploughing with a team of animals of different species (Deut. 22: 1 0). Although the Torah gives no explanation for this prohibition, it is usually assumed that the purpose is to spare pain to animals which are not evenly matched in strength and speed. The Mishna goes into great detail in determining which animals are of a common species and which are of different species, in order to teach us which maybe teamed together and which not. One would assume that if we have concern for the well-being of animals, we should have far greater and more sensitive concern for humans. Yet, the chapter of the Mishna which sets forth the detailed laws about mixing animals ends with the surprising rule that it is permissible to team man with any type of animal for pulling a wagon or ploughing or similar labors – ואדם מותר עם כולם למשוך ולחרוש ולהנהיג. It is hard to imagine a greater indignity to a person than to be teamed with an animal to do labor in the fields. Yet, the same body of law which has put so much emphasis on human worth and dignity has no problem about this ruling, which seems to show less concern for man than for animals. What is particularly Instructive is the fact that this ruling is stated baldly, without an explanation or justification that might mitigate its negative connotations. It is explained in another tannaitic source, which reads the biblical verse in a restrictive manner to refer only to animals of different species, but not to men— בשור וחמור אי אתה חורש אבל אתה חורש באדם ובחמור. (Sifre Deut. 231, ad Deut. 22: 10.) It would appear that we cannot claim that even so fundamental a moral value as human dignity is operative always and in all cases. The law goes its own way, uncontrolled by what we would consider moral values.

What we have seen so far casts doubt on any claim that the Mishna recognizes and implements a fixed set of moral rules and values. Instead, it would appear that what prevails generally is the law itself, a law which usually accords with what we today would think of as moral concerns, but does not always do so. It is not an independent morality or axiology which motivates the Sages of the Mishna. They teach the law as they understand it, even when it seems to run contrary to our (perhaps even their own) moral tastes. This becomes particularly clear when we consider those cases in which the law has profoundly painful human consequences for which no relief is provided. Most familiar are those laws which result in great family tragedy.

Consider the sad case set forth in M. Yevamot 10:1. A man goes off on a distant journey, leaving his wife behind. Some time later she is informed that her husband has died, and she remarries. Although the later discussions of this Mishna introduce various details concerning the number of witnesses and the other circumstances which led to her remarriage, the Mishna gives us no such information. All we know is that the testimony about her husband's death appeared to be reliable, and she proceeded to remarry in good faith and with no interference from the authorities. After some time the husband, who was presumed dead, returns. The law provides no remedy for this unfortunate woman. Both the first and the second husband must divorce her. Her children from both marriages are *mamzerim.* She has no financial claims against either husband, and is thus deprived of the economic security that marriage would normally have provided for her. In short, although she is the victim of an honest mistake, she is treated under the law as if she had deliberately committed adultery. No tender moral concerns are introduced to mitigate in any way the harsh consequences of a purely legal, even legalistic, ruling. This is in remarkable contrast to the strenuous efforts of the Sages to formulate the rules of evidence in such a way as to save women from becoming *agunot.* Reflection on these cases forces us to conclude that we cannot readily formulate a principle that determines when the law is controlled by "moral" considerations and when not.

In the case before us, we seem to have an instance of R. Akiva's principle that in matters of law considerations of compassion should not be introduced – אין מרחמין בדין. R. Akiva, known to be a person of great human concern and compassion, nevertheless takes the position that the law must stand firm and may not be changed, even in the interests of sympathetic concern for a seemingly innocent victim. He expresses this principle with respect to property rights, in cases where his opponent wants to favor those who are weakest. The principle, even when not explicitly stated, seems to be applied in many problematic cases where moral sentiment might impel us to find a solution that would reduce or eliminate human suffering. Thus, in M. Eduyot 4:9, the gentle House of Hillel imposes a rule which is so painful that the Mishna states explicitly that when the Sages considered the consequences they expressed deep sorrow and anxiety, saying – אי לו על אשתו ואי לו על אשת אחיו.

In some cases there is an internal debate in a Mishna based on considerations of fairness and compassion. M. Ketubot 13:5 records a case in which a man promised a dowry of a certain sum to his prospective son-in-law at the time of *the kiddushin.* By virtue of the *kiddushin,* the young woman is tied to her groom. The father went bankrupt and failed to pay the promised sum, and the young man, in turn, refused to marry the girl. The Mishna rules that she has no recourse, and may be required to live in her state of limbo "until her hair grows white" – תשב עד שילבין ראשה. Admon, a mishnaic figure who often rallied to the cause of the innocent victim, defends the girl. He argues that she is not responsible for her father's promises or his failure to keep them. Therefore, she can force the man either to marry her or to free her from her bonds to him. The Mishna records that Rabban Gamliel expressed his satisfaction with Admon's ruling. Here we have a seemingly harsh law tempered by equity and compassion, but this is certainly not always the case. What the Mishna exhibits is not a fixed pattern of moral concern, but, rather, diverse modes of response to each individual instance.

There are certain types of mishnaic legislation which seem to come closer to reliance on moral concerns for the determination of the law, but even these prove problematic when subjected to careful study. In contemporary discussions, the institution of the *prozbol* by Hillel the Elder is often treated as an example of a law being set aside because of moral concerns. This claim is not substantiated by the text of the Mishna in question. What Hillel confronted was a situation in which the Torah lays down a rule followed by a strong exhortation. The rule is that personal debts are canceled by the sabbatical year. The exhortation (Deut. 15:9-1 1) is that a person should not close his heart or his purse to the needy just because the onset of the sabbatical year is imminent and he fears that he will no longer be able to collect the loan he has made. The exhortation ends with the repeated positive command to give whatever is needed to the poor – נתון תתן לו, and not to hold back out of selfish concern. The Mishna teaches us that Hillel introduced the *prozbol,* not to meet some moral concern that he had arrived at independently, but in order to meet the requirements of the Torah. "Hillel instituted *the prozbol* when he saw that the people had stopped giving loans to one another and were thus violating the teaching of the Torah which cautions us, 'Beware lest you harbor the base thought, the seventh year, the year of remission is approaching, so that you are mean to your needy kinsman and give him nothing.'"

What we have in this case is two obligations set forth in the Torah that are potentially in conflict, the remission of debts and the injunction to provide for the poor, even at the risk of not being repaid. When social circumstances put these obligations in actual conflict, Hillel acted so as to preserve both the provision for the poor and the integrity of the sabbatical year. In this case, the need for a resolution is explicit both in the Torah and in the text of the Mishna. There are other cases of resolution of value conflicts in the law where we do not have explicit scriptural justification. In M. Bava Metzia 4:2, we are presented with the following case. The law specifies that in acquiring title to moveable property, the sale is only completed once the buyer has performed some act of taking physical possession. The Mishna rules, therefore, that if an agreement was made for the purchase of fruit and the money was paid, either the buyer or the seller may withdraw from the sale so long as there has been no act of taking possession. Although the Mishna does not spell out the reason for the decision to withdraw from the sale agreement, it is reasonable to suppose that we are dealing with a case in which a change in the market conditions makes it advantageous for the buyer or the seller to change his mind. We have here an established law concerning the acquisition of property, yet the Mishna is most unhappy with the results. Having established the right of either party to cancel the sale, the Mishna goes on to note that the Sages have pronounced a curse on anyone who takes advantage of this legal right. They are reported as saying, "He who punished the generation of the flood and the generation of the dispersion will also punish this person who does not keep his word." A provision of the civil law has come into conflict with the rule that requires us to remain faithful to our promises and commitments. The exemption given by the civil law stands, but the Sages urge that one should not take advantage of this exemption because the obligation to keep one's word should take precedence. They did not invent the moral rule about honesty; they simply decided that it should supersede any loophole in the law that permits one to violate a promise. If one chooses to interpret this as an instance of moral concern overriding mere legality, it should always be remembered that this moral concern is itself part of the law.

In another model we have an open internal debate about a value concern. The Torah sets forth rules of inheritance by which one's property is bequeathed to one's nearest relatives in a fixed order. May a man ignore the rules of the Torah in order to distribute his property as he chooses? From M. Bava Batra 8:5, it appears that one may not do so, at least not under the rubric of inheritance. A man may not, for example, deny a double portion to his first-born son. This would be contrary to the teaching of the Torah, שהתנה על מה שכתוב בתורה, and such conditions invalidate the will. There is, however, a legal way to get around this, by drawing up a document which distributes one's property as gifts, not as inheritance, A person may give a gift to whomever he chooses, and his decision is valid. Our Mishna notes that if a man drew up such a document distributing his property to others, while cutting his sons off, his act is legally binding. The Mishna then records its disapproval, noting that this is a violation of the spirit, if not the letter of the law. They condemn a person who does this, observing that, אין רוח חכמים נוחה הימנו; the Sages are very much displeased by his behavior. The value decision is clear. As in the case of withdrawing from a sale agreement, the law stands, but the act is condemned because it violates a norm set by the Torah.

Yet, in our Mishna, no less a figure than Rabban Simeon ben Gamliel adds a contrary approving note. He assumes that the father would not have chosen arbitrarily to cut off his sons from inheriting his property.

They must have misbehaved in serious ways in order to deserve this rebuff from their father, whose decision to punish them is praiseworthy – אם לא היו בניו נוהגין כשורה זכור לטוב. Both views rest on value considerations. The condemnation is concerned, above all, with preserving the intent of Torah law against legal loopholes. The approval is concerned with supporting the decision of a father deeply pained by the misbehavior of his sons. He considers it his Torah-given responsibility to correct and chastise them, not only in life, but even after his death. This is not an arbitrary value judgment or the introduction of external moral values into Jewish practice. It is, rather, a confrontation between the Torah's laws of inheritance and the Torah's broader rules of behavior which were violated by these wayward sons. The legal decision stands, but the value debate is unresolved.

In some other cases we find rulings which appear to depend on value preferences, but without any explicit statement. The Torah sets forth extensive rules concerning one who is afflicted with *nega,* a skin eruption which requires that the person be examined by a priest and then quarantined if he has the disease. A treatise of the Mishna is devoted to an exposition of the details of these laws. In M. Negaim 3:2 we find a striking exception to the Torah rule that when a person shows the symptoms of this skin eruption he should be brought immediately to the priest for examination. The Mishna text rules that if the eruption appears on a bridegroom, we delay until the end of the seven days of the marriage feast before bringing him to the priest. Similarly, for any person, if what appears to be a *nega* erupts during a festival, the examination by the priest is delayed until the end of the festival. No explanation is given here, or in the parallel tannaitic source in *Torat Kohanim* for this delay, but the reason seems obvious. The decision is to spare the bridegroom and his bride the pain of interrupting the festive celebration of their marriage, and to spare the householder and his family the pain of interrupting the celebration of the festival if it should turn out that they must be quarantined. Here we have a case where nothing is explicitly stated in the texts before us in justification of the value decision which gives priority to the completion of the festive celebrations. In fact, we can only infer that this is the reason. In any case, however, a choice had to be made as to whether the Torah's rules about quarantining the person suffering from this skin eruption should be immediately enforced, or to give prior status to the Torah's rules concerning the celebration of a marriage or a festival. Here again, even if we conjecture that the decision is based on humane moral considerations, we should remember that these considerations are not imposed from without, but reflect a choice between competing values in the Torah itself.

In another setting, and in a different mode of response, the Mishna advises us, in certain cases, how to benefit a householder by evading the stringencies of the law. In M. Maaser Sheni 4:4 the text begins with the permissive statement, מערימים על מעשר שיני, "We may circumvent the laws of the second tithe." The situation here is that the householder is required by the Torah to bring the second tithe to Jerusalem and eat it there. If it is difficult for him to bring the actual produce to Jerusalem, he is permitted by the Torah to redeem it for its monetary value and bring the money of redemption to Jerusalem to spend there.

In this case the Torah requires that he add one fifth of the value to the sum of redemption. Our Mishna goes on to teach us how to circumvent the duty to pay this added fifth. The technical details of the procedure are of no direct interest for our purpose. What matters is that we have an open invitation to evade the law, and a detailed procedure outlined for doing so legally. Here we seem to have a case in which the Sages gave preference to their concern for the protection of the farmer's financial interest against the explicit teaching of the Torah. Understandably, they sought and found a technically legal method, but even they themselves call it הערמה an evasion or circumvention of the law.

We have a similar case in M. Temurah 5:1, which opens with the question, "How can we circumvent [or evade] the law of the first-born animals?" – כיצד מערימים על הבכור. The concern is to evade the restriction which the Torah imposes against dedicating a first-born animal for sacrificial use other than that specified. The owner would like to use it for a sacrifice which he already owes, and thus save himself added expense, since the first-born animal must be given to the priest in any case, and the owner will derive no personal benefit from it. The text before us outlines a procedure for evading the law so as to benefit the owner of the animal. As in the former case, no direct justification is given for this legalized circumvention of a Torah-given obligation. These are cases where it would appear that the Sages gave priority to their concern for the financial interests of the farmers, even if it had to be achieved by designing a legal mode of evasion. In an unusual move, they sacrifice straightforward honesty and fulfillment of duty to the desire to save expense. We may well have here cases in which the value of saving money is given priority in the legal system without any justification in the system itself.

Far clearer are those instances in which the Sages used their authority to issue edicts whose purpose was to protect the value system of the Torah from forces which threatened it. I am referring to the various types of *takkanot* whose purpose is specified in the text of the Mishna. In M. Gittin 4:2, we are taught that, originally, a husband might send a bill of divorce to his wife by way of a messenger, and then appear before a court to annul the document. This meant that the wife might receive the divorce document without knowing that it had been annulled, and would remarry being unaware that she was not legally divorced. This could cause incalculable harm to her and to any children she might bear. Rabban Gamliel the Elder issued a decree forbidding this practice in order to protect the general welfare, מפני תיקון העולם. He instituted a number of additional *takkanot* with respect to the rules of divorce procedure, all of them justified with the same reason. In all these cases the aim is to protect the wife from arbitrary or negligent actions which would endanger her and increase the number of *mamzerim* in society. Since it was possible under the letter of the law to cause such harm, whether maliciously or not, the Sage instituted restrictions which would protect the innocent wife from being victimized. Although these *takkanot* prevent the husband from exercising certain rights which are his under the law, they can hardly be said to be introducing new moral values into the legal system. Concern for the general welfare, fairness, and compassion are all an established part of the system. The purpose of the *takkanot* is to make certain that these established values prevail against the machinations of thoughtless, malicious, or unscrupulous husbands.

Sometimes we find legislation. which clearly is aimed at the public welfare, although the point is not made explicitly. Thus, in M. Avodah Zarah 1:7, there is a prohibition against selling to gentiles bears or lions or anything else which might be a public danger – וכל דבר שיש בו נזק לרבים. Now, it is not stated explicitly that gentiles cannot be trusted to prevent such animals from becoming a danger to the public, but the inference is obvious. The rule simply gives practical effect to the established values of the legal system concerned with the preservation of life and limb.

There are other instances of legislation מפני תיקון העולם which do not appeal even implicitly to established values of the system, but simply invoke wise public policy. This is the case, for example, with respect to the *takkanah* which decrees that we may only ransom captives or redeem sacred scrolls from gentiles for a reasonable price. To pay them excessively would encourage them to take more captives or to steal more scrolls. It is not at all clear that this is a question of moral values. It appears, rather, to be a practical decision in order to reduce the danger of generating greater suffering, as well as preventing greater demands on the wealth of the Jewish community. Similarly, Rabban Simeon ben Gamliel instituted legislation in order to combat a contemporary explosion of price gouging at the expense of poor women who wanted to fulfill their ritual obligations (M. Keritot 1:7). Contrary to the established rules, he reduced drastically the number of doves certain women had to bring as offerings to the Temple. This had the effect of creating a large surplus of supply over demand, which drove the price down to a fair level. This concern for the poor and for fair business practices is not an imported moral value. It is deeply rooted in the legal system.

In M. Gittin 4:5, on the other hand, we have a case where the value justification for a *takkanah* 'is taken directly from the Torah. The problem is generated by the status of a person who is half-slave and half-free. The Hillelites see this as a problem of the legal distribution of property rights, hence they rule that this person should alternate, working one day for his master and one day for himself Nothing else in this situation seems to interest them. Yet the Shammaites see here a human problem of far greater concern than just money or property rights. They enter a vigorous protest at the idea of leaving the matter in this state, which provides for the master's property rights at the expense of the slave/free man's human rights. As they put it, תקנתם את רבו ואת עצמו לא תקנתם. Their concern is that a person in this ambiguous legal state can never marry. Being half-free, he cannot marry a slave, but being half-slave, he cannot marry a free woman. Here a biblical principle is invoked. Procreation is a primary duty for every person, as Isaiah 45:18 teaches us, and this must take precedence over the master's property rights. Based on this, the Shammaites ruled מפני תקון העולם that the master is coerced to free the slave so that he shall be fully a free man able to marry and fulfill his procreative duties. The freed slave, in turn, must give his former master a note for the amount of his half-slave worth, thus protecting the master's property rights. Here the value concern which is determinative is not invented or imported from the outside by the Shammaites. - It is an established biblical teaching which they invoke. Interestingly enough, the Mishna text records that the Hillelites subsequently changed their position to accord with the Shammaites.

The Mishna records a variety of rules מפני דרכי שלום, rules that were instituted for the purpose of reducing conflict and maintaining peaceful and harmonious relationships among Jews and between Jews and gentiles. M. Gittin 5:8, 9 records a series of these laws, but there are a number of other places in the Mishna where additional rules of this type are set forth. For example, the order of calling to the Torah first a Cohen, then a Levi, then a Yisrael was instituted to prevent disputes about who should be honored first. In another case we are instructed to greet and ask after the welfare of non-Jews whom we meet, despite the fact that there is a danger of using the divine name improperly when extending such a greeting. The ruling is made in order to promote harmonious and peaceful relations between Jews and non-Jews. The considerable body of such legislation מפני דרכי שלום gives concrete legislative expression to the high value placed by the Jewish legal system on peaceful and friendly human relations. It is by no means evident that this is a question of morality rather than law.

Particularly striking among the *takkanot* is one which is instituted in order to encourage sinners to repent, and set right the wrong that they have committed. M. Gittin 5:5 adjusts an established rule concerning the return of stolen property. If a person stole a beam and used it in the the building of his house, and then repented and wanted to make restitution, how should he proceed. The law entitles the original owner to receive the exact item that was stolen from him. In this case, it would require the penitent thief to dismantle his whole house in order to extract that particular beam. The Sages realized that this imposed an inordinately heavy burden that would discourage the thief from making restitution. They ruled that, in such a case, it was sufficient that the owner be paid the value of the beam that had been stolen and this would fully settle the obligation. The ground for this decision is מפני תקנת השבים, in order to encourage the sinner to repent. Penitence is judged here to be of such high value in the established Jewish axiology, that it takes precedence over the strict interpretation of the laws of property rights.

Finally, we consider a series of cases where the Mishna records the effect of changed social conditions on the law. We shall see that in these cases the law is responding to internal principles, not to external moral considerations. In the Torah (Deut. 21: 1-9) an elaborate ritual is ordained in the case where a murdered body is found in the field and the identity of the murderer is unknown. The elders of the nearest town expiate the sin by breaking the neck of a heifer. They then proclaim their innocence of the crime and they pray for God's forgiveness. Much of Chapter 9 of M. Sotah is devoted to setting forth the detailed rules for carrying out this expiatory ritual. In 9:9, however, a new note is introduced. The ritual is canceled because the incidence of murder has become so frequent and widespread – משרבו הרצחנים בטלה עגלה ערופה. The ritual is seen as mandatory and effective only so long as murder is a rare occurrence. Once unsolved murders are commonplace and widespread, there seems no longer to be any point to the expiatory act. Here the fact of the annulment of the ritual is simply recorded, but we are not told why the increase in the frequency of murder should have this consequence. It is almost as if the Sages are passing judgment on their society, and ruling that when there is so much wickedness it is no longer reasonable to seek redemption through ritual practice alone.

In contrast, the next section of this same Mishna provides us with a very different model. The Torah legislates that a wife who is suspected by her husband of adultery shall have her guilt or innocence determined by a trial by ordeal. Our Mishna records that, משרבו המנאפים פסקו המים המרים, when adulterers [note, not adulteresses] increased in number the trial by ordeal of ingesting the bitter waters was discontinued. In this case, however, we are told by whom and why. The Mishna says that Rabban Yohanan ben Zakkai was the one who canceled the testing of the suspected wife and the text goes on to record his reason. Scripture teaches that the trial by ordeal is only effective when the husbands themselves are innocent of wrongdoing and are above reproach. To establish this point, R. Yohanan quotes Hosea 4:14: "I will not punish their daughters for fornicating, nor their daughters-in-law for committing adultery; for they themselves turn aside with whores..." He construes this verse to mean that the effectiveness of the trial of the suspected wife is contingent on the virtuous behavior of her husband. Once adultery becomes widespread, then we can no longer proceed with the test of the bitter waters. Here again we do not have a personal moral judgment brought to bear on the law, but a judgment of Scripture which is applied when it fits the new circumstances.

We began this essay by raising the questions whether the Mishna contains the elements of an ethical theory, whether it provides us with a set of moral norms which can be validly generalized, whether it even recognizes the notion of ethics as a category separate from the law. In this study we have seen that there is no effort in the Mishna to address the general question of formulating an ethical theory. Furthermore, we have provided evidence that generalizations of the rules of the Mishna are hazardous. In almost every case, we are able to produce counter-instances which refute the generalizations. There seems to be very little evidence that the Mishna entertains any conception of a realm of the ethical which is independent of the law. The law itself contains much that is of moral interest from a contemporary point of view. These materials, however, are not viewed as a realm apart from mishnaic law, but, rather, as elements of the law itself. We need to study the whole of our literature to see if we can discover elsewhere a moral philosophy which will give grounding to a general Jewish ethical theory. We need also to see whether at any point in the canonical literature there emerges a generalized set of moral rules and values which is different from, if not fully independent of, the law.

27

THE ROLE OF PHILOSOPHY IN JEWISH STUDIES

In this essay I shall argue that without close attention to philosophic issues and methods, work in almost every area of Jewish Studies is deficient, although it is certainly the case that western culture has exhibited ambivalent attitudes toward philosophy and philosophers. In praise of philosophy it is claimed that it is the supreme architectonic science, the model of true wisdom, the fulfillment of the highest human aspirations. Plato is the classic source for this conception of philosophy, and his ideal man is conceived on the model of the philosopher. Plato's Socrates is presented as the best possible realization of the human ideal, which is to say, the true philosopher. Detractors of philosophy, on the other hand, have seen it as concerned with trivia and as threatening sound belief and even public order. This view, expressed by the accusers of Socrates in Plato's *Apology*, recurs throughout the history of western culture. Cicero makes the acerbic comment that, 'There is nothing so absurd that it has not been said by some philosopher."[1] Aristophanes in the *Clouds* pictures Socrates as a somewhat dangerous buffoon. While Thales is admired by some for his astute use of meteorological knowledge for personal profit, another tradition pictures him as so impractical that he fell into a well while gazing at the stars.[2] And Shakespeare's Romeo finds scant comfort in 'Adversity's sweet milk, Philosophy.' In his agony he asserts that, 'Unless philosophy can make a Juliet, Displant a town, reverse a prince's doom, It helps not, it prevails not.'[3] There is a similar ambivalence toward philosophy in the history of Judaism. Some medieval Jewish thinkers give to philosophic knowledge the highest place in their system of values, but their views can hardly be considered normative for all of Judaism. As is well known, there is a tradition of anti-philosophy within Judaism, which ranges from relative indifference to active hostility. The few direct references to philosophers in the rabbinic literature are on the whole uncomplimentary.[4] Philosophers are generally represented in Talmud and Midrash as heretics or as posers of rather foolish questions. There is little evidence that Greek philosophy had any significant influence on classical rabbinic thought. Professor Harry A. Wolfson said that he was "not able to discover any Greek philosophic term in Rabbinic literature," and Professor Saul Lieberman eliminates all doubt on this point when he adds, "I want to state more positively: Greek philosophic terms are absent from the entire ancient Rabbinic literature."[5]

Contempt for philosophy as a dangerous and misleading effort to substitute human wisdom for divine wisdom also occurs frequently in early Christianity. In a characteristic passage, Paul warns the Colossians against the dangers of "philosophy and empty deceit" which are mere human teachings and thus utterly unreliable.[6] The early church fathers considered certain Christian heresies to have their origins in "erroneous doctrines of the philosophers."[7] Tertullian expresses fierce opposition to philosophy as he depicts with delight the pleasures that await the faithful, when they will view, from a front row seat in heaven, the agonies of philosophers burning in Hell.[8]

Later periods in Jewish history exhibited some of the ferocity of the early Christian attacks on philosophy. The anti-Maimonidean controversy may have been the most extreme and extended case of such an attack, but it was by no means the only one. Suspicion of philosophy continued to manifest itself throughout the Jewish middle ages, and in certain circles the phenomenon continued in modern times. In some of the very yeshivot in which the study of Maimonides' *Mishne Torah* was mandatory, the study of his *Guide of the Perplexed* was frequently prohibited, or, at least, very actively discouraged. There are contemporary Jewish circles, as well, in which the rejection of philosophy continues to be considered as one mark of religious and intellectual virtue.

It is natural, therefore, to ask whether philosophy has any role in the study of Judaism. One immediate and easy justification is that there is, after all, a large literature of Jewish philosophic works, beginning with Saadia (if not with Philo) and continuing unbroken to the present. Surely, these are worthy of study, and they do constitute an appropriate segment of any curriculum of Jewish studies. While it seems pointless to argue against this claim, we can hardly ignore the argument made by some major scholars of our time. Leo Strauss held that the *Guide of the Perplexed* "is not a philosophic book."[9] Isaac Husik acknowledged that there was Jewish philosophy in the middle ages, but he was convinced that this discipline did not persist in the contemporary world. He ends his *History of Medieval Jewish Philosophy* with the melancholy observation that, "There are Jews now and there are philosophers, but there are no Jewish philosophers and there is no Jewish philosophy." Of course, neither Husik nor Strauss would exclude from our courses of study works which seek to interpret Judaism philosophically. They only want to argue that they are not works of philosophy.

Despite the existence of such extreme views, I doubt that any reasonable student of these matters will wish to assert seriously that there is no literature of Jewish philosophy. It exists and it is worthy of study. Without question such study constitutes one part of the role of philosophy in the Jewish Studies curriculum. In considering our topic, however, we must recognize how severely and needlessly we limit philosophy if we restrict it to the study of the history of Jewish philosophy. The thesis which I present here does not address itself to the question of the place of philosophy in Judaism. It does, however, argue that we are urgently in need of serious philosophic study and analysis of the whole range of textual materials which are the subject-matter of Jewish Studies, not only of acknowledged Jewish philosophic works, but also of every type of Jewish literature from antiquity to the present.

The very nature of philosophic thinking is such that it can and should be applied without exception to the entire corpus of Jewish literature. Bible, Talmud, and other major Jewish works are not systematic philosophic treatises, but they will never be fully understood if we do not approach them with the concerns and the techniques of philosophy. Opposition to philosophy at various times and places in Jewish history does not invalidate the propriety and usefulness of a philosophic study even of the very works in which such opposition is expressed. On the contrary, the texts which seem least philosophical are often the ones which most demand philosophical analysis.

I shall not attempt to offer here a definition of philosophy. Anyone familiar with the literature knows the range and complexity of the definitions that have been attempted. Yet we can set forth certain general characteristics of the philosophical approach to texts which is advocated in this essay. I suggest that in the study of any Jewish texts we must engage in philosophic work on two levels, substantive and methodological. Substantively, the texts are almost certain to contain specifically philosophical subject-matter. In one way or another, directly or by implication, serious works take some stand with respect to some of the 'ultimate questions' which are usually considered the subject-matter of philosophy. Even non-philosophical Jewish books contain both explicit and implicit metaphysical theses, fundamental claims about the ethical, philosophical or theological anthropologies, views about knowledge and truth, systems of logic, and other types of specifically philosophical teachings.

A proper philosophic study of these works will be concerned not only with subject-matter but also with method. Perhaps the least limiting characterization of philosophic method is that it is critical thinking about the theoretical foundations of whatever subject or text is being analyzed. A philosophic study of Jewish texts will thus be concerned with careful analyses of the foundations on which the doctrines set forth rest. It will give critical consideration to the arguments which are set forth and will uncover the premises of those arguments. Beginning with the assumption that the texts before us are the work of men who were both intelligent and serious, philosophical analysis will seek to provide a coherent and intelligible account of what was in the mind of each author.

Philosophical thinking stands at the center of all serious intellectual work. Any field of scholarship which ignores its own philosophical subject-matter and rejects any method of critical philosophical analysis, condemns itself to a certain narrowness of vision and extracts from its subject matter far less than it is capable of yielding. For philosophy is a universal and inescapable human activity. It is not the exclusive domain of the professional philosophers, but an ongoing task of every man. It is this which led G. K. Chesterton to assert that

> The most practical and important thing about a man is... his view of the universe. We think that for a landlady considering a lodger, it is important to know his income, but still more important to know his philosophy. We think that for a general about to fight an enemy, it is important to know the enemy's numbers, but still more important to know the enemy's philosophy. We think the question is not whether the theory of the cosmos affects matters, but whether, in the long run, anything else affects them.[10]

Our task is to uncover and explicate the philosophy, implicit or explicit, in the Jewish texts which are the subject of our study. If they are works which are relatively unsophisticated, they still have an important philosophical dimension which forms their foundation in thought. If they are highly sophisticated, but non-philosophical texts, they demand most careful philosophical study. And if they are genuinely philosophical texts, we need to learn to read them philosophically, not just as pieces to be moved around on the grid of the history of terms, arguments, and ideas.

Philosophic study of a body of materials is not a substitute for rigorous and specialized scholarship. Each field of Jewish Studies requires its own modes of scholarship and uses those tools of learning and those methods which are appropriate to it. Philosophic analysis and construction depends on that scholarship and can only be meaningful if it works with reliable texts, if it is fully informed about the cultural ambiance of those texts and their authors, if it is aware of the relevant social, economic and political data, and if it has access to as much as can be known of the inner life of the authors and the modes of thought which underlie the texts. Philosophic work is not done in a vacuum. Since it is unlikely that any one individual will have the whole range of learning that is required, the task of philosophy in Jewish Studies must result from cooperative scholarly efforts. Yet, having said this, we can proceed here to outline and illustrate some of the main features of the specifically philosophic enterprise within the various fields of Jewish Studies.

For anyone engaged in a philosophic study of the literary sources of Judaism, a first requisite is a highly sophisticated understanding of theories of interpretation. We are dealing with a literature much of which is, or claims to be, an interpretation of earlier works. We record differing interpretations of a text; we compare and contrast them; but we almost never ask the philosophic questions: What is the theory of interpretation which is being employed in each case? How do the interpreters understand their own activity? What are the principles which guide them? To take a typical case, the *Encyclopaedia Judaica* articles on "Hermeneutics" and "Interpretation" set forth certain general principles and discuss the details of various types and rules of interpretation, but never once do they raise the critical philosophic questions. In the discussion of rabbinic modes of biblical exegesis, the thirteen hermeneutical rules of R. Ishmael are classified into two groups, "Elucidative Interpretation"' and "Analogical Interpretation." There is then added to the thirteen principles a category named "Logical Interpretation." Shall we infer from this that the principles of R. Ishmael are not logical? If so, must we not try to understand the nature of the non-logical thinking that goes into their formulation and use? What shall we make, for example, of the rule of *gezerah shavah?* It is not enough to know that versions of this mode of interpretation, which in many cases seems to defy all logic, were used by Greek and Roman rhetoricians.[11] Neither does it solve our problem to be informed that the rabbinic authorities tried to limit the danger of abuses of this method. We need to enter into the minds of those who proposed what seem like far-fetched conclusions based on *gezerah shavah.* What was behind their thinking? What theory of interpretation were they following? How did they conceive their task as exegetes? What is needed is philosophical analysis. We may not be successful in every case, but we can surely hope to illuminate much that is now obscure and to emerge with some sense of a coherent systematic structure which informs particular modes of interpretation.

A philosophic mode of study and analysis has an important role to play in our understanding of each of the various types of Jewish literature. Whether it be Halakha or Aggadah, Mishnah or Midrash, there is a philosophic task to be done, but any study of the existing literature will show that the philosophic work has hardly begun. Let us consider a sample case. It is generally acknowledged that the Aggadah is a major source for Jewish religious thought. The point was made in tannaitic times in the well known statement that if one wants to know the Creator, he should study Aggadah, since this is the way to know God and to cleave to His ways.[12]

We see that Aggadah was thought of by some teachers as one important way to the knowledge of God. This certainly should make aggadic literature a major focus of philosophic interest, and one would expect students of Aggadah to treat the texts philosophically. However, the major works on the subject deal with everything but the philosophical dimension.

Yizhak Heinemann's, דרכי האגדה is an indispensable handbook for the study of this form of Jewish literature. It has the seeming advantage of having been written by one whose primary work was in philosophy. Yet the book deals with almost every aspect of the study of Aggadah, but pays no attention to the philosophical analysis of aggadic texts. The bulk of the discussion in Heinemann's book comes under the headings "Methods of Creative Historiography" and "Methods of Creative Philology." He discusses in one place what he calls הזנחת הלוגוס מהקיף in the Aggadah, but even here he does not confront the philosophic issues. It is hardly enough to list examples of the apparent lack of rational order and structure in the Aggadah, as he does. To take one case, Heinemann informs us that: חז״ל פירושו אמנם את שיר השירים כולו דרך משל, אבל בנוגע לנמשל

בולטת בפירושיהם אי עקביות גמורה.[13] He then goes on to list instances of this "total inconsistency." This should be the beginning, not the end, of the investigation. If we take the Aggadah seriously, then we must subject it to searching philosophical analysis. A pattern of thinking which appears to be patently irrational, but which is pursued by intelligent and serious men, must engage all our philosophic acumen. We need to penetrate beneath the surface to the intellectual foundations of their thought and to their conceptions of textual interpretation. Our task is to find the way to bring order out of the apparent chaos, to understand the seemingly incoherent texts in ways which penetrate philosophically to their depths and discover their inner principles of order and structure. Glib slogan-like solutions are insufficient. Heinemann does little to illuminate the obscurity when he gives us a capsule explanation to the effect that aggadic writers see the contradictions in Scripture as a reflection of the paradoxes of life. Just how do they conceive these paradoxes? Are they saying that the world is irrational and lacking inherent principles of order? Or is it human life which is irrational? If all is paradoxical, what role does God play in the world? And what is their conception of God? These are only a few of the philosophic questions which must occupy any student of this aspect of the Aggadah. If Heinemann wants to argue that certain literary forms are deliberate instances of art imitating reality, then we must have some clear and coherent notion of the view of reality which underlies these literary texts.

The achievement of a philosophic understanding of the Halakhah is an equally great and urgent requirement. Here philosophy has a major task in a field where hardly any serious work has been done. Although the centrality of Halakhah in Judaism is not subject to debate, little effort has been made to explicate the philosophic foundations of the law or to search out its philosophic meanings. The study of Halakhah with philosophical insight is perhaps the most important work that is required for any genuinely philosophical study of Judaism. In the limited context of the present discussion, I shall not attempt to show how this applies to the great and overarching questions. Before we are ready to deal with the most fundamental and comprehensive issues in the philosophical exposition of the Halakhah, we shall have to do much intensive work on the smaller questions. To illustrate the point, let us consider in a limited context some problems about ethics and Halakhah. This is a subject on which there is considerable literature, much of it apologetic and most of the rest selectively descriptive, which is only a subtler form of apologetics.

A mishnah reads as follows: "If one paid money for produce, but did not draw the produce into his possession (לא משך), he can nullify the purchase. But they (i.e. the Sages) said: He who punished the generation of the flood and the generation of the dispersion will punish whoever does not keep His word."[14] We have here a puzzling situation. The law is clear. There is no consummation of the sale without the act of drawing (משיכה). Payment of money does not constitute legal purchase. Therefore, even if money has been paid, the purchaser has full legal right to change his mind and to nullify the purchase. Nevertheless, the very mishnah which sets forth the law condemns anyone who take advantage of his legal rights. Neither the classical nor the modern commentators seem to be troubled by this paradox. They simply record the case, explain the main terms, and state that the sages invoked a curse on one who behaves this way. In the standard literature a number of specialized versions of this type of case are discussed, but no attention is paid to the curious logic of the situation. This is the point at which philosophical analysis must enter.

Certain basic questions present themselves for consideration. Does the invocation of the curse, with its stress on the importance of keeping one's word, imply that there are non-halakhic moral principles which are superior to the law? if so, how are such principles known and what is their source? Since the law is Torah and, from its own inner perspective, an expression of God's teaching, how can it be morally imperfect? Does not the suggestion of moral imperfection in this law open up the possibility of questioning the moral soundness of any other halakhah?

Investigation of the Halakhah as an ethical system forces us to deal with these and similar questions. These basic philosophic issues cannot be resolved (if they are in fact open to solution) if we restrict ourselves only to one specific case. What is required is a careful study of the whole group of parallel cases which occur in the Mishnah, Tosefta, etc. Each case needs to be examined in its individual setting, and then we must determine whether there is some pattern that emerges. The various expressions which are used to convey similar ideas need to be considered individually and in their interrelationships. For example, in a Tosefta which is parallel to our Mishnah, we find an additional statement,[15] אבל אמרו הכמים כל המבטל את דיבורו אין רוח חכמים נוחה הימנו. Does this have identical force to "He who punished," or is it less intense? When all such matters have been considered, there remains the major philosophic work. Until we determine whether there is an extra-halakhic criterion of the morality of the Halakhah, we shall not understand the Halakhah itself fully. By failing to clarify the ruling in the law itself that it is wicked to abide by the law, we leave the law without a meaningful foundation. It is not my task here to deal with the substantive issues, but only to cite a sample case in which philosophic analysis is required in order to illuminate the Halakhah.[16]

The ethics of the Halakhah is only one area in which philosophy has a contribution to make. The field is far wider than this. Once we recognize the Halakhah as a major source (and in the view of many the major source) of Jewish doctrine, we shall be moved to develop not only the ethics, but the metaphysics, epistemology and logic of the Jewish legal system.[17] Here we are in a field that is little explored and demands massive effort. We don't know for certain how to begin, what methodology to employ, or even exactly what we are expecting to find. Nevertheless, it is time to put to the test the classic Jewish emphasis on Halakhah as the core of Judaism. The pious often assert that there is more religious depth in שור שנגח את הפרה than in the great works of theology. It is a long way, however, from such folk piety to sophisticated and systematic philosophic explication of this thesis. We need to fashion appropriate philosophic instruments and then to approach the study of the law with a combination of the learning of the classical *talmid hakham* and the critical thinking of the philosopher.

One point which should be stressed is that we are far from ready to produce a comprehensive account of the philosophy of the Halakhah. It is not even clear that there is a single body of philosophic thought which is the basis of the Halakhah. We should be initially suspicious of any work which purports to reduce rabbinic thought to a single, neat, and orderly structure. So many strands need to be disentangled, so many specific issues need to be analyzed, that it will be a very long time before we can hope to be ready to develop a complete philosophical picture of halakhic literature.

The problem is many times more complicated if we want to address ourselves also to the Aggadah. What we can do, however, is to take up one by one smaller and more limited topics. Some examples were given above in the area of the ethics of the Halakhah. Other studies in this area might include philosophic examinations of such topics as freedom, personal responsibility, the individual and society, divine law and the political state, ideas of justice, hierarchies of values, and similar subjects within the Halakhah. Such studies, properly done, might give us the ground for a comprehensive account of ethical theory in the Halakhah. In a similar way we need to pursue a series of individual studies which could result in a sound account of the metaphysics and epistemology of the Halakhah. If these studies were also extended to the Aggadah, we might finally be able to speak responsibly and with insight about what we so glibly today call rabbinic thought.

While the Halakhah and Aggadah may constitute the first priority for serious philosophical analysis, the study of the Bible is no less in need of a sophisticated philosophical dimension. There are many books and chapters in books which purport to offer a philosophical account of biblical thought. We encounter such comprehensive titles as "The Philosophy of the Old Testament," "The Basic Ideas of Biblical Religion," "Philosophy and the Bible," or "Prophetic Philosophy." In almost every case these turn out to be collections of vague and undefended generalizations or highly selective concentrations on a few themes chosen arbitrarily. Frequently they fail to take into account the best available biblical scholarship on each particular point, and they tend to substitute preaching for sober philosophical reflection. For example, one writer construes the קול דממה דקה of Elijah's experience to mean that "the voice of God is heard in the inner recesses of the soul." According to Bible scholars the expression קול דממה דקה is obscure, but there is no ground whatsoever for identifying it with the familiar modern definition of conscience as "the voice of God in the soul of man." A passage such as this can only be interpreted soundly if we first take account of all that we can learn about its meaning from biblical philology, comparative studies of ancient Near Eastern religions, and similar disciplines. To these may then be added the special insights and analysis of philosophical study. If the passage is an important biblical instance of a theophany, then it deserves and demands both sound biblical scholarship and meticulous philosophical analysis. Comparison is required with the immediately preceding episodes in which the divine power is manifested in public actions as well as with similar episodes elsewhere in the Bible. We must consider a number of philosophic questions. What conceptions of God are expressed in the various episodes in I Kings 18 and 19? How are these conceptions related? Do they form a systematic whole or are they separate and even contradictory? What shall we make of the God who shows his power publicly through the אש ה' which consumes the sacrifice and who proclaims only a few verses later לא באש ה'? Is there a difference in theological meaning between the expressions אש ה' and לא באש ה'?

Careful comparative studies are required to understand the religious meaning of these terms and of the episodes they portray. For, in addition to the questions arising directly out of the manifestations of God in the fire or His failure to be known through the fire, there are other more general problems that have to be worked through. For example, what is the status of the kind of empirical test which Elijah proposed?[18] How shall we understand in this episode the role and power of the prophet? Does God respond to his prayer as a free agent or is the prophetic force that of צדיק גוזר והקב"ה מק? These are some of the philosophic questions which would occupy us in any serious analysis of this biblical passage. Similar philosophic questions confront us in the study of almost any biblical passage chosen at random.

What is called for, within the framework of sound biblical scholarship, is serious philosophical work. As Nahum M. Sarna, a distinguished Bible scholar, puts it, "No study of biblical literature can possibly claim to do justice to the subject if it fails to take account of the world-view of the biblical writers, or if it ignores their ideas about God and man and pays no regard to their deep sense of human destiny."[19] Sarna goes on to take note of the tendency, in the enthusiasm for parallels, to draw easy and imperceptive comparisons. "Scholarly integrity," he says, "demands that the conclusions drawn from the utilization of the comparative method to be recognized for what they are-generalizations of limited value. One has to be sure that one is not dealing with mere superficial resemblances... There always remains the possibility that we have touched upon purely external characteristics... Further, we may have torn a motif right out of its cultural or living context and so have distorted the total picture." We must move with great care in this field and with an acute sense of the integrity of cultures and the central role which philosophic ideas play in these cultures.[20] This requires us to overcome the temptation to premature and unfounded generalizations. Instead, we must be prepared to work carefully on individual passages, particular themes, or special and limited topics. Out of these studies we may hope, at least, for philosophic insight into the small subjects to which we address ourselves. As in the case of rabbinic literature, we must leave open the question as to whether we may be able to achieve that grand synthesis which could legitimately be represented as biblical philosophy. So much more limited work must first be done that it is pointless to speculate on the final outcome. Unless we proceed more or less in this way, we shall simply be multiplying the arbitrariness and the intellectual irresponsibility which is typical of so much of the existing literature in this field.

Even careful and philosophically sophisticated scholars seem to lose control of their material when they generalize about biblical thought. In a major book by one of the greatest students of Jewish philosophy of the last generation, there is a discussion of basic ideas in the Bible which includes the following statement:

> Jewish thought is not oriented towards metaphysical questions. The sloughing off of mythological cosmogonies eliminated all potential starting points for the growth of metaphysics. The notion of a Creator provides no occasion for a theoretical interpretation of the world. This may well be the answer to the question: Why did Judaism not develop its own philosophic system?[21]

I find it impossible to offer an intelligible explication of this passage and am utterly perplexed by its claim to represent biblical thought. What can it mean to say that "the notion of a Creator provides no occasion for a theoretical interpretation of the world?" That notion is a theoretical interpretation of the world, just as is the notion that the world is eternal and uncreated, or the notion that the world came into being when eternal matter was given form by the demiurge or the notion that that world came into existence as the result of a "big bang." Can we accept a reading of the first chapter of Genesis that concludes that biblical thought has no concern with metaphysics? The first verse of Genesis makes a metaphysical claim, no less than the first verse of the Gospel of John. Both verses leave much unsaid, but what they say is more than enough to generate intense philosophical reflection.

In the study of the Bible, as in other Jewish literature, we must free ourselves of easy generalization, romanticization, and homileticization. To know the bible in its full depth and importance, we must reflect on its philosophical dimension. To begin with the familiar, biblical ideas of creation, revelation, and redemption await sober analysis. We are lacking serious philosophical analyses of the main aspects of biblical ethics, of the relationship of ethics to law, and of both to divine commandment. We need to determine whether the Bible anywhere recognizes a natural moral law which is not derived from divine commandment. These questions are typical of the work that remains to be done in a philosophic study of the Bible. As in the case of rabbinic literature, the work can only be done initially in small segments. From these studies we may expect a considerable degree of philosophical illumination which will raise our understanding of the Bible to new levels of sophistication.

Another area which awaits serious philosophical study is medieval and modern biblical commentaries. With some exceptions, the vast literature of *Parshanut* has been treated as if it were of little or no philosophical interest. It is usually thought that only commentaries by philosophers contain philosophic elements, while others stand beyond the boundaries of philosophy. In his admirable little book, *Parshanut haMikra,* M. Z. Segal has one section entitled "Philosophical Commentaries" and another headed "Modern Philosophical Commentaries." The implication is that the figures discussed in these sections are the only ones who offer commentary which is philosophically interesting. Thus, he tells us with respect to Rashi that,[22]

אין אצלו כלום מהפרשנות הפילוסופית.
השאלות שהטרידו את חכמי ישראל בארצות הערביות...לא העסיקו כלל
את רש"י....אמנם הוא יודע שאין לקחת את דיבורי ההגשמה כפשוטם.....
והוא משתמש הרבה בדיבור "כביכול" ....אבל בכלל הוא מפרש דברי
ההגשמה כפשוטם ,ואינו מרגיש בתמימותו .....וצדקותו שאפשר
להתקשות בהבנת הדברים כהויתם. למרות חירות הדעות שלו, נשאר

Or, speaking of R. Yoseph Bekhor Shor, he says:[23] ר"י בכור שור נאמן למסורת
של האסכולה הצרפתית ולתמימותה באמונות ודעות. הרציונליות שלו
היא מיוסדות על השכל הישר, ולא על שום השקפה פילוסופית כדרך
הפרשנים הספרדיים.

There are certainly important distinctions to be drawn between the French and Spanish schools of commentators, among them the fact that the latter dealt directly and explicitly with philosophical issues while the former did not. But it is precisely at this point that we see the important and unfulfilled role of philosophy in the study of this literature. Philosophy is not contained only in packages that are explicitly labeled; every instance of human thought has a philosophical dimension. The commentaries of Rashi and Rashbam may not be discussed in histories of Jewish philosophy, while Kaspi and Gersonides claim their rightful place there. However, a proper understanding of the "non-philosophical" commentators demands no less philosophical insight and sophistication than is required for the study of the "philosophic" commentators.

Consider the hidden implications in the observations of Segal that were just quoted. First, there is a theory of textual interpretation implicit in Rashi's method. This is a philosophical issue and can be fully exposed and explicated only by methods of philosophical analysis. Second, if, as Segal says, Rashi does not take anthropomorphisms literally, then he has a philosophic stance on this point. Third, if he has no hesitation, nevertheless, about using anthropomorphic language, we must try to grasp the principles that are the basis for his method. When Segal tells us (in the passage cited above) that במקומות ...שעוררים תמיהה לא עלה על דעתו שצריך לעקם את הכתוב כדי לקרב אותו אל מושגינו, he has presented us with a question, not an answer. Perhaps it is a question which can be answered by cultural historians who will help us to see why in Rashi's setting this way of speaking about God posed no problem. Even then we shall still need the perceptions of the philosopher to clarify just what Rashi is doing and how it differs from the way of other commentators. Fourth, if "temimut" is a proper characterization of Rashi and his disciples, that too is a philosophic stance. I confess that I do not know with certainty what it means, but I do know that philosophical innocence is also a form of philosophy. Fifth, if Bekhor Shor is both loyal to the "temimut" of the French school and also a "rationalist" (as Segal seems to say), then we surely need a philosophical account of this interesting combination of rationalistic simple-mindedness. Sixth, we need a philosophical exposition of a rationalism "which is based on common sense and not on any philosophical perspective." These are some philosophical issues which arise from a cursory reading of a few lines in a major secondary work on the biblical commentators. How much more is likely to emerge from a close and sensitive reading of the commentators themselves!

As examples, I shall mention only two types of commentary which in every case demand philosophic study. One is the treatment of contradictions in Scripture. Most, if not all, commentators deal with this problem at some point, the philosophically "innocent" Rashi no less than the philosophically "sophisticated" Abraham ibn Ezra. Contradictions are an offense to human reason, and methods for their resolution are always of interest to the philosopher in his role as logician. However the resolution is achieved, it presupposes some logical theory which may be implicit rather than explicit, but which is the controlling intellectual force. A comparative study of the ways in which individual commentators deal with contradictions would be extremely valuable. Do they all follow some standard version of Aristotelian logic, whether they know it as such or not? Are there different logics at work? Do we have adumbrations of multi-valued logics? Is contradiction always held to be inadmissible, or do we have commentators who glory in paradox? In the latter case, on what metaphysical-logical ground do they rest? There is much philosophic work to be done here, even in the study of supposedly nonphilosophical commentators.

A second example may be found in the problem which is posed by the multiplicity of interpretations of a single passage, interpretations which differ widely and frequently contradict each other. The critical philosophical issues which this phenomenon raises stand at the heart of the whole commentarial enterprise. How is the biblical text understood by each commentator? Does he suppose that it has one and only one true meaning, or that it is laden with many layers of meaning? When a commentator openly rejects midrashic explanations in favor of his own version of the *peshat,* what theory motivates him? Is he affirming the authority of his own intellect against that of the official literature of the tradition, and if so on what ground? What of the cases in which midrashim which soften extreme anthropomorphism are rejected in favor of a crudely literal interpretation; as, e.g., Rashi to Genesis 3:8? Is he moved by a theory of literal meaning even at the price of questionable theological consequences? Why in this case are "helpful" midrashim rejected while in other cases, e.g., the previous verse, rather fantastic midrashim are accepted? Answers to these questions will not come from purely philological studies. They are, at their depth, philosophic questions and they demand philosophic answers.

The cases we have cited to illustrate the role of philosophy in the study of various types of Jewish literature and subject matter are by no means an exhaustive account. There is no area of Jewish learning that does not have need for this kind of philosophical analysis. One more area, however, does require our explicit attention, and that is the relationship of philosophy to the study of Jewish philosophic literature. Put this way the matter sounds either absurd or paradoxical, but it is neither. At the beginning of this discussion, we indicated that our main concern was to show the extent to which philosophy has a productive role in the study of various non-philosophical types of Jewish literature. Now we must reflect briefly on the role of philosophy in the study of the literature of Jewish philosophy itself.

The reason that this is neither absurd nor paradoxical is the fact that there are many non-philosophical ways of studying philosophic texts.

At their best these are valuable propadeutics to genuinely philosophical studies. We must know the uses and meanings of the key technical terms employed in a philosophic work. We need to know all that we can about the historical-cultural setting in which the work was written and about the audience for whom it was intended. We need to know what the main influences were on an author, and to what extent he is reproducing the ideas and arguments of his predecessors. Scholars who provide us with this information have performed an invaluable service. Without their work no responsible study of these texts is possible. But we must stress again that such studies are (in addition to their intrinsic interest) a necessary but not a sufficient condition for the philosophic study of philosophic texts.

The required work of preliminary scholarship has been so massive that it has occupied most of the energies of the available specialists in Jewish philosophy. And that work must continue. It will be a long time before we have a complete set of thoroughly reliable scientific texts, which we lack for many important works in medieval Jewish philosophy. However, as scholars continue to pursue these and similar studies, they should not lose sight of the philosophic purpose of the enterprise. The immense and remarkably productive scholarly effort in this field is intrinsically valuable and needs no further justification. Nevertheless, from the perspective of true philosophical interest, this work matters most because it provides us with the accurate learning without which no philosophical understanding of these philosophical works is possible.

In our enthusiasm for philological and historical research, we sometimes forget that we are dealing with works of philosophy. It is at least as important to read a philosophic argument critically as it is to know its history. The great Jewish philosophers, from Saadia to our contemporaries, have offered us profound philosophical interpretations of Judaism. Their works contain rich philosophic treasures. Read analytically, they include theories of textual interpretation, cosmologies, theologies (in the literal sense of the term), ethical theories, theories of knowledge, theories of prophecy, accounts of the nature and purpose of the mitzvot, eschatologies, and more. Read synthetically, they integrate these disparate elements into coherent and systematic philosophies of Judaism.

One of our greatest needs is genuinely philosophical study of these great works. With sound knowledge of the meanings of terms and with a thorough grasp of the intellectual background of each work, we are in a position to devote ourselves to the kind of philosophic reading which is rarely done. We need critical philosophical analyses (not only historical accounts) of the doctrines which are advanced and of the arguments by which they are supported. It is our philosophic responsibility to ask if these doctrines are true and if the arguments are sound. It is equally our responsibility to determine whether the teachings of the philosophers, even if they should be sound, are authentic versions of Judaism. We must first decide, of course, whether the notion of an "authentic version of Judaism" is itself tenable and meaningful. A decision in its favor requires us to produce criteria of authenticity. A decision against forces us to ask whether 'Judaism' stands for anything at all.

Much profound and subtle philosophic work has to be done in order to gain a perceptive philosophic understanding of the Jewish philosophers. Each had his own vision which informed his work, giving it structure, unity, and direction. The kind of philosophic approach which we take for granted when we study Plato or Aristotle, Descartes or Spinoza, Whitehead or Wittgenstein, should be adopted in our studies of Jewish philosophy. To do anything less is to transform great philosophic works into textbooks for linguistic and historical studies. We can only claim to understand a serious Jewish philosopher when we are able to provide a systematic formulation of his philosophy of Judaism. That important goal is yet to be achieved for most of the major figures in the history of Jewish philosophy. It is a goal which should be the culmination of our philosophic efforts, following on the philosophic reading of the non-philosophic Jewish materials.

There is no area of Jewish studies, just as there is no area of human endeavor, to which philosophy is irrelevant. Philosophical ideas abound and must be identified and comprehended if we are to have an intellectually sound grasp of any Jewish text which we study. Furthermore, the philosophic methods of critical analysis are an indispensable tool in all serious reflection on the great achievements of the human spirit which abound in the Jewish tradition. The role of philosophy is central here as it is in the study of the human achievement embodied in every culture and in every literature.

NOTES

[1] Cicero, *De Divinatione*, II, 58.

[2] Plato, *Theaetetus*, 174A.

[3] *Romeo and Juliet*, III, 3, 55-60.

[4] See, for example: *BT*, Abodah Zarah, 54b, Shabbat, 116a; *PT* Shabbat, III, 6a; Gen. R, 1:9, and similar references.

[5] Saul Lieberman, "How Much Greek in Jewish Palestine?," *Biblical and other Studies,* ed. A. Altmann, (Cambridge, Mass., 1962), p. 130. Lieberman notes that, "Whereas we have no Greek philosophic terminology in Rabbinic literature, the situation is quite different with regard to Greek and Latin legal terms." *(Ibid.,* p. 132).

[6] Colossians, 2:8.

[7] Harry A. Wolfson, *The Philosophy of the Church Fathers,* Cambridge, Mass., 1956), p. 16.

[8] Tertullian, *De Spectaculis,* Chs. 29f. See the comments on this passage by Nietzsche in *Zur Genealogie der Moral,* Sec. 15.

[9] Leo Strauss, *Persecution and the Art of Writing,* (Glencoe, Ill., 1952) pp. 42-43.

[10] G. K. Chesterton, *Heretics*, (New York, 1927), pp. 15-16, as cited by Lewis White Beck, *Philosophic Inquiry,* (New York, 1952), p. 6.

[11] On this point see the discussion in Saul Lieberman, *Hellenism in Jewish Palestine.*

[12] *Sifre Debarim,* 49, ed. Finkelstein, p. 115: דורשי אגדות אומרים, רצונך להכיר את מי שאמר והיה העולם למוד הגדה שמתוך כך אתה מכיר את מי שאמר והיה העולם ומדבק בדרכיו. Some texts read דורשי רשומות. For our purposes there is no need to deal with the problem of the differing terminology, The main point is unaffected.

[13] P. 137.

[14] M. Baba Mezia, IV, 2.

[15] T. Baba Mezia, III, 14.

[16] For some useful discussions of the general problem in recent literature see: Aharon Lichtenstein, "Does Jewish Tradition Recognize an Ethic Independent of Halakhah?" in *Modern Jewish Ethics: Theory and Practice,* ed. M. Fox (Ohio State University Press, 1975); Shmuel Shilo, "On One Aspect of Law and Morals in Jewish Law: *Lifnim Mishurat Hadin,*" *Israel Law Review,* 13, No. 3 (1978); Saul J. Berman, "Lifnim Mishurat Hadin," *Journal of Jewish Studies,* 26 (1975) and 28 (1977); Moshe Silberg, "Law and Morality," Ch. VI of his *Talmudic Law and the Modern State,* (New York, 1971).

[17] For a study of some aspects of the logic of the law, see Louis Jacobs, *Studies in Talmudic Logic,* (London, 1961).

[18] This problem is discussed by Emil L. Fackenheim in *Encounters between Judaism and Modern Philosophy,* (New York, 1973), Ch. 1.

[19] Nahum M. Sarna, *Understanding Genesis,* (New York, 1966), p. xxiv.

[20] *Ibid,* p. xxvii.

[21] Julius Guttmann, *Philosophies of Judaism,* (New York, 1964), p. *15.*

[22] M. Z. Segal, *Parshanut ha-Mikra,* (Jerusalem, 1952), p. 66.

[23] *Ibid.,* p. 76.

28

PHILOSOPHY AND RELIGIOUS VALUES IN MODERN JEWISH THOUGHT

Professor Katz has argued the thesis that religion served, in modern times, to unite the Jews over against the non-Jewish world, while dividing them internally into various sects or denominational groupings. We might anticipate that philosophy would have the opposite effect. As an expression of the human intellect, unfettered by the restraints of a particular revelation, philosophy should serve to unite all men as rational creatures. This means that, in practice, it can be expected to divide Jew from Jew. For those Jews who affirm the soundness of philosophical thought will become citizens of a general intellectual world, while those who reject philosophy will be separated from their brothers who have joined the wider world. In short, religion separates the Jews from the rest of society, making them one entity, and, at the same time, divides them internally; philosophy, we might conjecture, unites them with the general society, but may also divide them internally. In this paper I shall examine several versions of this pattern in order to see whether our conjecture turns out to be verified by the facts. We shall consider three model thinkers, each of whom relates to philosophy and to specifically Jewish religion in a special way. These models are Moses Mendelssohn, Samson Raphael Hirsch, and Hermann Cohen.

Before we can reflect on these modern instances fruitfully, however, we must give some attention to certain background questions. First, we must ask whether a Jew, qua Jew, can be a philosopher. Despite the familiar claims in Jewish sources that philosophy originated among the Jews and was lost to them during their wanderings, no sober historical judgment supports such a view.[1] It is clear, beyond much doubt, that Jews pursued philosophy primarily in response to external forces which challenged their thinking and even their faith, Must we view philosophy, therefore, as an alien growth which stands outside the sphere of Jewish religious life and thought? Is it legitimate for a Jew to philosophize only in defense of his faith, or may he seek in philosophy basic truths which are not available to him from within the religious tradition? Does he stop being a Jew when he becomes a philosopher?

An important contemporary writer has taken exactly this position. Attempting to characterize the work of Maimonides, Leo Strauss argues that Maimonides "obviously assumes that the philosophers form a group distinguished from the group of adherents of the law and that both groups are mutually exclusive. Since he himself is an adherent of the law, he cannot possibly be a philosopher."[2] Maimonides had very great admiration for Aristotle, and goes so far as to say that Aristotle had achieved the highest and most perfect knowledge open to a human being, short of that which is known through prophecy.[3] Yet, he is at great pains to distinguish regularly the views of a faithful Jew from those of the philosophers. Often, in the *Guide of the Perplexed,* he lists various approaches to a subject, a list in which the views of the philosophers are distinguished from those of the adherents of the law.[4] This differentiation of the Jewish views from those of the philosophers occurs, for example, when Maimonides deals with such topics as creation, prophecy, God as free cause, providence, and God's knowledge of the world. In each of these instances Maimonides differentiates the Jewish teaching from that of the philosophers and associates himself with the Jewish doctrine. To take just one case, in talking about his view of divine providence, he says, "In this belief that I shall set forth, I am not relying upon the conclusion to which demonstration has led me, but upon what has clearly appeared as the intention of the book of God and the books of our prophets."[5] Even if we consider the formulation of Strauss too extreme, it is, at the very least, evident that for Maimonides philosophy and Judaism are not co-extensive, and that at certain points one must choose between the doctrines of the philosophers and the teachings of the Torah.

This leads to the second of the background questions, namely, whether philosophy is by itself a reliable or sufficient source of religious truth. We have seen that Maimonides has clearly answered the question negatively. The instance that has been cited is by no means unique, or even unusual. There are many points at which Maimonides explicitly recognizes the limits of philosophy and feels bound to take his stand on the ground of Torah alone.[6] This is a characteristic stance, not only of Maimonides, but of Jewish philosophers from Philo through the Middle Ages, who tended to distinguish themselves from the non-Jewish philosophers by stressing those doctrines which are affirmed by the Torah and denied by philosophical teachings

When the approach to philosophy is restricted in this way it poses no threat to internal Jewish Life. The Jewish thinker does not see himself as philosopher, but as Jew. He does not derive his doctrines from philosophy, but from the Torah. Viewed this way, philosophy becomes either a means for explicating the Torah, or a means of acquiring knowledge of matters which are not directly dealt with in the Torah. Philosophical activity does not transfer its Jewish practitioners into the world of general thought. We can learn from the case of Ibn-Gabirol's *Mekor ha-Hayyim,* which passed for centuries as the work of a non-Jewish author because it lacked any Jewish references and had no visible connection with Jewish teaching. It simply became a work of pure philosophy, which was widely accepted and admired in non-Jewish circles. On the other hand, when Jews engaged in philosophical reflection from within the limits of Jewish religious thinking, they and their works remained separated from the wider philosophical world.

One might have expected, as a result, that such philosophic work among Jews would not cause any internal divisions. Yet, we know the extent to which bitter controversies arose over the study of philosophy, ranging from the anti-Maimonidean controversy, which tore Jewry apart, to the prohibitions against philosophy, which continued into modern times. R. Moses Isserles felt constrained to defend himself against the charge that he studied philosophy, and assured his critic that he depended only on Jewish sources, that even these he consulted only on occasions when other men engage in recreational activity, but never at the expense of the study of Torah; moreover, he went on to affirm that all true wisdom and knowledge are contained in the Torah so that no Jew ever has any need to look beyond.[8] The Gaon of Vilna, in the eighteenth century, explains an alleged aberration of Maimonides as due to his having been misled and confused by his study of philosophy.[9] Through the nineteenth century and up to our own time there were still those, at least among the Orthodox, who considered the study of philosophy tantamount to heresy. Even the observance of the most careful limits with respect to philosophy was no remedy for the prevention of internal divisions among the Jews. The ancient and medieval Jewish thinkers may never have seen themselves as philosophers; they surely were never fully united with the community of all thinking men; they never claimed that philosophical thought rather than the Torah was the source of religious truth; yet even this restricted philosophic activity generated deep internal controversies, and served to divide Jew from Jew, community from community.

For Moses Mendelssohn, the first truly modern Jewish thinker, philosophy played a much more central role and one which was designed deliberately to overcome the barriers that separate the Jew from the rest of humanity. The basic strategy with which Mendelssohn worked was to invoke the universality of human reason and to represent Judaism as a purely rational religion. It was Mendelssohn's policy to represent himself as first and above all a man, a member of the admirable society of enlightened rational humanity, and it was as such that he was perceived in the non-Jewish circles which accepted him as one of their own. As Jacob Katz has put it, despite the fact that Mendelssohn had very deep Jewish roots and was profoundly affected by his Jewish education and Jewish learning, "he appeared in non-Jewish society, not in his special character as a Jew, but rather as a philosopher, a writer, or simply as a human being."[10] In fact, it was one of the bitter disappointments of his life that even those who were most warmly disposed toward him among his non-Jewish friends could never understand the seriousness of his attachment to Judaism. Perhaps, however, it would be wrong to blame them, since hardly anything mattered to Mendelssohn more than that Jews should be universally accepted as free and equal members of the general society.

If Mendelssohn had simply fought for Jewish rights without in any way compromising Judaism, his distress might have been more justified. It seems clear, however, that his own way of understanding and interpreting Judaism was itself calculated to remove Jewish distinctiveness at a most crucial point. It is no surprise, therefore, that his non-Jewish contemporaries found it difficult to grasp the seriousness with which he continued to hold to his Jewish faith.

Mendelssohn presents us with the classic case in which Jewish religious values are completely replaced by, or swallowed up in, a set of philosophical principles. He was so much the child of the Enlightenment, so committed to its characteristic doctrines, that he could not approach Judaism through any other perspective. If it was to be defended as a religion, then it would have to be reduced to a set of universal doctrines completely available to the unaided natural reason. But such doctrines can never claim to be the distinctive property of any particular community. Reason is universal. Its teachings are equally available to all men by virtue of their humanity. What reason teaches is the common property of the whole of mankind, never the private possession of a privileged elite. Just as there can be no Jewish mathematics, so, says Mendelssohn, can there be no Jewish religion. True mathematics is purely rational in character, and is knowable with equal facility and opportunity to every man who makes the effort to think soundly. True religion is of exactly the same character. There is only one true religion of reason that is apprehended by every right-thinking man. If Judaism is a true religion, and Mendelssohn believes that it is, then it can have no distinctive doctrines. It can only be a version of natural religion, and that is exactly what Mendelssohn takes it to be.

In effect, Mendelssohn replaces religion with philosophy. In so doing it is his deliberate intention to break down any doctrinal walls that separate Jews from non-Jews. As he himself expressed it, "We have no doctrines that are contrary to reason... the fundamental tenets of our religion rest on the foundation of reason. They are in consonance with the results of free inquiry, without any conflict or contradiction."[11] In the light of this conviction he writes elsewhere, "With regard to the teachings of reason... there is no distinction between Israel and any other people."[12] True philosophy knows no national or communal boundaries. In representing Judaism as doctrinally nothing more than such a rational philosophy, Mendelssohn was attempting to guarantee that Jews would be united with all enlightened men, and his philosophy was calculated to serve as the force which would realize this objective.

Even Maimonides, thought by many to be the supreme rationalist among the Jews, never claimed that all Jewish doctrine was simply pure rational philosophy. As we noted earlier, he explicitly distinguished Jewish doctrine from the teachings of the philosophers at many crucial points. In so doing, he also separated the Jews from the world of general philosophic thought. No Jew could be a pure Aristotelian, according to Maimonides, even though he held that Aristotle had reached the summit of all true philosophic knowledge. The reason for this was simply the fact that, on the one hand, Aristotle had failed to demonstrate certain basic doctrines, while Jews, on the other hand, were ultimately instructed in such matters by the Torah. Whatever the eminence of the philosopher, the prophet surpasses him. The greatest of the philosophers is, Maimonides holds, inferior to the greatest prophets. With all our regard for Aristotle, we are dependent only on Moses for instruction about certain fundamental religious matters.

Mendelssohn, in contrast, was so completely dedicated to his principle that he treated of the purely philosophic issues in works which bore little or no trace of his Jewishness. It is revealing that as a contemporary of Immanuel Kant he still occupied himself with demonstrating on purely rational grounds the existence of God and the immortality of the soul, and this in works which are in no respect Jewish in content. In the age of Maimonides, proofs for the existence of God were part of the common intellectual baggage of all thoughtful men. This is why he could so readily offer such proofs, and do so without claiming any originality for his work, for this was a point at which philosophy unified men of different persuasions. But Mendelssohn was living as a contemporary of David Hume, and he was in fairly close contact with Kant. Here were the two philosophic giants of the age (though, admittedly, not fully acknowledged as such by their contemporaries), both of whom had argued vigorously against any possibility of proving the existence of God by way of philosophic arguments. It is true that Mendelssohn was by no means alone in opposing them. Yet it is certainly a measure of the intensity of his concern with preserving natural religion that as his last major work, after *Jerusalem*, he composed his *Morgenstunden,* in which he seeks again to rehabilitate the proofs for the existence of God. Though the work is not a direct response to Kant, we know that Mendelssohn did have the *Critique of Pure Reason* in his hands at the time that he worked on the *Morgenstunden*.[13] At a time when proofs for the existence of God were under serious philosophic attack, Mendelssohn thought it was necessary for him to defend them anew. Without such proofs the very foundation of his natural religion would be destroyed, and there would no longer be any possible way in which Judaism might be represented as a version of the universal natural religion.

In the area of ethics, Mendelssohn also took great pains to deny to Judaism anything unique or specific. Here, too, he wanted to use philosophy to unify the Jews with the rest of humanity. No special moral code or moral knowledge could be allowed for the Jews, if this unification was to be realized. A special moral code might suggest that some virtues were designated as particular and peculiar to the Jews, and this was, for him, in principle unacceptable, since it ran counter to his program. Moreover, if virtue is a condition for salvation, a Jewish claim to special virtues would also entail a claim to special opportunities for salvation. Nothing could have been more offensive to the universalism which Mendelssohn's doctrine consistently advocated than the suggestion that salvation was not equally open to all men.

To avoid these undesirable consequences, Mendelssohn again made use of his philosophy as a bridge joining the Jews with all men. To do so he was forced to deny that there is a special internal Jewish moral teaching. Even while advocating the doctrine that Judaism is not revealed religion, but only revealed legislation, he continued to affirm that the principles of morality are universal and are known through natural reason alone. The principles of ethics, according to Mendelssohn, can be demonstrated "with geometric rigor and force."[14] The question of how he attempted this demonstration, and the evaluation of its soundness, does not concern us here. All that matters is that he was determined to offer such a demonstration, and thus to argue that all morality derives from a rational, natural moral law. In developing his line, Mendelssohn was assuring his contemporaries that Judaism can make no distinctive claims to moral knowledge. Rather, the Jews, like all other men, must approach the basic principles of ethics through the light of reason, and in so doing they exhibit again their unity with all humanity. The fact that their revealed legislation includes moral prescriptions does not seem to disturb Mendelssohn. Though he never directly confronts this question, it is apparent that he would argue vigorously against the claim that the moral rules themselves are derived from revelation. One can only conjecture how he would explain their presence among the revealed laws.

To appreciate the full force of Mendelssohn's effort to ground morality in reason, we might find it instructive to contrast him with Maimonides. The medieval thinker explicitly excludes all moral principles from the sphere of reason.[15] Early in the *Guide* he labels as a major error the notion that good and bad are among the things which are known by the intellect.[16] In a later discussion he states explicitly that only the first two of the ten commandments are knowable by reason. These are, of course, the affirmations concerning the existence of God and his unity. With respect to the remaining eight commandments, he tells us that "they belong to the class of generally accepted opinions and those adopted in virtue of tradition, not to the class of the intellecta."[17] Since Jews are hardly willing to assign these commandments to the realm of pure convention, they have no choice but to understand them as derived from the revelation which was made known to us through the prophecy of Moses. Here we see in a striking way how the earlier thinker limits the sphere of reason and in so doing separates the Jew from the rest of mankind, while the modern thinker extends the sphere of reason so as to deny to the Jews any claims to moral preeminence or to special moral instruction. The role of philosophy is to bring about the unification of the Jews with all other men, even if it has to be done at the cost of severely limiting all Jewish claims to special revelation.

That this is, in fact, Mendelssohn's aim is underscored by his great anxiety over the way in which Maimonides treats the Noachide commandments as a condition for the salvation of all righteous gentiles. Mendelssohn wants to identify the Noachide commandments with the natural moral law, which is known to all men by way of reason. If ethical principles are geometrically demonstrable, as he claims, then the identification of the seven Noachide commandments with the natural moral law is only another way of saying that they are demonstrable. Again, all humanity is united by a philosophical understanding of an area of basic concern. In his letter to Lavater, Mendelssohn lays great stress on this point. While the Jews have their special legislation, he writes, "All other nations were enjoined by God to observe the law of nature and the religion of the patriarchs."[18] This law of nature he then identifies with the Noachide commandments, and it is these rational rules which unify all men on a common moral ground. Mendelssohn expressed intense distress over the fact that Maimonides rules that gentiles who observe the Noachide commandments merit salvation only if they observe them out of the conviction that they were commanded by God through Moses at Sinai. If they claim to know these commandments by way of reason, and to observe them because they believe that their reason instructs them to do so, they have no status as righteous gentiles, and no claim to *olam ha-ba*.[19] Mendelssohn found this ruling both painful and unacceptable.[20] He rejected it because he could not tolerate the introduction of a Jewish claim to special revelation that separated Jew from non-Jew, and, even worse, one that would force gentiles to submit to the special Jewish revelation as a condition for their ultimate bliss. Maimonides felt no embarrassment at this separation of Jew from gentile. Mendelssohn found it utterly intolerable, and could only overcome it by invoking a philosophy which stands above all sectarian differences.[21]

Finally, we must note that the very philosophy which Mendelssohn introduced as a device for unifying the Jews with the rest of humanity, had the effect of dividing the Jews among themselves. We know that Mendelssohn wanted very much to preserve the law and with it the distinctiveness of the Jewish people, at the very same time that he wanted to unite them in doctrine with all thinking men. What he achieved, however, was quite different. For many his teaching became an open invitation to abandon Judaism altogether, since it was evident that there were no specifically Jewish religious doctrines. If that was the case, they felt, then there was little reason to pay the high cost of remaining a Jew in a society which still denied basic rights to members of the Jewish faith. Among those who remained within the fold, some rejected Mendelssohn's teachings about Jewish doctrine. They could not accept a Judaism which, so far as doctrine goes, was merely a form of general philosophic teaching. They sought to develop instead a Jewish philosophy which was distinctive, or, at the very least, to see in Judaism the highest development of general philosophy. This was particularly true of such nineteenth-century Jewish thinkers as Samuel Hirsch, Formstecher, and Steinheim.[22] By way of their philosophical understanding of Judaism they divided the Jews from other religious communities. At the same time, because they rejected the law, wholly or in part, they helped create serious internal divisions among the Jewish people.

It was, in some measure, as a reaction against those who affirmed the centrality of philosophy for Judaism that Samson Raphael Hirsch developed his own position. While maintaining the outer appearance of positive attitude toward the main elements of Western culture, Hirsch rejected any understanding of Judaism that based itself on alien philosophies. As he saw it, the very philosophy which might serve to unite the Jews with enlightened humanity would also serve to tear down and destroy all that is essential to Judaism. Such philosophical approaches to Judaism undermine true faith, and divide the Jews from their own heritage and from each other. He does not hesitate to criticize Maimonides severely for his reliance on Greek and Arabic thought, even though he has high regard for him as an incomparable halakhic authority. Whatever credit is properly due Maimonides for his contributions to the preservation of Judaism, Hirsch holds that along with the good that he did, he was also responsible for the "evil which afflicts us."[23] His great error was that "he sought to reconcile Judaism with the difficulties which confronted it from without, instead of developing it creatively from within."[24] Similarly, Mendelssohn failed because he "had not drawn his mental development from the wellsprings of Judaism, [and] was great chiefly in philosophic disciplines, in metaphysics and aesthetics."[25] The interpretations of Judaism offered by both these great figures are so heavily dependent on philosophy (which is essentially non-Jewish) that they distort and misrepresent the inner nature of Judaism. Their practical effect, Hirsch claims, was to persuade many Jews that there was no longer any need to remain within the Jewish fold, and no need to continue to observe the law, since higher philosophical understanding had now taken the place of the parochial religious views which characterize traditional Judaism. There is no suggestion here that they intended to make the exit from Judaism easy, but only the insistence that this was the practical consequence of equating Judaism with philosophy. In an especially sharp expression, Hirsch says that those who have been misled by Maimonides and Mendelssohn "Should have asked themselves, 'Is Moses the son of Maimon, or Moses the son of Mendel, really identical with Moses the son of Amram?'"[26]

As his ideal, Hirsch stresses that Judaism must be understood only from within, that it can be properly known only out of its own sources. These do not include philosophy, which claims to be universal, but only the classic Jewish texts and historical Jewish experience. There is, he believes, a specific Jewish view of the world and of man, a view which can be known only through a proper and creative insight derived from within Judaism itself. Jews are separated from the rest of mankind, for the Jew is properly "Mensch-Jissroel,"[27] a person whose whole nature is formed by his Jewishness. Philosophy can only divide such a man from his roots, can only serve to weaken and obscure his specifically Jewish perspective. However much we may admire the achievements of human culture, they can never take the place of our unique Jewish *Weltanschauung.* The independent human intellect has its admitted uses, but it is no substitute for the understanding and sensitivity that is formed exclusively by the Torah. For the Jew, "Nature should be contemplated with the spirit of David; history should be perceived with the ear of an Isaiah, and then, with the eye thus aroused, with the ear thus opened, the doctrine of God, world, man, Israel and Torah should be drawn from the Bible, and should become an idea, or a system of ideas, fully comprehended."[28] No external categories or concepts can be properly applied to Judaism. "Torah" is absolutely unique; it is *sui generis,* and can only be misunderstood when it is explained in terms that are common to philosophy or religion generally.[29]

Though there is in the work of Hirsch an outer show of Western culture, he basically rejects every source of knowledge except that which comes from Torah. Philosophy, in his view, can never lead us to a true knowledge of God. That can come only from a proper study of Torah, and even in that context the best source is not theoretical speculation, but the deepest possible understanding of the divine commandments. In one of his essays on education, he cries out passionately, "What is the use of torturing the youthful minds with 'proofs' of the existence of God, with doctrines about the essence of God and His attributes, such as eternity, unity, incorporeality, with metaphysical speculations and demonstrations of why God must be eternal, indivisible and spiritual, and all the rest of what is called rational religion or rational theology? In reality the maturest mind of a philosopher knows no more about the essence of God than the simple mind of a child; nor is it necessary for the moral behavior of man in this world to know more than the Torah tells us about God."[30] The very topics which concerned Mendelssohn so deeply strike Hirsch as inconsequential. Mendelssohn, seeking to unify Jews with enlightened mankind by way of a universal philosophic truth, needed to stress the positive value of these basic theoretical questions. Hirsch, who was only interested in preserving the internal integrity of Judaism, rejected the claims of philosophy, not only because he held them to be theoretically unsound, but also because he saw in philosophy a threat to Jewish uniqueness, to the one source of Jewish truth.

It is illuminating to realize that the one philosophy which Hirsch and his school valued was that of Kant. They valued it particularly because they saw in the Kantian critique of metaphysics a strong source of support for their position. Kant had announced as his program the intention to limit knowledge in order to make room for faith.[31] He denied that we can have any philosophical knowledge of that which goes beyond the limits of human experience. As Hirsch and his disciples understood this position, it meant that one could appeal only to extra-philosophical sources for religious truth, that it was intellectually legitimate, even mandatory, to go beyond the limits of philosophy in order to know the ultimately true. In a remarkable statement, Hirsch's grandson and spiritual heir, Isaac Breuer, proclaims, "God caused to rise among the nations the exceptional man Kant, who, on the basis of the Socratic and Cartesian skepticism, brought about that 'Copernican turn' whereby the whole of man's reasoning was set in steel limits within which alone perception is legitimized. Blessed be God Who, in His wisdom created Kant! Every real Jew who seriously and honestly studies the *Critique of Pure Reason* is bound to pronounce his 'Amen' on it."[32] Because Kant made philosophy impossible (we cannot here comment on the adequacy of this way of understanding Kant), he is the one philosopher to be fully accepted. If the only proper appeal of man is to experience, then, Hirsch holds, the Jewish people rest their claims on the most powerful and most fully attested of all historical experiences, the revelation at Sinai. Following Judah Halevi, whom he most admired among the medieval Jewish philosophers, Hirsch sees in the Sinai moment the key and unquestionable historical fact on which all Judaism rests.[33] Given the certainty of that fact, we need only devote ourselves to a proper understanding of the Torah in order to get at all the truth which we need and which is available to us. He criticizes certain patterns of Jewish study, not because they are insufficiently philosophical, but rather because they are insufficiently deep and penetrating in their study of the Torah. Philosophy must be rejected because in the process of unifying the Jew with other thinking men it separates him from his own religious tradition and substitutes error for truth.

One can see the full force of this position when we consider the point at which Hirsch rejects Kant. So long as Kant makes metaphysics impossible, he is to be admired. However, when he tries to make ethics rest on reason alone, when he insists on absolute moral autonomy and attacks all heteronomous moral laws, then he, too, is in error, and Hirsch can no longer follow him. For all moral laws, for every notion of human duty and obligation, we are dependent directly on divine commandment. Mendelssohn also spoke of morality as dependent on acknowledging God; however, he meant this only as a general condition for recognizing the rationally given moral law.[34] Hirsch holds, on the contrary, that there are, strictly speaking, no rational moral laws. There are no moral rules which could be known to us through the unaided operation of reason without any dependence on divine commandment. Some of the rules of morality will strike us as socially useful while others may not. However, even the former are known and can obligate us only because of our recognition that God has commanded them. Contra Mendelssohn, there is no natural moral law.[35] The medieval distinction between so-called rational commandments *(sikhliyyot)* and the ceremonial commandments *(shim' iyyot)* is a mistaken and even dangerous way of interpreting the law. Addressing himself to this distinction, which the Reformers invoked to justify their emphasis on the moral law and their rejection of the ceremonial law, Hirsch says that "it is thoroughly wrong, e.g., to understand the prohibition of theft as a duty which is taught to us by our reason alone, just as, in general, it is an unfounded claim that reason by itself teaches us anything about any duty."[36] Here, again, philosophy is in error, and the appeal to a rational morality, while it may unify us with other men, divides us from each other and separates us from the true ground of duty and obligation.

While Mendelssohn saw in the Noachide commandments an instance of the natural moral law, known to all men without any dependence on revelation, Hirsch firmly refuses to follow this line. In his comment on Genesis 2:16-17, he sets forth his view explicitly. This is the biblical text on which the Talmud bases the Noachide commandments, and about it Hirsch says, "It is a prohibition, and it is not a so-called 'rational prohibition,' no *mitzvah sikhlit,* but rather one which all the human means of judgment would speak against.... Of oneself one would never have come to forbid it, and even after the prohibition no other reason for it could possibly have been found than the absolute will of God... This was to establish the condition for all morality as being: subordinating the dictates of our senses to the expressed will of God. According to the teaching of our sages, the codex of the laws of morality for mankind in general, the seven Noachian laws, also rest on the Divine revelation."[37] What offended Mendelssohn, because it ran counter to his aspirations for a unified humanity, seemed to Hirsch axiomatic. Without divine commandment there can be no morality for anyone, whether Jew or gentile. If this means that all mankind is dependent on the revelation to the Jews, so be it.

Both Hirsch and Mendelssohn stressed the importance of the commandments, and both saw them as divine revelation. For Mendelssohn, the law was the only content of divine revelation, while all doctrine was part of the teaching of reason to all humanity. In thus using philosophy to join the Jews with the world, Mendelssohn stripped Jewish religion of any doctrinal base, and his appeal to the binding force of revelation on the Jews turned out to be largely ineffective. Hirsch, on the other hand, saw in the Torah the only source of Jewish self-understanding. In it he found that the law stood at the center, and it was only through the proper understanding of the law, Hirsch believed, that we could arrive at sound doctrinal as well as sound legal norms. As is well known, in his rejection of philosophy and of the independent claims of reason, Hirsch not only separated the Jews from their non-Jewish neighbors; he also divided them from each other by creating a community of his own, a community which remained so committed to the purity of its Torah-based doctrines that it felt forced to distinguish itself formally from the general body of Jews.

Still another form of the relationship between philosophy and Judaism emerges in the thought of Hermann Cohen, who is essentially a nineteenth century figure, despite the fact that his most important Jewish writings were composed in the early years of the twentieth century. There is much evidence to support the view of those interpreters who hold that there was a significant change in Coben' s thought as he entered the last period of his life. For the early Cohen, philosophy provided the total systematic structure for all human knowledge, and in this structure there was no specific place for religion. At this stage, his God was no more than the God-idea, and while this idea had a very significant role to play in philosophy, it had little to do with the God of Judaism, who is both loving father and the ultimate being. During this period of his thought, Cohen retained certain emotional ties to the Judaism of his home, but he saw no ground for maintaining the distinctiveness of Judaism. Franz Rosenzweig records an often-repeated anecdote in which this point is underscored. F. A. Lange, Cohen's senior colleague at Marburg, asked him whether it was not the case that, although they agreed about most philosophical matters, their opinions about Judaism and Christianity divided them. Cohen answered, "No, since what you call Christianity, I call prophetic Judaism."[38] At this point of his life, Cohen was the pure philosopher who could see in Judaism little more than a set of philosophic theses which it shared with liberal Christianity. We have here an echo of the pattern which we first saw in Mendelssohn, a pattern in which philosophy unifies Judaism with world thought by robbing it of any distinctive teaching of its own.

Cohen shifted his thinking in a very significant way, though it is not clear whether he was himself aware of the depth and force of the shift. In his later thought, religion is assigned a separate status, though it is still tied to ethics and is still understood as derived from reason. Moreover, Judaism is now understood as distinctive, as the prime instance of the religion of reason. At this stage, he is extremely critical of Mendelssohn for his reduction of Judaism to the commandments alone and his denial that there are any specifically Jewish doctrines. Commenting on Mendelssohn's restriction of revelation exclusively to the law, Cohen asks when, within Judaism, Torah was reduced to being merely the law. Torah, he holds, is that basic doctrine which is the source of religious love, which in turn gives to the law its inner meaning and its truth. To reduce it, as Mendelssohn did, to nothing but law, is to rob it of its deepest significance.[39] Moreover, as Cohen argues, the law itself is also not restricted to the Jews. Pointing to the ambivalence in Mendelssohn's position, Cohen asks whether the ten commandments, which are the classic text of revelation, are not directed to all men, whether the Noachide commandments are not directed to all men, even though they were taught by Moses.[40] Mendelssohn's universalism is too extreme. He has robbed Judaism of all that makes it significant by limiting it to the law and assigning all doctrinal matters to general philosophy-

This is not to say that Cohen was ready to follow Hirsch in affirming the truth of the historic revelation as the sole ground on which we stand. The very title of his major book on Judaism tells us otherwise. *Religion of Reason* is a title which indicates that we are dealing with a conception of religion which is never in opposition to reason. More important, as Cohen never tires of saying, true religion derives from and is intimately connected with reason, and like every product of reason it must be universal. Yet he does not reduce religion to philosophy, as one might expect with such a doctrine, nor does he simply sweep away the distinctiveness of Judaism by absorbing it into a universal rational religion.

Religion is a separate sphere from philosophy for Cohen because it makes possible a level of moral reality which philosophy cannot provide. Philosophical ethics, "in its systematic opposition to everything sensual and everything empirical in man, arrives at the great consequence that it must first tear away from man the *individuality* of his I... In ethics *the I of man becomes the I of humanity*..."[41] Ethics alone does not make possible that compassionate relationship between man and man in which my neighbor becomes my fellow-man with whom I identify. In philosophical ethics, says Cohen, the other man is still a He, not yet a Thou. This latter, which is the highest level of genuine morality, is achieved only in the sphere of genuine religion. Here religion carries the life of reason to its highest fulfillment in a way that philosophy alone is incapable of doing. "The Thou is a classification within the notion of humanity, which humanity itself is unable to achieve; nevertheless, because of the Thou, all the methodological doubts about the share religion obtains in the tasks of reason which might have arisen disappear."[42] We see here how Cohen treats philosophy as insufficient in itself to fulfill the highest needs of man, which are, at the same time, the highest demand of reason. This is, however, a problem for all men, certainly not a peculiarly Jewish problem.

What is of interest for our purposes is that Cohen turns to Judaism for the solution of the problem, and in so doing justifies the continued existence, the important function, and the distinctiveness of Judaism. He is, of course, very careful not to offend by making exclusive claims for the truth or moral superiority of Judaism. This much one would expect from a Jewish philosopher of his generation and background. However, even while limiting his claims, he exposes his conviction that Judaism is the one ideal and fully sound religion. He leaves the door open to the possibility of a variety of religions under the aegis of reason. "Insofar as they attest themselves as religions of reason on the basis of their sources, they prove their religious legitimacy. The sovereign concept of reason opens the possibility that many religions may be collected under it." Yet, he goes on, "I do not assert that Judaism alone is the religion of reason. I try to understand how other monotheistic religions also have their fruitful share in the religion of reason, although in regard to *primary origin* this share cannot be compared with that of Judaism. This primary origin constitutes the priority of Judaism, and this priority also holds for its share in the religion of reason... Primary origin bears the mark of purity. And *purity* in creativity is the characteristic of reason."[43] While Mendelssohn denied to Judaism all doctrinal content and merged it with philosophy, Cohen restored the doctrinal content and insisted, at the very least, that Judaism is the highest and most pure version of the religion of reason, if not the only one. In effect, if a philosophical understanding of religion is to bring about a unification of mankind, it would operate, in Cohen's view, by bringing all men to the teachings of Judaism. This is best illustrated by another story recorded by Franz Rosenzweig. When Cohen returned from his visit to the major Jewish centers of Eastern Europe he told of his visit to a heder in Vilna where he asked one of the children, "Well, what will happen *b'acharis hayomim,* at the end of days?" To which the child replied without a moment's hesitation, "Well, all men will become Jews." When Cohen repeated the story, he added with pleasure, "What more do we want?"[44]

While it is admittedly hazardous to draw serious conclusions from anecdotes, this is one case where the sense of the story is borne out by Cohen's most serious theoretical work. For what he sees as the highest goal of religion, a goal that is not given in pure philosophy, is Messianism, and that, in turn, he believes, has its source, above all, in the teachings of Judaism. By Messianism he means the aspiration toward the unity of all mankind, and the confidence that it can and will be achieved in history. This hope and this confidence reside most of all in their original home, namely, Judaism. Pure monotheism, such as we have only in Judaism, is the necessary condition for this Messianism. "The unity of God becomes the model for the peoples of the world so that they set their unity in mankind as the goal of their historical existence. The unity of men is the eternal value of the human race. Messianism is the straightforward consequence of monotheism."[45] To whom is this task of the teaching which aims at the realization of Messianism properly entrusted? "Monotheism required a continuous development beyond the Bible, which could not be entrusted to those peoples who did not produce the ancient Bible. The continuity of the spiritual power of one people was necessary in this case."[46] After all that he says about the religion of reason, Cohen still returns to Judaism as the primary source and the continuing historical model of this true religion. Here the philosopher, while still appealing to a reason which should be universal in its scope, uses his philosophy to unify the Jews and to set them apart from other peoples.

In the three model cases that we have examined, we can see a variety of patterns relating philosophy and Jewish religion, as well as the diverse effects of these patterns. Mendelssohn affirmed a universal philosophy, leaving for Jewish religion only the law. In the process he succeeded in achieving a theoretical union between Judaism and all other enlightened religions, but only at the cost of dividing the Jews among themselves and, even worse, of tearing Jews away from Judaism. Hirsch, in turn, also affirmed a positive attitude toward general culture, but he rejected philosophy as a source for Jewish self-understanding. For him Judaism could only be known from within, which is to say from a penetrating study of the law and commandments. His quasi-philosophic Judaism had no bridges to unify it with the world of general philosophic thought. It was able to serve as a center of internal unification, but only for those Jews who were prepared to submit to the full discipline of the law. The story of how this doctrine, in fact, divided Jews among themselves is well known. Cohen, while keeping all the outer appearances of philosophy, developed a theory of religion which makes it transcend the limits of pure philosophy. This served to divide religion from philosophy, and, since Judaism was his instance of the highest religion, also had the effect of dividing Judaism from other religions. Because Cohen's doctrine never became the basis for a school or community of Jewish thought and practice, it is difficult to attribute to it any specific practical effects. However, since he opposed Jewish nationalism and was ambivalent about the extent to which the law was binding, it is easy to predict what kind of divisive effects his doctrine would have wherever it might be adopted as a policy and pattern for the ordering of Jewish life.

NOTES

[1] For typical instances of the opinion that philosophy originated among the Jews but was lost to them due to their unhappy history, see, e.g., H. A. Wolfson, *Philo* (Cambridge, 1947), Vol. 1, pp. 141 f., Maimonides, *Guide*, I, 71, and the references on this point in the works of R. Moses Isserles, which are cited in Asher Siev, *Rabbenu Moshe Isserles* (New York, 1972), pp. 242-43.
[2] Leo Strauss, "The Literary Character of the *Guide of the Perplexed,*" in *Persecution and the Art of Writing* (Glencoe, 1952), p. 43.
[3] Letter of Maimonides to Samuel ibn Tibbon, *Kobetz* (Leipzig, 1859), 11, 28d.
[4] Cf. *Guide*, II, 13; 11, 32; 111, 17; these are only some typical instances.
[5] *Guide*, III, 17.
[6] For typical instances, see *Guide*, I, 31 and 32; II, 24; III, 9; Letter to R. Hasdai Halevi, in *Kobetz*, II, 23.
[7] Philo affirms the doctrine of divine providence against the views of the philosophers; cf. *De Opificio Mundi, passim.* Similar instances of open opposition to the teachings of the philosophers are common and easily identified in medieval Jewish philosophy.
[8] References in Siev, *op. cit.*, pp. 238-39, 241.
[9] *Be'ur ha-Gra, Yoreh De' ah,* 179:6.
[10] Jacob Katz, *Die Entstehung der Judenassimilation in Deutschland und deren Ideologie,* reprinted in *idem., Emancipation and Assimilation* (Gregg International Publishers, 1972), p. 244.
[11] In a letter to Elkan Herz, cited in Moses Mendelssohn, *Jerusalem and Other Jewish Writings,* trans. and ed. by Alfred Jospe (New York, 1969), p. 137.
[12] From *Biur* to Exodus 20, cited in *Ibid.*
[13] For a discussion of the composition and contents of *Morgenstunden,* see Alexander Altmann, *Moses Mendelssohn: A Biographical Study* (Philadelphia, 1973), pp. 671-97.
[14] See his *"Abhandlung über die Evidenz in Metaphysischen Wissenschaften," Gesammelte Schriften,* Jubilämsausgabe, Vol. 11, pp. 315-30. For a discussion of this topic, see my paper, "Law and Ethics in Modern Jewish Philosophy: the Case of Moses Mendelssohn," in *PAAJR, 1974.*
[15] I have discussed this topic extensively in my paper, "Maimonides and Aquinas on Natural Law," *Dine Israel* (Tel-Aviv University, Faculty of Law), III (1972).
[16] *Guide,* I, 2.
[17] *Ibid.,* II, 33.
[18] In Jospe, *op. cit.,* pp. 116-17.
[19] *M. T., Melakhim*, 8:11.
[20] See his letter to R. Jacob Emden, in *Ges. Schr.,* Jub. A., Vol. XVI, pp. 178 f.
[21] Despite the vehemence of Mendelssohn's objections, one cannot help but be struck by the poor quality of his arguments.
[22] Cf. Jacob Katz, "Jewry and Judaism in the Nineteenth Century," reprinted in *Emancipation and assimilation,* pp. 12-13.
[23] S. R. Hirsch, *The Nineteen Letters* (New York, 1960), p. 119.
[24] *Ibid.*
[25] *Ibid.,* p. 123.
[26] *Ibid.,* p. 125.

[27] *Ibid.,* p. 29; German edition (Frankfurt, 1901), p. 9. The term is an invention of Hirsch' s, which he uses frequently, and has become something of a trademark.
[28] *Ibid.,* pp. 127-28.
[29] See, e.g., *Judaism Eternal, Vol.* I, pp. 88 ff.
[30] Quoted in Grunfeld's introduction to the English edition of *Horeb,* p. xiii. It should be noted that this statement, which is cited by Grunfeld as continuous, actually occurs in a number of paragraphs in the German original from which he collected the relevant sentences.
[31] *Critique of Pure Reason,* Bxxx.
[32] Cited by Grunfeld in *Horeb,* pp. xxiv-xxv.
[33] Hirsch follows Judah Halevi in making the certainty of the divine origin of the Torah rest on the fact that God's presence was directly experienced by the multitudes of Israel who stood at the foot of Sinai. In his comment on Exodus 19:4 he says, "The two fundamental truths on which the whole of Judaism rests, the exodus from Egypt and the Lawgiving on Sinai, stand firmly on the actual evidence of your senses, and as they were seen, heard, felt, and experienced simultaneously by so many hundreds of thousands of people, every possibility of deception is ruled out." This is a theme which recurs frequently in Hirsch' s writings.
[34] Cf. *Jerusalem,* p. 38.
[35] For a general discussion, see Grunfeld, *op. cit.,* pp. lxii-lxiii.
[36] *Erste Mitteilungen aus Naphtali's Briefwechsel* (Frankfurt, 1920), p. 10.
[37] *Commentary on the Torah, ad loc.*
[38] Franz Rosenzweig, Introduction to Hermann Cohen' s *Jüdische Schriften, Vol.* 1, p. xxv.
[39] *Ibid.,* Vol. II, 258-59; see also the comment on this point by Jacob Katz, in *Entstehung,* p. 245.
[40] *Ibid.*
[41] *Religion of Reason,* tr., Simon Kaplan, (New York, 1972), p. 13.
[42] *Ibid.,* pp. 15-16.
[43] *Ibid.,* p. 34.
[44] *Jüdische Schriften,* I, xii.
[45] *Religion of Reason,* p. 255.
[46] *Ibid.,* pp. 252-53.

29

THE HOLINESS OF THE HOLY LAND

The Land of Israel has long carried the designation "the Holy Land." While the expression itself is not biblical, it surely may be said to express biblical attitudes towards Eretz Israel. There are numerous biblical expressions associating holiness with the temple and the temple mount.[1] Twice in Scripture the phrase "holy ground" occurs. The area of the burning bush is called *admat kodesh,* and the prophet speaks of the portion of Judah as in *admat hakodesh.*[2] In rabbinic literature and in later Jewish literature the holiness of the land is a widespread theme. As the Mishna expresses it, "The land of Israel is holier than all other lands."[3] This theme recurs in the writings of poets and philosophers and has for many centuries been a standard expression in common usage. Palestine is in many languages of the western world simply the "Holy Land."

It is surprising that little effort has been made to clarify the meaning of the concept "holy land." Just exactly what does it mean to say of a particular place that it is holy. Beyond the purely honorific elements in this expression, we need to know what the full significance is of this usage. We have fairly clear ideas about the halakhic meaning of holiness as it refers to the land as a whole and to more limited areas within the land. Here we are able to work out a whole set of rules of behavior which give operational meaning to the idea of the holiness of the land. What is lacking and what I shall attempt in this paper, is a philosophical-theological elucidation of this idea.

It is important, for clarity of thought, not to confuse the specific concept of holy place with all the other laudatory things that are said about the land of Israel Such modern accolades to the land as that it is a national home for the Jewish people, a cultural center, a place of assured refuge for Jews in need, and similar characterizations may all be true. Moreover, they are legitimate occasion for feelings of pride in the land, attachment to the land, and high praise for the land and its settlers, but it is not immediately evident that this has anything to do with holiness as such. Even the ancient rabbinic praise of the land as the first place to be created and as the center of the world do not necessarily lead to the idea of holiness. In fact, the biblical references to Jerusalem and the land of Israel as the center of the world do not clearly carry with them the notion of holiness. Ezekiel, in affirming the geographical centrality of the land, appears to report a fact which indicates that Jerusalem is important, but it does not follow from this that it is holy. Thus said the Lord God: I set this Jerusalem in the midst of nations, with countries round about her." (5:5) There is no direct reference to holiness as connected with geographical centrality. Similarly, in the passage where Ezekiel speaks of the Israelites as "living at the center of the earth" (38:12) there is again no specific connection to the idea of the holy. The term *tabbur haaretz* is probably an instance of the widespread ancient practice of identifying the favored land as the *omphalos,* the navel of the earth from which all the rest of the world emerges.

There is no question that the Jewish doctrine of the holy land frequently includes these special claims about the land as the center of the earth and the beginning of creation. We must, however, take care to avoid any confusion between these elements, which may enter into the concept of the holiness of the land, and the core of the concept itself. A contemporary scholar seems to see this point clearly when he notes that there is a specific line of development from the *omphalos* doctrine to the doctrine of a holy land. Speaking of the eschatological hope for a rebuilt Jerusalem, he says, "The eschatological Jerusalem which had been envisioned by Ezekiel... as the center of a recreated earth in a radically transformed nature became a geographical *hieros topos.*"[4] The notion of the centrality of the land is not by itself identical with the notion of the holiness of the land, nor is it evident that it is even a necessary element in the idea of holiness.

Something of this same pattern can be discerned in the rabbinic materials. There are many midrashim and aggadic passages which do not assert a necessary connection between being first or being the center and being holy. Sifre *Deuteronomy,* for example, goes on at great length to establish the principle that what is created earlier is more beloved. In its list of proofs for this principle it notes that the land of Israel, which is more beloved than other lands, was created first.[5] Yet, no direct association with holiness is evident in this passage. There are other well-known talmudic and midrashic passages which praise the land as the first, the center, or the highest of lands, without making any clear connection between these properties and the holiness of the land.[6] It is likely that at some point, when the idea of a holy land was fully developed, these other praiseworthy characteristics were integrated into the concept of holiness, or were seen as somehow connected to or derived from the fact of holiness.

Before we approach directly the task of elucidating the concept of holy place in Judaism, we need to consider a preliminary question. Whatever we may mean by holy land, how does the land become holy? Is holiness an intrinsic quality, part of the essence of this particular place, or is it an acquired characteristic, a property infused into a place which previously had no special holiness? Having been acquired, if it is not an original property, does the holiness then reside permanently in that place, or is it subject to removal? The cultures and religions of the Ancient Near East have many parallels to the biblical and rabbinic claims about holy place, but they appear to be, in certain key respects, radically different. A widespread doctrine of the religions practiced by ancient Israel's neighbors taught that each temple site was inherently sacred. Its holiness was part of the cosmic order. It was built into the original creation. Beginning with the doctrine of a primeval hill which is the beginning point of creation, each temple is then perceived as sharing in the original holiness of the primeval hill "Each Holy of Holies throughout the land could be identified with the primeval hill... Each sanctuary possessed the essential quality of original holiness; for, when a new temple was founded, it was assumed that the potential sacredness of the site became manifest."[7] This doctrine of the intrinsic holiness of each holy place was widespread in the religions of the Ancient Near East. Yet, as we shall try to show, it has no exact counterpart in biblical or rabbinic doctrines concerning the holiness of the land of Israel, or even of the temple site itself.

Some modem scholars have tried to argue for the idea that the holy land is intrinsically holy, this quality being present from the very moment of creation. Rabbi Hayyim David Halevi asserts that there is just such a natural holiness in Eretz Israel that dates back to the day of the creation of the world. He argues that at the very creation God chose the land of Israel as His special place, and "it is, therefore, certain, that from the time of creation He infused into the land of Israel its natural holiness, and He chose it from the very beginning as the place where His Shekhina would dwell."[8] In his view the holiness of the land of Israel entails that the land is essentially different in its nature from all other lands. It is qualitatively distinct from every other place. Halevi bases his claim largely on a *Tanhuma* passage which hardly seems to support his position The passage expands on the idea that, "The land of Israel is especially beloved, because the Holy One, Blessed be He, chose it as His own." The point is then made that at the time of creation God assigned the various lands to the control of supernal beings who would guide the destinies of each of the nations, but He retained the land of Israel for himself.[9] However high the praise that this implies for the land of Israel, it does not directly associate it with intrinsic holiness, nor does it provide us with any notion of what might constitute the nature of that holiness.[10]

The extreme opposite position has been championed most vigorously in recent times by Professor Yeshayahu Leibowitz. He categorically denies the attribution of intrinsic holiness to the land of Israel. In his characteristically acerbic style, he charges that anyone who holds this view is guilty of idolatry. There is no intrinsic holiness in the created world, according to Leibowitz. Only God is intrinsically holy, and all holiness derives from Him. If there is any sense in which we can properly speak of the land of Israel as holy, it is only in respect of the fact that God commanded us to observe a large number of mitzvot which are specifically tied to the land. Other than the commandments which are to be fulfilled there, there is no special association of the land with God which makes Eretz Israel in any way distinctive or qualitatively of another order. As he expresses it, "The fact that Eretz Israel is called 'God's special possession' (*nahalat haShem)* does not imply that there is any special quality in this land. For, 'The earth is the Lord's and the fullness thereof; the world, and they that dwell therein.' From the standpoint of their relationship to God, Paraguay and Cambodia and their peoples are equal to Eretz Israel and its people." The only true distinction is that there are special commandments which obligate the people of Israel in the land of Israel to serve God in a particular way.[11]

There is more than a small measure of truth in Leibowitz's contention. Unfortunately, his extreme way of formulating his position tends to obscure those elements in it which are sound. While Leibowitz claims to find his position fully articulated in the classical Jewish sources, he often cites, as his basic support, passages from *Meshekh Hokhma* by R. Meir Simha Hakohen of Dvinsk, a rabbinic authority of the late nineteenth and early twentieth century. Although Leibowitz goes too far in the way he uses these materials, a careful study makes clear that R. Meir Simha opens for us a sound and insightful way of understanding the idea of the holiness of place. The major source of his discussion is in his comments on Exodus 32:19, the verse in which we are told that Moses broke the tablets of the law which he had received from God. The problem is that having received these tablets from God, and knowing that they were formed and written by God, we would have expected Moses to treat them as supreme holy. Instead, in his anger, he threw them down and broke them.

It is in this context that R. Meir Simha sets forth his view of the nature of holiness. Nothing is intrinsically holy in the created world. Not even the temple in Jerusalem or the sanctuary in the desert possess any intrinsic holiness. Only God is holy in His essential nature, and everything else which is holy achieves that state only in relationship to God. What makes the sanctuary holy is the Divine Presence which dwells in it. If, through our sins, we cause the Divine Presence to withdraw, there is no holiness whatsoever in the physical place itself. That is why, according to the talmudic tale, Titus was able to enter the Holy of Holies, cohabit there with a harlot lying on a Sefer Torah, and yet emerge unharmed.[12] The place itself had no holiness at that point, and thus posed no special danger to the tyrant. God alone is holy in his very being, and only he is worthy of worship. "Every other instance of holiness acquires that property only by virtue of the Creator's commandment. Thus, He commanded us to build a sanctuary and to offer sacrifices there to Him alone." This is what makes the sanctuary holy, not anything intrinsic to its nature or its geographical location. The tablets of the law, similarly, forfeited their holiness when the Israelites worshipped the golden calf. This is why Moses could break them with impunity. "No created thing is holy in itself. It is only by virtue of our observance of the Torah in accordance with God's will that anything can be said to be holy."[13] Let us now begin our investigation of the idea of the holiness of the land with the perspective that we have gained from R. Meir Simha.

The first element in Jewish idea of the holiness of a place is that it is in a special way associated with God or with the Divine Presence. The burning bush episode is the first occasion in the Bible in which a particular place is designated as holy. Moses is instructed by the voice which addresses him, "Remove your sandals from your feet, for the place on which you stand is holy ground." Immediately afterward the voice identifies itself as the God of Abraham, Isaac and Jacob. In a similar encounter Joshua is also told to remove his sandals because "the place where you stand is holy." This is also followed immediately by a direct address from God.[14] It seems clear that what makes a place holy is just the fact that God appears there to man. It is important to note that neither of these sites acquired permanent holiness, since their direct association with the Divine Presence was not an ongoing reality. Similarly, Mount Sinai is designated a holy place; during the period of the revelation Moses is commanded to "set bounds about the mountain and sanctify it."[15] As the place of revelation, the place where the Divine Presence becomes manifest, the mountain is sacred and the people are forbidden to ascend it. However, once the revelation is complete and God no longer reveals himself there, it loses all its holiness. At the end of the revelation a ram's horn sounds to indicate the withdrawal of the Presence. Then the people may ascend the mountain.[16] We know, of course, that Mount Sinai has no special status as holy in subsequent Jewish history, there being no further association with God. What is fundamental to all claims about the holiness of the land of Israel is the affirmation that God is in some special way present in this land. This is a metaphysical claim whose implications we shall try to clarify.

We can gain useful insight into the general notion of holiness of place from the work of Mircea Eliade, one of the most distinguished contemporary historians of religion. "For religious man," says Eliade, "space is not homogeneous... some parts of space are qualitatively different from others."[17] In Eliade's account there are two basic factors in the idea of sacred space. The first is that, "Revelation of a sacred space makes it possible to obtain a fixed point and hence to acquire orientation in the chaos of homogeneity."[18] The second point is that the sacred represents that which is objectively real in the fullest sense of the term. The sacred is true being. "Religious man's desire to live *in the sacred* is in fact equivalent to his desire to take up his abode in objective reality, not to let himself be paralyzed by the never-ceasing relativity of purely subjective experiences, to live in a real and effective world, not in an illusion."[19] It may be that Eliade overestimates the philosophical sophistication of ancient man when he expresses the idea of the sacred in such abstract terminology. Yet, he seems to have discovered essential features of sacred place which can help us understand and illuminate the biblical-rabbinic view.

The metaphysical claim that a sacred place is one where God is present in a special way is supported consistently by scriptural and rabbinic texts. We already cited some of these texts with respect to temporarily holy places outside the land of Israel. The evidence for the sanctuary, the Temple, Jerusalem, and Eretz Israel is widespread and familiar. The first commandment with respect to the sanctuary makes the point unmistakably clear. "And let them make Me a sanctuary that I may dwell among them."[20] It is in the sanctuary that God will meet Moses and speak to him directly.[21] The fact that it is the place where God is present is what makes it holy. "For there I will meet with you, and there I will speak with you, and there I will meet with the Israelites, and it shall be sanctified by My Presence. I will sanctify the Tent of Meeting and the altar... I will abide among the Israelites, and I will be their God."[22] Solomon prays that his Temple be consecrated as a place where the Divine Presence is located, "a place where You may dwell forever."[23] God, in turn, informs Solomon that his prayer is answered. "I consecrate this house which you have built and I set My name there forever. My eyes and My heart shall ever be there."[24] Maimonides explicitly associates the holiness of the Temple and of Jerusalem with the Divine Presence. It is because of the Shekhina which is there that these places are holy. More precisely, it is the presence of the Shekhina which constitutes their holiness.[25] As to the land itself, the presence of God there is a recurring theme in scripture and in rabbinic literature. It is the land in which God dwells, and by virtue of that it is holy.[26]

In Eliade's terminology this is space which is "qualitatively different" from all other space. Its difference consists in the fact that in a way that is unique God is present here and may be encountered here as nowhere else. This is what is implicit in the view that prophecy is only possible in the land of Israel. Rabbinic and philosophic sources strongly support this claim, even while fully cognizant of those instances of recorded prophecy that took place outside of the land of Israel.[27] Insofar as prophecy is a form of direct encounter between man and God, it is in the land of Israel, where the Shekhina dwells, that such a meeting can be expected to take place.

God is, of course, not restricted to any one place. To speak of Him in spatial terms generates serious philosophical/theological problems. Yet, once we allow ourselves to use such language, we are accustomed to think of God as omnipresent. Nevertheless, it is one of the central doctrines of classical Judaism that the omnipresent God concentrates his Presence in a metaphysically special way in the sanctuary and in all the land of Israel. The Mishna seems to be sensitive to this point when it states that, "The land of Israel is holier than all other lands."[28] Note that it does not assert that the land of Israel is the only holy land. Since God is present everywhere, and since He may reveal Himself wherever He chooses, we cannot restrict holiness a priori only to the land of Israel. Mount Sinai was holy during the time of the revelation, and the same is true of the other places where God revealed Himself to man. Each such place is *admat kodesh* for as long as it serves as the site of revelation or theophany. What distinguishes the land of Israel is that the Shekhina is there not only for a brief moment, but as an ongoing metaphysical reality. Those who dwell there live in the immediacy of the Divine Presence in a way that is distinct from every other place. If we accept Eliade's identification of the sacred with objective reality, then it is evident that to live in God's Presence is to live in objective reality in the fullest sense. The God of Israel identifies Himself as "I am that I am," i.e., as pure being.[29] He alone is objective reality, the Being from whom all other existence derives. In Him there is no illusion, no mere appearance, no relativity, no subjectivity. To live in His Presence is to live in the fullest reality.

We might ask why the universal God should permit Himself to be represented in so limited a way, why He should associate Himself with the seeming restrictions of a particular place. Solomon gives voice to the problem at the consecration of the Temple. He asks, "But will God really dwell on earth? Even the heavens to their uttermost reaches cannot contain You, how much less this House that I have built!"[30] And Isaiah, transmits the divine message, saying, "The heaven is my throne and the earth is my footstool; Where could you build a house for Me; what place could serve as My abode?"[31] From the Bible and rabbinic sources it seems clear that designating a single locale as *the* holy place—sanctuary, Temple, Jerusalem, the land of Israel—is a concession to a profound human need.

The sin of the golden calf is the key to understanding this point. Judaism put an inordinately heavy burden on the people in demanding faith in and loyalty, to a God who is totally abstract. We are forbidden to make any concrete images which purport to be icons of the divine, or even simply reminders of the divine. The God of Israel, conceived in absolute metaphysical purity, is being as such, the ground of all being. How can man relate to such a God? Perhaps the original hope was that the Israelites would be the bearers of this philosophically pure faith despite its difficulties. As the biblical chronicle teaches us, however, history conquered philosophy. So long as Moses, the living concrete bearer of the divine message, was present among them, the people were able to maintain their faith. After the revelation at Sinai, the people plead with Moses, "You speak to us, and we will obey; but let not God speak to us, lest we die."[32] Moses reassures the people and seeks to calm their fears. He tells them that God has only come to test them "in order that the fear of Him may be ever with you."[33] Obedience to God, trust in Him and loyalty to Him will be required of the people, not only when they stand at the foot of Sinai and experience His Presence directly, but always and in all circumstances, even when He is not evident.

That high standard exceeds their grasp. With Moses absent, they lose their confidence in the omnipresent, but incorporeal, God. They respond to their own doubt and perplexity by creating a concrete physical image. Commentators differ in their interpretation of just exactly what the Israelites intended in proclaiming, as they danced around the calf, that this was their god who had brought them out of the land of Egypt. At the very least, they must have felt that they had captured in the image of the golden calf some concretization of the divine power which had saved them from slavery. They could not accommodate themselves to a religion which demanded of them absolute trust in a God who could not be seen or imagined. Metaphysical abstraction had become the enemy of a vital religious faith.

The sanctuary should be understood, in the biblical context itself, as a divine concession to the fact that even this people could not fully escape the limitations which their own finitude put on them. They may not have gone the way of their pagan neighbors, nevertheless, they faced a problem which continually confronts biblical religion. The later Christian solution is to concretize the divine in a single human figure. Whatever theologians then do to try to preserve the spirituality and incorporeality of their God, it is undeniable that the concretized human figure serves the needs of the people who cannot live with the pure abstraction. Christianity can focus its attention on a man (even if he be, metaphysically, one person in the trinity) who has a name, who lives at a certain time and in a certain place, who has a history, and to whom members of that religious community can relate without any extraordinary effort of intellect or imagination. They can, and do, produce concrete symbols, representations in painting and sculpture; in short, they have those aids to the religious imagination which are denied to the Jew as a matter of non-negotiable principle.

Yet, even Judaism, albeit with the greatest of care and restraint, had to make some concession to man's limitations. The Jewish concession takes the form of the legitimation of holy place. No figures of God, no images of God, but yet a place which is consecrated as the special locus of Divine Presence. The clue to the accuracy of this claim is openly present in the Bible itself. Ignoring the chronological sequence of events, the biblical text sets the episode of the golden calf directly in the center of the chapters that deal with the building of the sanctuary. It is almost as if the sanctuary chapters are a protective wrapping around the sin of the golden calf, providing the one legitimate alternative to the totally illegitimate way in which the people fulfilled their need to concretize the divine.

The point is made most explicitly in a midrashic comment to Exodus 38:21. In summing up the accounts of all that went into the building of the *mishkan*, the sanctuary in the desert, it is referred to there as*mishkan ha'edut,* the sanctuary of testimony. Rashi cites in his commentary to this phrase a midrash which, in his version, reads, "The tabernacle was a testimony to Israel that God had shown Himself indulgent to them in respect to the incident of the golden calf, for through the Temple He made His Shekhina dwell amongst them."[34] This comment follows out the clue which is present in the text of the Torah and makes its point explicit. Recognizing that the sin of the golden calf was not an act of malice, but a result of the people's inability to relate to a divine Being who is totally abstract, God legitimated their need by providing them with a holy place. The root characteristic of that holy place is that it is a focus of Divine Presence, not simply in the way in which God may be said to be present everywhere and always, but with a special intensity reserved for that chosen place. It is there that man may encounter God and be assured of his reality in a manner unlike that which is possible in any other place. God has answered the people's need and Solomon's question with an act of gracious self-limitation. No image of Him may be made. The people must never again profane the Divine Being by reducing it to works of human art and imagination. In turn, God will respond by making Himself present to them in their sanctuary, in their holy city, in their holy land. His holiness makes the place where He is specially present also holy.

Some thinkers (and some midrashic texts, as we noted earlier) see an additional element in this metaphysical holiness of the land which has become holy by virtue of the Divine Presence concentrating itself there. They argue that this means that the density of the land of Israel is determined by God alone, never by any other supernal forces. Nahmanides, commenting on Leviticus 18:25, makes this point explicitly in his account of the cosmic order. In his view, God assigned to each land and the nation dwelling therein a supernal power which controls the destiny of the people and the land. This doctrine, rooted in astrological principles, conceives human destiny to be determined in large part by the various heavenly bodies. According to Nahmanides, only one people and one land are exempt from the control of these powers, namely, the land of Israel and the people of Israel. They stand directly and exclusively under God's providential care. No other power has any control over them. This is one more aspect of the doctrine that the people and the land of Israel are holy, that is, they are in a special and intimate connection with God. Where He is present no other power can be present,

This account of the metaphysical meaning of the holiness of the land is extended and intensified by Rabbi M. M. Kasher in a polemic against those who argue that the contemporary Zionist settlement of the land and the establishment of the State of Israel are the work of satanic and demonic powers. Rabbi Kasher bases his views on Nahmanides and on the Zohar where he finds strong confirmation for his position. "it is an established principle which is set forth in the holy Zohar that in the land of Israel the *sitra ahara* (i.e., the satanic forces) have no power whatsoever at any time... The land of Israel is specially consecrated to His Name, and all that occurs there occurs under His direct guidance without the intervention of any other powers... It follows that we cannot attribute any event in the land of Israel to the power of the *sitra ahara*."[35] This is a natural extension of the metaphysical principle that God is present in a special way in Eretz Israel. The presence of the ultimate power excludes all lesser powers, and certainly excludes any powers which are hostile to the divine intent and purpose.

From the biblical materials on there is an additional corollary of the holiness of the land. It is always conceived as a place of great material abundance. It is the land which flows with milk and honey. It is as if the Divine Presence guarantees not only spiritual elevation but also material prosperity. Even the faint-hearted spies, sent to report to the tribes in the desert on the state of the land they are about to enter, admit that the crops are incomparable in quality and richness. This theme is so common through out scripture and tradition that there is no need to cite sources. For the present, it is sufficient for us to record this added element of the holiness of the land, an element which is directly associated with its having been selected by God and endowed with His special providential came. "It is a land which the Lord your God looks after, on which the Lord your God always keeps His eye, from year's beginning to year's end."[36]

The holiness of the land is not inherent or automatic. Despite those authorities whom we cited earlier, the weight of evidence seems to make clear that the land becomes holy only when the Jewish people do certain things to make it holy. If it is true that there is some kind of holiness inherent in the land from the time of creation—a point which we are not prepared to grant—it is nevertheless the case that the land of Israel does not become effectively a holy place until it is properly consecrated by the Israelites. This involves first the conquest of the land by Joshua, and at a later time the return of the land to Jewish control in the time of Ezra. Until man has done his work, the special divinely blessed character of the land will not be evident. This work consists not only of the initial conquest, but of the ongoing reconsecration which is implicit in the observance of those special mitzvot which are directly connected with life in the land of Israel, the *mitzvot hateluyyot ba'aretz.* Setting aside tithes and heave-offerings, observing the sabbatical year, leaving the gleanings of the yield and the comers and the forgotten sheaves for the poor, these and all the other agricultural laws which are peculiar to the land of Israel are man's contribution to the holiness of the land. They are man's way of affirming the divine claim on the land and its produce. This land is rich and abundant only because God is specially attached to it. However, until and unless man does his part, there will be no true holiness in the land. The point is made earlier respect to the sanctuary. "And let them make me a sanctuary that I may dwell among them."[37] Unless man does his work, i.e., building the sanctuary, God will not be present. Although no place is holy unless God makes it a center of his holy Presence, it appears that God does not choose to dwell in land or sanctuary until man has first done his work.

This brings us to the second major element in the idea of the holiness of the land. There is in this holiness a moral dimension which is the direct counterpart of the metaphysical dimension. For the land to be holy it must be a center of specially intense and focused divine indwelling. However, God has made clear to us that His presence is contingent not only on His choice of the place and on our performance of the specifically cultic and agricultural commandments. It is equally dependent, in addition, on our fulfillment of all His commandments. The Torah teaches us that the people must be holy for the land to be holy, that is that God will only dwell in the land if the people who dwell there are god -like. "Ye shall be holy, for I the Lord your God am holy."[38] *Imitatio dei* is the necessary condition for the children of Israel to merit God's special love, His special concern, and His presence in their land. We can imitate God only by observing His commandments. To be holy, in imitation of the divine holiness, means for man to fulfill the terms of the covenant at Sinai. There it is stated explicitly that, "If you will obey Me faithfully and keep My covenant, you shall be My treasured possession among all the peoples. Indeed, all the earth is Mine, but you shall be to Me a kingdom of priests and a holy nation."[39] The penalty for disobeying the law and breaking the covenant is that the land will turn barren, the people will be exiled, and God's presence will be hidden. The main elements of the holiness of the land will be hidden from all public awareness. God may continue to dwell in the holy land even when Israel has been exiled, but at such a time He hides His presence and is no longer readily and intimately known to those who continue to make their home in his land.[40]

This moral dimension of holy place is in accord with Eliade's point that it is through sacred space that we "acquire orientation in the chaos of homogeneity." The orientation which is acquired here constitutes the value structure for all of human life. Wherever man is in the presence of God he is in a holy space. That relationship demands of man abandonment of all relativity of values, the denial of any subjectivity in morals. God provides the general principles as well as the specific rules of appropriate human behavior. We relate to Him through the acceptance and fulfillment of His commandments, through orienting ourselves to all of life's concerns using the divine perspective as our guide. As divinely oriented beings, we can live in His land. When we choose to reject His way, we become unworthy by virtue of that choice to be in His presence. Under those conditions, the Torah makes clear, the holy land can no longer suffer even our physical presence.

The archetypal model which teaches us the essential elements of this divine-human relationship may be found in the Garden of Eden episode. Man, in his primal state, first establishes and exemplifies all the points that we have made about life in the holy land. Adam lives in a setting which prefigures in detail the later holy land situation. He is in the immediate presence of God. The Divine Being is there; He is readily accessible; He makes Himself manifest to Adam directly. The place itself is one of great abundance. It contains every kind of fruit, all the produce that one can possibly want, and it is available freely and with little effort. Finally, although the abundance is the gift of God, it requires some work on the part of man. There is initially no vegetation, no fruit and no grain, because God had not yet sent rain to the earth, and also because "there was no man to till the soil". Man must do something to supplement God's acts in order to produce the fruits of the earth. That is why even in the Garden of Eden man is expected "to till it and to tend it."[41] Adam's life is given form and structure through the duty which God imposes on him. From the first moment that he is situated in Eden, God commands him not to eat of the fruit of a particular tree. Man can only be man, which is to say he can only become the bearer of the image of God, if he accepts and fulfills the divine mandate. He must orient himself in his space in accordance with the divine perspective. He may be totally perplexed by God's commandment. He may not understand why this one tree is forbidden to him. That is of no consequence. All that matters is that he should recognize that he cannot live with the holiness of the divine unless he commits himself fully to the divinely given commandment. For Adam, God's perspective provides the only true source of values, the divine orientation which gives axiological form to his otherwise relativistic and subjective world.

When Adam and Eve choose to sin, they have broken the terms of their covenant with God. They give priority to their moral subjectivity over the divine objectivity. The consequences follow necessarily. They are banished from that special place because they are no longer worthy or able to live in intimate relationship with the Divine Being. In place of the ready abundance which graced their lives with so little labor on their part, they will now have to struggle for a living. Thorns and thistles will result from their labors, and they will have to earn their living by the sweat of their brows.

In Eden, the best of worlds, man is granted all that he truly needs, all that he aspires toward. The highest material and spiritual blessings are his, and all that is asked is that he be faithful to God. The children of Israel about to enter the promised land, are in precisely the same situation They are offered a chance at a life of holiness in a holy place. If they observe God's commandments, they will be worthy to live in the land where He is uniquely present. They will be blessed with that special fellowship with God which is man's deepest need and highest aspiration. They will also be granted material prosperity with little effort so that they can fully enjoy their spiritual rewards. The penalty for breaking the covenant is banishment from the Divine Presence and a life in exile characterized by pain and struggle for survival. A profane people cannot have its home in a sacred place. "You must keep My laws and My norms, and you must not do any of those abhorrent things... for all those abhorrent things were done by the people who were in the land before you and the land became defiled. So let not the land spew you out for defiling it, as it spewed out the nation that came before you."[42] Just as a person who is defiled, in a state of uncleanness, may not enter the sanctuary, so people who are morally defiled may not be present in that larger sanctuary which is the holy land.

These are the main features of the concept of the holiness of the Holy Land. First, it is the place in which there is a special metaphysical reality. God is uniquely present in that place. Second, its holiness is not inherent, but requires specific acts of conquest by the Israelites and ongoing reconsecration through observing the commandments that are specifically tied to the land. Third, the people must be God-like in their own behavior. They must be holy to be worthy to live in the presence of the truly Holy. In practice this means that they must honor the covenant by doing all God's commandments. If they fail they defile themselves and the land. It will lose its material abundance and become barren. The people will be exiled. And God's presence in the land of His special choice will no longer be discernible. Living in the Holy Land under God's covenantal care is a kind of return to the primeval Paradise. The conditions for being there, the rewards and the dangers, are essentially the same.

We may ask, finally, whether this classical conception of the holiness of land of Israel can have any meaning for us today. We live in largely secular societies in which ideas of the holy in general are alien. The idea of a holy land may seem even more alien to contemporary man. Our problem is aggravated by the fact that contemporary Israel is largely the creation of Jews who do not see themselves as bound by the ancient covenant Is there anything left today then of holiness in the land of Israel? Can we understand the restoration of the people of Israel to its ancestral soil as more than a political act? Is there in this great event which has transformed Jewish existence in our time anything of restoration of the holiness of the land?

A proper religious clarification of the question must itself come only from inside the tradition. As we noted earlier, there are those contemporary religious teachers, especially among the extreme right of the Hasidic world, who accept the distinction between the religious and the secular that was implicit in the questions raised above. They view secular Jewry, so-called, as the embodiment of the evil and demonic forces which are aimed at destroying Judaism, the Jewish people, and the holy land.

From this perspective the questions answer themselves. Contemporary Israel is a satanic temptation which has pushed us to the edge of the abyss. There can be no talk of holiness in such a setting. It is the terrifying model of total defilement.[43]

This is, however, a minority view. The vast majority of contemporary Jewish religious authorities view the modem Yishuv and the State as a positive development which sets us on the way toward spiritual rebirth as well as national sovereignty. Relatively few of them, however, have developer a clear and coherent theory which addresses our questions in the contemporary setting. Among those who did deal with the question the most eminent by far was the late Chief Rabbi Abraham I. Kook, and we shall try here to summarize his views. They seem to revolve around two major points. The first is a rejection of the now common distinction between religious and secular Jews. The second is his conviction, based on his reading of all the sources, that today, as in antiquity, full spiritual development is possible for a Jew only in the land of Israel. It is the center of holiness in the world, the truly holy place, and there alone can a Jew fully encounter the divine and thereby become what he properly should be as a person.

The categorization of some Jews as "secular" as over against others who are "religious" is in R. Kook's view a total distortion of reality. Every Jew is in the depths of his soul oriented towards restoring the convenantal bond of holiness. Although a Jew may not be conscious of this deep religious concern, it is present in him as part of his essential nature. Writing to a critic who chastises him for his "Zionism", R. Kook defends himself by appealing to the special nature of the Jew, the special nature of the land and the effect of their being joined together. He explains that he supports the Zionist effort because Eretz Israel is "God's land which he chose and loves above all other places on earth. It has the special holy power to induce prophecy and to cause the holy spirit to dwell in us. By virtue of being present in that land one merits a place in the world-to-come. Its special virtues protect even the wicked... Whoever tried to turn toward the path of virtue and to speak good concerning Israel, even if that person is not engaged in doing God's will, is to be praised. It is certain that even in the least pious Jew—every one without exception—there are many gems of good deeds and virtuous character, far more than we can imagine. There can be no doubt that the land of Israel serves to elevate and to sanctify them. If all this is not immediately evident in our contemporaries, then it will become evident in their children and grandchildren."[44] Every Jew is in the depths of his soul oriented toward a life of holiness, and in the Holy Land alone can that orientation come to its full expression

This conviction that the land of Israel is still holy today, i.e., that the Divine Presence and the divine power continue to function there, leads R. Kook to his repeated assertion that only in the land of Israel can each individual Jew discover his own true nature and his own spiritual power. As he puts it "It is impossible for a Jew to be as devoted and true to his own deepest inner thought and imagination in the Diaspora as he can in Eretz Israel. Manifestations of the holy of whatever degree are relatively pure in Eretz Israel, while in the Diaspora they are heavily mixed with dross and impurity. Indeed, the greater one's yearning for and attachment to Eretz Israel, the purer his thoughts become, because they are rooted in the atmosphere of the land of Israel."[45] This doctrine is encapsulated in a single remarkable statement. "The hope for redemption is the stabilizing force of Diaspora Jewry, while the Jewry of Eretz Israel is the very redemption itself."[46] Since redemption is not simply a matter of physical return to the land, but at the same time the achievement of spiritual fulfillment, it is evident that R. Kook believes that the land of Israel continues to be holy in the classical meaning of the concept. It is still the land of the indwelling of the Shekhina. Jews who are there have by virtue of that very fact already been blessed with a great measure of redemption

This contemporary restatement of the meaning of the holiness of the holy land is not universally accepted even in religious circles, as we already noted. Militant secularists who deny the deeply hidden religious motivations which R. Kook ascribes to them also reject such a view. There is, however, one aspect of contemporary Israel whose holiness must evoke near universal assent. In Jewish teaching one of our highest duties is to do all in our power to save human lives. One who devotes himself to this duty with all his being is certainly fulfilling, at least, a most important aspect of the covenant. A place that makes such saving action possible must be seen as a place which is itself an instrument of the covenant. In the eloquent language of Abraham Joshua Heschel, "No act is as holy as the act of saving human life. The Holy Land, having offered a haven to more than two million Jews—many of whom would not have been alive had they remained in Poland, Russia, Germany, and other countries—has attained a new sanctity."[47] As these lines are being written we have just learned of the remarkable rescue of thousands of Ethiopian Jews who were dying of starvation and neglect. These Jews, as well have been given life and a home in Israel. The life saving activity that was begun much earlier in this century continues to be a central commitment of the land and its people. Whether they know it or not, they are doing God's work in a way in which no Jew could hope to do it anywhere else in the world. The people are doing their part to sanctify the land, and we believe that the Divine Presence in the land does its part to sanctify the people.

NOTES

[1] See, e.g., Ex. 15:13; Is. 11:9,64:10; Ps. 78:54. The idea is a biblical commonplace which is repeated in various forms throughout the Bible. Extensive discussions of the place of the land of Israel in Judaism are contained in W. D. Davies, The *Gospel and the Land* (University of California Press, 1974), and W. D. Davies, *The Territorial Dimension of Judaism*, (University of California Press, 1982). See the comprehensive bibliographic in these books for a survey of literature in the field.

[2] Ex 3:5; Zech. 2:16.

[3] M. Kelim, 1:6.

[4] S. Terrien, "The Omphalos Myth and Hebrew Religion," *Vetus Testamentum* 20 (1970), 334.

[5] *Sifre Deut., Ekev,,* 37, ed. L Finkelstein, p. 70.

[6] See, e.g., b. Taanit, 10a, and other parallels noted by Finkelstein in his notes to Sifre Deut.

[7] H. and H. A. Frankfort, "Myth and Reality", in H. and H. A. Frankfort, et al., eds. *The Intellectual Adventure of Ancient Man,* (The University of Chicago Press, 1977), 21. For a general discussion of this topic see Richard J. Clifford, *The Cosmic Mountain in and the Old Testament,* (Harvard University Press, 1972), The subject has been taken up anew most recently in Jon D. Levenson, *Sinai and Zion,* (Winston Press, 1985).

[8] Hayyim David Halevi, *Mekor Hayyim*, Vol. 5, Sec. 266. Similar views, though not well developed, are present in the *Kaftor va-Ferah of* R. Estori ha-Parhi of the early fourteenth century. Echoes of such views appear in more recent rabbinic authorities, but they are rarely restricted to the purely metaphysical claim that the land of Israel has a natural holiness which was infused into it at the time of creation.

[9] Tanhuma, *Re'eh*, 8; see also Tanhuma, *Bemidbar*, 17. In these and similar texts priority of creation centrality in the world, even being beloved by God are not directly associated with intrinsic holiness of the land.

[10] For a similar position to that of Halevi using similar sources, see *E. T,* 2, 213-214b, s.v., Eretz Yisrael.

[11] Y. Leibowitz, *Emunah, Historia, ve-Arakhim*, (Akademon, Jerusalem, 1982), 133. See also, ibid., 213. This theme recurs frequently in the published work and in the public addresses of Professor Leibowitz. For a sharp attack on Leibowitz's views see, *Shelila Lishmah: Kelapei Yeshayahu Leibowitz*, (El Hashorashim, Jerusalem, 1983). In this collection many aspects of Leibowitz's thought are subjected to severe, often *ad hominem*, criticism. For a sustained attack on his views concerning the holiness of the land of Israel see the article by M. Hen, pp. 257-266.

[12] b. Gittin 56b.

[13] *Meshekh Hokhma,* (Jerusalem 1927), 94-95.

[14] Joshua 5:15-6:5.

[15] Ex. 19:23, cf. Ex. 19:12.

[16] Ex. 19:13. Elijah's experience of revelation at Sinai (Horev) is also a temporary phenomenon that confers no ongoing sanctity on the place. Cf. I Kings 19:8 ff.

[17] Mircea Eliade, *The Sacred and the Profane,* (Harper & Row, 1961), 20.

[18] Ibid., 23,

[19] Ibid., 28.

[20] Ex. 25:8. Here the emphasis is that God will dwell *betokham,* in the people, rather than in the place. However, see the passage cited from Ex. 29:42-45 for the clear case of holiness of the place.
[21] Ex. 25:22.
[22] Ex 29:4245.
[23] I Kings 8:10-13.
[24] I Kings 9:3.
[25] M. T., Bet Habehira 6:16.
[26] Num. 35.34. The association of God's presence with the sanctuary, the holy city, and the holy land is a theme that recurs throughout the Bible, and it is regularly related to the holiness of place.
[27] See, *e.g., Mekhilta d'Rabbi Yishmael,* Pisha 1, ed. Horovitz Rabin, p. 2, 11. 10ff. See notes there for the parallel rabbinic sources. For a classic case of the philosophic treatment of this topic see Judah Halevi, *Kuzari,* II, 12-14, 50 and passim.
[28] M. Kelim 1:6.
[29] Ex 3:14.
[30] I Kings 8:27.
[31] Is. 66: 1.
[32] Ex 20:16.
[33] Ex 20:17.
[34] Rashi to Ex 38:21. Tanhuma, Pekudei 2 has slightly different language but conveys essentially the same idea. The version in Tanhuma Buber is much fuller and even more explicit than that in Rashi or the regular Tanhuma text. The same is true of the text in Ex. Rabbah, Pekudei 51, 3 which is almost exactly parallel to Tanhuma B.
[35] Menahem Mendel Kasher, *Hatekufah Hagedolah,* Jerusalem, 1969), 287-288. Much of this book is directed against the doctrines of R. Joel Teitelbaum of Satmar and his followers.
[36] Deut 11:12.
[37] Ex. 25:9. There is a well-known talmudic debate over the question whether Joshua's conquest conferred permanent holiness on the land for all future time, but no one normally holds that the halakhic status of holy land was present in Canaan before it was conquered and became the land of Israel.
[38] Lev. 19:2.
[39] Ex. 19:5-6.
[40] Deut 31:17-18; Ex. 39;23-24. *Hester panim,* the withdrawal of the Divine Presence, is consistently viewed as the greatest of curses. See, e.g., Ps. 13:2. The theme is one of the most persuasive in the Book of Psalms as it is throughout Scripture and rabbinic literature. The terminology of *hester panim* does not occur in the two long passages of *tokhaha* in Leviticus and in Deuteronomy. There is no doubt, however, that it is an important underlying element.
[41] Gen. 2:5; 2:15.
[42] Lev. 18:26-28.
[43] This is the continuing theme of much of the writing of R. Joel Teitelbaum of Satmar.
[44] R. Abraham Isaac Hakohen Kook, *Iggerot HaR'i YaH,* Vol. 2, Jerusalem, 19621 194.
[45] Idem., *Orot,* (Jerusalem, 1961). 10. Here and in the next quotation I follow largely, although not completely, the translation of Arthur Hertzberg in his *The Zionist idea.*
[46] *Ibid., 9.*
[47] Abraham Joshua Heschel, *Israel: An Echo of Eternity,* (Farrar, Straus and Giroux, 1969), 113.

30

NATURALISM, RATIONALISM AND JEWISH FAITH

Despite the gratifying growth of many fields of Jewish learning in recent decades, the important area of Jewish thought has been sadly neglected. There are hardly any contemporary works in Jewish philosophy and theology that begin to equal in scope and depth the great studies that have appeared in such fields as rabbinics and Jewish history. Though we live in an age when all religious faith is under fire, and when Judaism, in particular, is little known or understood, very few serious books have appeared which analyze, explicate, and defend the fundamentals of Jewish faith. One of the small number of serious scholars in this field is Professor Emil Fackenheim whose penetrating essays in Jewish philosophy and theology have been published during the past twenty years in various learned journals and general periodicals. The appearance of these studies in a single volume[1] is an important and welcome event.

Though they appeared during a span of two decades, and though they deal with a variety of subjects, the essays are unified by their concern with a central theme, namely, the explication of the foundations of Jewish faith. Fackenheim remains even today a product of his liberal background in many respects, but he came early to the conclusion that, in its extreme versions, liberal Judaism is indefensible. His deepest objection is that it is not really Judaism at all, but rationalism and scientific naturalism with a dash of Jewish flavor. A first requisite for any legitimate version of Judaism is that it should give primacy to the sources of the Jewish tradition and that it should judge the values of any society and the doctrines of any competing faith or philosophy by purely Jewish standards. Instead, the radical reformers reversed the order, judging and evaluating classical Jewish faith by the philosophic and scientific standards that were dominant in their own time.

Fackenheim notes that what they created could no longer be recognized as authentically Jewish at all. "At one time," he tells us, "the great question may have been how to make Judaism modern. Today, the great question is how to save it as Judaism." An authentic Jewish theology must have as its primary and authoritative sources of religious insight the classical Jewish texts and the substance of Jewish historical experience. Nothing less will produce specifically Jewish religious thought.

In addition, Fackenheim rejects the religiously destructive claims which follow from extreme rationalism and naturalism. He has profound regard for reason and for the natural sciences, and he affirms unhesitatingly his own strong commitment to the way of reason and science. Yet, he is emphatic in his vigorous opposition to the view that reason and natural science are in themselves sufficient to provide answers to man's ultimate questions. He admires science, but not scientism, and has regard for a "critical rationalism which knows what it is doing," but not for "a rationalism expanded into uncritical dogma." The limits of reason are not necessarily the limits of reality, nor are the boundaries of the empirically verifiable the boundaries of what can be known. The deepest human concerns, those to which religious faith speaks, transcend discursive reason and empirical verification. In confronting the ultimate questions, we must seek out the illumination of faith. In Fackenheim's view, "Faith may be defined as the sole positive answer to questions of ultimate importance, the asking of which is still reason's prerogative, but which reason is no longer able to answer." Any version of Judaism which is historically and theologically sound must rest on this faith which transcends the limits of rationalism and naturalism, otherwise it will be neither legitimately Jewish nor legitimately religious. Professor Fackenheim protests repeatedly against those reductions of Judaism which have robbed it of religious depth and stripped it of its historical roots. "Our naturalists and rationalists thought to improve Judaism; they made it more 'systematic' and 'scientific.' As becomes ever clearer today, they sucked the life out of it, and transformed profound insights of religious existence into platitudes."

That version of liberal Judaism which rests primarily on rationalism and naturalism emerged in an intellectual climate which posed seemingly irrefutable challenges to the ancestral faith. Radical reform was a serious attempt to save Judaism by purifying it of those beliefs and practices which were no longer acceptable in an enlightened scientific age. Now, a century later, we live in an even more naturalistic climate. How, then, does Professor

Fackenheim propose that we should return to the traditional Jewish non-naturalistic and trans-rational position of faith? It is obvious that neither he nor most of his readers are prepared to give up modern science. They accept its factual claims and consider its theoretical foundations to be sound. Neither are we ready to give up philosophical claims concerning the reliability of reason and the existence of a fixed rational world order. How, then, can we find room for the God of Israel, for revelation, for commandment, for all that is Jewishly distinctive and essential? Fackenheim's answer is that modern man can discover and confront God as the ultimate reality only when he makes serious efforts to understand himself and his own humanity. In the search for self-knowledge man learns that his very humanity is both impossible and unintelligible without God. "The analysis of the human condition constitutes the necessary prolegomenon for all modern Jewish and, indeed, all modem theology."

What does that analysis show? Man is both an observer of nature and a participant in nature. As participant, he is like all other creatures in the world of nature, but as observer he differs from them radically. For he is a member not only of the realm of nature, but also of the realm of spirit. His natural needs are morally neutral or amoral, but in judging them as such he is forced to seek a non-natural moral standard. Like every natural thing that lives he must inevitably die, but in confronting this inevitability he forms concepts of death and deathlessness which are not given in nature. In each case of self-confrontation he is driven beyond the natural data. "Man appears to be mere nature; but in order to recognize himself as 'mere' nature he must be spirit also."

Man is the one crucial exception to that uniformity of nature that we take for granted as the foundation of naturalistic empiricism. In all other cases we reject the seeming exception as impossible in principle, since otherwise we would be forced to deny the very uniformity which we are affirming. Any event or phenomenon which does not conform at once to the fixed patterns of the natural world as known by science is treated by us, not as some miraculous break in the uniformity of nature, but rather as a case of our own ignorance. We think of it as only a seeming deviation, not an actual one, and we are convinced that further scientific investigation will be able to assimilate this phenomenon into its pattern of uniformity. Fackenheim has no quarrel with this position, on the whole. Only when it comes to the analysis of the nature of man does he refuse to acknowledge that scientific naturalism is adequate. For here our self-knowledge makes it impossible for man to treat himself as nothing but a natural phenomenon. Spirit, thought, aspiration, hope, duty, moral striving are so vividly present to any man who confronts himself that only through sheer tendentiousness can he deny them or reject their implications.

Essentially, Fackenheim follows a Kantian line. It is in the moral necessity and subjective certainty of human freedom that he find the basic ground for affirming the reality of a dimension in man which transcends nature. Kant also provides him with the philosophical tools for explicating and defending such a move. Kant's critical rationalism treats human reason as a specifically human way of looking at the world, not as a way of penetrating to the ultimate reality. He held that the world which is known through human thought and experience must conform to, and is conditioned by, human ways of experiencing and understanding. Whatever becomes cognitively available to man is filtered through the apparatus of human sensation and thought, through the forms of intuition and the concepts of the understanding. That is why we can be certain *a priori* that anything that we may experience, think, or know will have a specific structure and will conform to certain fixed patterns. Kant argued, however, that these uniformities are restricted to the phenomenal world, to the world viewed as appearance. As to the character of things-in-themselves, that ultimate reality which is beyond the appearance, Kant was not prepared to say anything definite so long as he remained within the framework of natural science. The moment he shifted to moral philosophy, however, he moved in a radically different direction. Kant found himself forced beyond the limits of naturalism and dogmatic rationalism by the inescapable fact that man has moral awareness, that he recognizes himself as having duties and as bound by obligations. In reflecting on morality Kant came to see the limits of dogmatic rationalism and simple-minded scientism. It is to this that he alluded in the famous passage in which he tells us (speaking of his own highest philosophic achievement) that he had "found it necessary to deny knowledge in order to make room for faith." Though he cannot offer any evidence for God, freedom and immortality in his speculative philosophy, precisely because they transcend the limits of natural human experience, he introduces them as necessary postulates of the moral life. Taking moral awareness as an immediate and undeniable datum, he is led to conclude that without these postulates moral decision and moral choice are neither possible nor intelligible.

Professor Fackenheim follows Kant a considerable way. He accepts the Kantian restrictions on the claims of reason and science. In the light of these restrictions he finds particular force in man's subjective awareness of his own moral freedom. Without this freedom there can be no moral responsibility, but when we affirm that man is free we are also affirming that there is a break in the fixed uniformity of nature and in the chain of natural causation. "For while *qua* observer man may view himself as a mere instance of law, *qua* responsible agent he must act as if he were free and unique. Nor can this belief be a mere illusion. If it were, all responsibility would lie in shambles."

Fackenheim stresses a second break in the order of nature, one which is as significant as the first. We not only recognize ourselves as free agents, but we also claim to know other men as free and morally responsible beings. As anything less they would lack that dignity and worth which is essential to their humanity. Though I do not experience another's subjectivity, I affirm it categorically. If I were to deny the possibility (and the actuality) of interpersonal relationships, I would be forced to reduce all other men to things, to morally neutral objects of my experience. None of us can honestly accept such a conception of ourselves, nor of other men. So it is that we break out of the rigid confines of pure naturalism, forced by our own subjectivity to recognize a reality which stands beyond the realm of nature. It is this recognition, according to Fackenheim, which opens up to us the theoretical possibility and tenability of religious claims. "If it is necessary to admit the free human other, as a quasi-miraculous breakthrough of the fixed world of objects governed by laws, is it possible to admit a miracle of miracles—a break-through of a free Divine Other into that world?" The central line of argument in this book is Fackenheim's affirmative answer to that question.

The God whom we know through faith is not described in detail, nor is any attempt made to prove his existence. Fackenheim accepts the Kantian view that God's existence can neither be proved nor disproved since He stands beyond the limits of all natural experience and speculative thought. We cannot describe or define Him since we have no language in which we can speak about Him literally. We only encounter Him and know Him, in so far as it is given to us, through direct and intense personal involvement. Our response must be expressed in some fashion, however inadequate and even misleading our language may be. Professor Fackenheim makes the point eloquently and clearly:

> But to be unable to speak literally cannot mean to remain silent: for, to faith, that relation itself is a reality, demanding participation

> on the part of man. Man addresses God, obeys His law, prays for and trusts in His mercy; he must treat God as if he were literally Person, Judge and Father. Man must speak, but speak symbolically; or (if we wish) anthropomorphically; for he speaks from his finite situation. But anthropomorphic language, not being absolute truth, is not therefore falsehood; it is the truth about the God-man relation as it appears from the standpoint of man; and that relation is itself a reality. How it appears from the standpoint of God man cannot fathom, nor is it his business to fathom it.

The substance of man's relation with God depends on revelation, that direct encounter with the Divine Being for which naturalism cannot account, and which it, therefore, dismisses as illusion, a kind of psychological aberration or self-deception. That a man may in fact be deceiving himself when he claims to have confronted God, is a danger from which there is no escape. This is precisely why every positive response to such a claim involves a decision of faith, a decision which is its own verification. That which is known in faith is immune from empirical-naturalistic criticism, since the methodological presupposition of all empirical science is precisely the contrary of the attitude of faith. Science requires the observer to remain detached from the data before him, but the neutral detached observer can never know the reality which is the divine-human relation. "For man either participates in that relation, responding to the presence of divine power in his human freedom, or else he does not know it at all." Of course, there are some false prophets who proclaim, "Thus saith the Lord God, when the Lord hath not spoken" (Ezekiel, 22:28). But the very possibility of false prophets suggests the possibility of true ones as well, For the man who participates in his own relation with God—and this he can never do as a detached outside spectator—the force of the experience is such that it is beyond all denial. Given a believing attitude, faith opens up the world of the divine, a world which otherwise remains closed and inaccessible. "Faith, to be sure, is a 'subjective attitude;' but because it is a believing attitude, it takes itself as receptive of an objective truth accessible only in the believing attitude and inaccessible otherwise." For those who lack eyes which see and ears which hear no objective evidence is possible. For those who do see and hear, no objective evidence is necessary. They decide for faith, as they must, because their own existential situation demands it. "Decision," says Professor Fackenheim, "stems from the insight that existence is inescapable. The decision of faith stems from the insight that God is inescapable. Man surrenders his neutrality in the realization that he cannot be neutral; he surrenders authority over his existence in the realization that he cannot be his own authority."

For Fackenheim revelation is far more than a moment of glorious exaltation. It creates and confirms human responsibility, thereby making us what we uniquely are as men. Revelation occasions commandment and duty. In relation to God every man becomes personally and morally responsible. In that same relation the Jew also becomes Jewishly responsible, for it is not as man in the abstract, but as specifically Jewish man that he stands before God. Fackenheim is not bothered by the "scandal of particularity" and sees no reason for being anxious about the tension between the universal and particular elements in Jewish faith. God is the Lord of all nature and of all history, but He is also the God of Israel. The Jew is a man immersed in all the concerns of humanity, but he is at the same time a very particular man, one who is confirmed in the covenant which binds Israel to God. As such, his responsibility extends beyond the moral obligations of all men to particular obligations of *homo Judaicus,* to that all encompassing divine law which is the Halakhah.

Predictably, Professor Fackenheim's views about the nature and scope of Halakhah are not acceptable to Orthodox Judaism. He is close to the position of Rosenzweig in stressing that all revelation is humanly interpreted. Consequently, no revealed text can be taken as God's word containing God's law and teaching in any literal sense. Yet, the customs, ceremonies, and sanctified practices of the Jewish people are all potentially laden with true religious significance that can reflect the presence of the divine in our lives. Fackenheim would reject no traditional mitzvah out of hand, since each may be an occasion for giving oneself to God in a concretely Jewish way. Neither would he accept any set of *mitzvot* as categorically binding, for their religious significance depends, not on the text from which they are derived, but on what we make of them.

> Halakhah is Jewish custom and ceremony mediated through the leap into Jewish faith; and it thereby becomes the divine law to Israel. In themselves, all customs, ceremonies and folklore (including those Jewish, and those contained in the book called Torah) are mere human self-expression, the self-expression of men alone among themselves. But through the leap of faith any one of them (and preeminently those of the Torah) have the potency of becoming human reflections of a real God-Israel encounter. And thus each of them has the potency of becoming Halakhah, commanded and fulfilled: if fulfilled, not as self-expression but as response on the part of Israel to a divine challenge to Israel; as the gift of the Jewish self to God.

Fackenheim's conception of the nature of divine commandment flowing from revelation leaves us unsatisfied. It is pointless to enter into tendentious polemic, repeating once again the standard set of Orthodox moves. They are well known, and, except for their apologetic value, do not serve to advance materially the discussion of the issues. It would, however, be extremely valuable to have a direct and searching confrontation of Orthodox Jewish thought with the halakhic position advanced by Professor Fackenheim. There is so much in his theology that we can share and from which we can learn, so much that illuminates the stance of classical Jewish faith, that we could only benefit from a careful mutual examination of this issue which divides us most deeply. For in these essays it is not clear exactly how Fackenheim conceives Halakhah. One gets the uneasy feeling that he himself still needs to work out his own position, and that at present he may occasionally be inadvertently resorting to a rhetoric which is beautiful, but not very illuminating. We need to know what it is that makes a custom or bit of folklore into a genuinely religious duty. How does one avoid arbitrary selection: When is the ceremony appropriated as a gift to God, and when does it become a specifically Jewish gift? May any practice invented by the Jewish people at any time in its history become Halakhah? If not, then which, when, and how? What weight is to be placed on those laws and practices enjoined in the Torah, and how do we avoid judging them by an external non-Jewish criterion? These are only a few of the questions which require and merit careful exploration.

Professor Fackenheim has produced a work in the field of Jewish theology which is worthy of the careful attention of every serious and thoughtful Jew. He has set forth with eminent skill and insight an analysis and explication of major aspects of Jewish faith which intelligent Jews, of whatever persuasion, should find instructive and stimulating. However we may differ on particular points, and most especially on the nature of Halakhah, we can only be grateful to him for this book which teaches us much, opens up new religious perspectives, and is an eloquent and effective exposition of Jewish faith.

NOTE

[1] Fackenheim, Emil L., *Quest for Past and Future: Essays in Jewish Theology,* (Bloomington & London: Indiana University Press, 1968).

31

CONTINUITY AND CHANGE IN JEWISH THEOLOGY

It was fashionable until recently in certain Jewish circles to assert that Judaism has no dogmas, that what is required of a Jew is only the proper observance of the law, without any prescriptions concerning belief. That fashion has, happily, passed. No serious student of Judaism would want to assert today that there are no fixed elements of Jewish faith. It is obvious that Judaism requires us to affirm the truth of certain doctrines, else the observance of *mitzvot* would be meaningless and without any foundation. We are, however, suffering today from an extreme reaction to the 19th century conception of a "dogmaless" Judaism. Certain circles have now adopted as their standard the view that the dogmas of Judaism are completely fixed, that we can state precisely and unambiguously just exactly what are the fundamental and binding principles of the Jewish faith, and that we have a single official interpretation of the meaning of each of these fundamental principles. This latter view seems to me a misrepresentation of the very nature of Jewish religious belief. In addition, it seems to me to be destructive and self-defeating, since it has the effect of driving out sincere and faithful Jews who find that they cannot honestly subscribe to whatever fixed and "official" version of Jewish dogma happens to be offered to them. In this essay, I want to show that while there are fixed parameters to Jewish faith, and also certain fixed terminological formulas, there is, at the same time, a refreshing openness within those parameters. The normative and authentic Jewish tradition has accommodated a remarkable variety of basic religious ideas over the centuries. There is no reason that it cannot continue to do so in our own day.

Contrary to the position of those who fear and discourage careful inquiry into the foundations of our faith, one can show easily that a Jew has the right, and even more the duty, to use his intellect to its fullest capacity in order to reflect on fundamental religious ideas. The point is stated with striking force and clarity in Bahya's *Duties of the Heart*, a treatise which is accepted as a sound guide in even the most conservative circles. "On the question whether we are under an obligation to investigate the doctrine of God's Unity or not, I assert that anyone capable of investigating themes by rational methods, is bound to do so according to his powers and capacities... Anyone who neglects to institute such an inquiry is blameworthy and is accounted as belonging to the class of those who fall short in wisdom and conduct... It has thus been demonstrated by arguments drawn from Reason, Scripture, and Tradition that it is our duty rationally to investigate every topic on which we can, by the exercise of our mental faculties, attain clearness."[1] Bahya was giving full expression to a view that was widely held in the Middle Ages and which continues to be valid in our own time. Judaism does not require us to sacrifice intellectual concern and integrity. On the contrary, it requires us to serve God with our minds as well as with our bodies.

Any serious study of the problem of the fundamental principles of the Jewish faith forces one to the conclusion that there never has been a single officially fixed creed. In fact, it was not until medieval times that anyone had proposed formal creedal formulas. The well-known first Mishnah of *Perek Helek* in *Sanhedrin* can be taken, at most, as pointing to certain elements of Jewish belief. It certainly is not a full and fixed formula of the Jewish creed. Moreover, in that very Mishnah there are differences of opinion, and in the *Gemara* which follows it, there are differing interpretations of the meaning of the Mishnah. When, in later times, attempts were made to establish an exact creedal formula, there emerged instead a variety of creeds which differed in number of articles and in contents. The popular impression that the thirteen principles of Maimonides are the one universal formulation of the basic and mandatory beliefs of Judaism is, of course, mistaken. We have had creeds with three articles, seven articles, and even Abravanel's insistence that each of the 613 commandments should be viewed as an article of faith. At the other extreme is the frequently quoted talmudic passage in which the 613 commandments are seen as resting finally on a single principle, the statement of Habakkuk, "but the righteous shall live by his faith."

It is not even clear that Maimonides himself kept consistently to the formula of the thirteen principles which he set out as a young man. (It is worth noting, in passing, that the version of the creed which we have in the siddur is certainly not identical with the version in Maimonides' commentary on the Mishnah.[2] Nor, as has been pointed out by various scholars, including R. Joseph Kapah in his recent new Hebrew translation, is the usual printed version identical with the original.) At the end of that formula Maimonides takes an absolutely uncompromising line. He asserts that if a Jew should doubt even one of these thirteen principles, he has excluded himself from *k'lal yisrael*, and is a denier of the faith, a heretic, one who should be despised and reviled. Yet, when the same Rambam in his *Mishneh Torah* sets forth the procedure for converting a non-Jew to Judaism, he says specifically, "We must inform him (i.e., the convert) of the fundamental principles of the faith, namely, the unity of God and the prohibition against worshipping idols" (*Isueri Bi'ah* 14,2). One wonders why the convert should not be required to learn, accept, and affirm all thirteen principles if they are absolutely essential to the Jewish faith. This is not the place to attempt to interpret, or to interpret away, the apparent difference in Maimonides' position. All that matters is that we should see how even in the mind of a single Jewish thinker, and a remarkably systematic one, it is not evident that there is a single permanently set creed.

We may take it as certain that any legitimate version of Judaism must affirm the existence and the absolute unity of God. This is a fundamental without which no system of belief can conceivable be identified as Jewish. Yet, while all authentically Jewish thinkers accept these principles, they attach a variety of meanings to them. The most familiar division of opinion is that between Rambam and Rabad. Rambam rules that the one God must be absolutely incorporeal, else his unity would be compromised. As a result, he holds that whoever claims that God has a body and physical shape is a heretic. To this Rabad replies that "greater and better men" than Maimonides believed in God's corporeality, basing themselves on Scripture and Aggadah, and clearly, Rabad holds, they were not heretics (*Teshuvah*, 3, 7, and gloss ad loc.).

While most Jewish thinkers conceive of God as transcendent, there are those who view Him as immanent, and there are even views which can only be seen as approaching pantheism. Is the *Zohar* to be considered less Jewish than Maimonides because of its clearly pantheistic tendencies?[3] Must we choose between a totally transcendent God and the God of whom R. Shneor Zalman of Liadi wrote, "There is truly nothing besides Him"? Have we any ground for asserting that only one view is to be accepted as fitting the requirements of the Jewish creed? To deny that God exists, or to affirm that there are many gods, is to reject what is essential to Judaism. Nowhere is there any clear evidence that within the parameters set by the existence and absolute unity of God there is only a single authorized conception of Him. The point is well put in the Midrash which teaches that God must be understood by each person in accordance with his own powers of apprehension and conceptualization, "young men according to their understanding, the aged according to their understanding, and children according to their understanding" (*Ex. R., Yithro* 29, 1).

In recognizing the range of possibilities that are open to us within the framework of authentic Jewish faith, we can return to the intellectual openness of some earlier Jewish generations. Unlike them, we too often adopt fixed positions which leave no room for difference. We tend to cry "heretic" much too readily, and to suppose that we cannot differ with mutual respect and with mutual recognition of the legitimacy of alternative views. Yet, our ancestors knew how to engage in the sharpest kind of intellectual combat without losing respect for their opponents or considering them destroyers of the faith. What a marvelous model we can find in the relation of the Ramban to the Rambam. The frequent criticisms which he levels are, at times, unmitigated in their intense ferocity. One need only cite the passage in Ramban's commentary on the Torah where he discusses at length a position taken in the *Guide of the Perplexed*, only to conclude that, "These doctrines directly contradict Scripture. It is forbidden to listen to them, much less to believe them." (ad Gen. 18:20). We know how frequently and strongly Nachmanides disagreed with Maimonides. Nevertheless, he always evidenced enormous respect for the man whom he opposed, and while he may have differed with him on particular points, he explicitly defended him from charges of heresy.

The same Ramban, who is often more conservative than Maimonides in his treatment of theological questions, adopted certain positions which would undoubtedly seem radical to some of our contemporaries. A Jew who expressed a doubt today concerning the precision of the number 613 as the number of the commandments would be labeled heretical in certain contemporary Jewish circles. The number 613 has been treated as sacrosanct. We know how mightily various Jewish thinkers labored in order to produce a precise list of 613 commandments. Yet, Ramban seemed to feel no danger of heresy, or even of serious non-conformity, when he chose to question the reliability of that number. In his first gloss on Maimonides' *Sefer ha-Mitzvot* Ramban expressed his own serious doubts concerning the number 613, despite the fact that he knew, as he says, "that everyone accepts it as a simple established truth." The substance of the argument which he develops is of no intrinsic importance for our discussion. What is important is that it was possible for a Jewish thinker to question seriously what was universally accepted, and to do so without feeling that he must apologize for holding a different view. It is instructive to note the fact that he refers to the Rambam, with whom he is differing, as "*ha-Rav ha-Gadot.*"

Even with respect to matters which are treated with fear by many of our contemporaries, we find a combination of fearlessness and intellectual integrity in our classical tradition. Perhaps no area of contemporary life is considered as dangerous to Jewish faith (by some) as the claims and achievements of the natural sciences. Here, too, there are those who would ignore, and even suppress, scientific knowledge. They see in many scientific claims, however well established, a threat to traditional Judaism. Commonly held views concerning the age of the world, the theory of biological evolution, and similar matters are seen by conservative religious forces as so perilous that they must be labeled false on purely religious grounds. In their opinion, the Torah can only be understood in one way, and that is a way which necessarily excludes most modern scientific doctrine. It is difficult to reconcile this with the position which emerges at many points in the tradition. When dealing with an astronomical question, the Talmud itself records that our sages noted a contradiction between the established Jewish view and that of the non-Jewish astronomers. After careful investigation R. Judah ha-Nasi concluded that the Jewish view could not stand up under critical investigation and that the non-Jewish view was more acceptable (Pesahim 94 b). In commenting on this Talmudic discussion, Maimonides teaches that those who accepted the non-Jewish view were correct. "For everyone who argues in speculative matters does this according to the conclusions to which he was led by his speculation. Hence the conclusion whose demonstration is correct is believed."[4] In his letter to the scholars of Marseilles, Maimonides rejects all astrological claims as false, despite the fact there are numerous passages in the Talmud and later literature which teach that the stars do affect our lives and destinies. He assures his readers that they need feel no anxiety over the fact that in such a matter (in contrast, of course, with questions of Halakhah) they are rejecting the views of certain respected rabbinic authorities. As he says explicitly, we should never give up a position which is based on the strongest evidence available in favor of opposed and undefended views held by individual rabbis of the Talmud. Even with respect to the Torah itself this is not required of us. "For you see that certain verses of the Torah are not to be understood literally. Because it was known through sound intellectual evidence that it was impossible for things to be as they were represented in a literal interpretation of these verses, the translator (i.e. Onkelos) translated them in a manner which accords with our knowledge. A man should never cast intellectual apprehension behind him, since man's eyes are in front and not behind."[5]

Precisely the same attitude is taken by Malbim in the introduction to his commentary on the book of Ezekiel. Though he has profound reverence for Maimonides, he announces, at the outset, that we can no longer accept the latter's interpretation of Ezekiel's Chariot Vision. It must be rejected because it is based on astronomy, physics, and philosophy all of which are outdated. The foundations on which Maimonides' views rested have been shown to be unsound. "They have all been undermined by developments in scientific research in the last generations. This research has built astronomy and the other natural sciences on other foundations which are both stronger and more reliable." Here we see giants of the authentic classical Jewish tradition who do not fear science, philosophy, or any other source of human knowledge. They are convinced that the Torah does not require faithful Jews to close their minds or to withdraw from the world. On the contrary, for the Torah itself must always be read in the light of the best current knowledge.

Characteristically, they did not claim to know or understand what was beyond them, but readily admitted their own ignorance. Given such an admission, they did not proclaim dogmatic certainty about that which they were in principle incapable of achieving basic understanding. A single instance will suffice to make the point. In their opposition to the theory of evolution and to geological claims about the age of the earth, various contemporary religious circles proclaim that we know exactly when and how the world was created. One need only read the first chapters of *Bereshit* literally, they say, and it is all crystal clear. Now, it may well be that the theory of evolution and the claims about the great antiquity of the earth are false, but they cannot be refuted by a literal reading of the Torah. Nor should we feel constrained to attempt such a refutation.

The Ramban was among the profoundest students of the Torah that our tradition has produced. He had insights into the meaning of very obscure and difficult passages which have illuminated the way for all succeeding generations. Yet, with respect to the opening chapters of the Torah, the Ramban writes that he does not claim to understand them. "The narrative concerning what was created on the first day, and what was made on the second day, and on the remaining days, the long description of the creation of Adam and Eve, their sin, their punishment, the story of the Garden of Eden and of Adam's expulsion therefrom, none of this can be understood fully and clearly from the scriptural text. This is even more the case with respect to the story of the generation of the flood and the generation of the schism" (*ad* Gen. 1,1). In a similar manner, Maimonides concludes, after careful study, that the question of the eternity of the world or its creation in time is not subject to resolution by either scientific or philosophical evidence. However, he stresses that he does not feel constrained, even in such a case, to affirm the doctrine of creation in time merely because it would seem to be required by a literal reading of Scripture. He will not allow himself to become the prisoner of a literalistic fundamentalism even in the case of such an absolutely basic issue. He affirms that God is the creator of the world in time, but bases that affirmation on deeper and more defensible grounds.

I fail to understand why we should feel obligated to reject science where our very illustrious teachers of earlier generation did not. I fail even more to understand why we should be prepared to accept a simple literal reading of the most obscure and complex scriptural passages when they, with all their depth, held that no meaningful literal interpretation was possible or intelligible. Granted that the belief in the divine creation is a fundamental principle of Jewish faith, and one must grant this, it does not follow that we can interpret that principle in a single, literal, and universally binding way. Did not the Ramban (following a long-established tradition) teach us that "*ma'ase bereshit* is a profound mystery which is not capable of being understood from the scriptural verses and cannot be known and grasped clearly except by way of the oral tradition that extends back to Moses who received it from the Almighty. Those who know this secret doctrine are duty-bound to keep it secret" (*ibid.*). Yet, we insist that every six-year-old can be taught the whole of this mystery and in terms which are simple, literal, and present no special difficulty!

Let us consider briefly one final example. The doctrine of divine revelation, specifically that the Torah was given by God at Sinai, is surely among our basic principles of faith. Without this doctrine we lose the essential foundation on which rests the whole of our religious practice. No formula which denies *Torah min ha-Shamayim* can be admitted as normatively Jewish. But who would want to claim, as some do, that we understand precisely and literally what it means? Do we understand how the eternal makes itself temporal; how the purely spiritual becomes manifest in physical form; how God speaks and man hears? Does any spiritual advantage accrue to us when we yield to the temptation to present such subtle and mysterious matters in childishly simple versions? For that matter, does any intellectual or tactical advantage accrue to us? Why then should we speak as if we know and understand such matters clearly and unambiguously?

Even with respect to the text of the Torah things are not as clear and unambiguous as we might like them to be. The most extreme interpretation of the doctrine of *Torah min ha-Shamayim* is that of the Baraitha (Sanhedrin 99a) which rules that whoever believes that there is even one word of the Torah which is not directly from God, but was spoken by Moses on his own, is a denial of *Torah min ha-Shamayim* (based on Num. 16:31; see Maimonides' Teshuvah 3, 8). This is the generally accepted view in Orthodox circles today. It is remarkable (if also disturbing) that even with regard to this most delicate and sensitive issue different views were expressed and recorded. I am fully aware that one can find ways to interpret (or interpret away) these differing views so that they will not threaten the traditional structure. That is not my task here. What is instructive for our purpose is the fact that these views were expressed, recorded, and permitted to stand openly in our official literature. In making the halakhic ruling that the section of curses in the Torah must be read as a single uninterrupted section, the Talmud distinguishes between the curses in Numbers and Deuteronomy. Abbaye holds that the former must be read as a unit, but the latter need not be. His reason is that "the former are in the plural and were spoken by Moses at the dictation of the Almighty, while the latter are in the singular and were spoken by Moses on his own authority, מֹשה מפי עצמו אמרן (*Megillah* 31b). Rashi in his comment on Deuteronomy 28:23 quotes almost these exact words. However one interprets them, they are a startling contrast to what we take to be the official view, as it is formulated by Maimonides who, of course, bases himself on the above Baraitha. The mere fact that Rashi did not feel constrained to explain, justify or apologize for his (and the Talmud's) formulation is already instructive, no matter how we ourselves interpret this passage. The same can be said of ibn-Ezra's explicit statement, in his explanation of the differences between the Ten Commandments in Exodus and Deuteronomy, that the former were the very words of God while the latter were the words of Moses (*ad* Exodus 20, 1). A similar statement can be found in a midrashic comment on Exodus 32, 26-28. There the Midrash goes so far as to call heaven and earth as witnesses that the words which Moses spoke were not dictated to him by God, but were his own (*Seder Eliyahu Rabba*, ch. 4). Such statements, heterodox as they may seem, are contained in our official literature without in any way threatening the integrity of our faith. They bear witness to the wide range of possibilities which exist within that framework which we call Judaism.

What I have tried to establish in this brief essay is the claim that, on the one hand, Jewish faith rests on certain fixed dogmas such as the existence and unity of God, the divine origin of the Torah, God's role as the Lord of history as well as the Lord of nature, and others. On the other hand, however firm and unyielding our commitment is to these articles of faith, and even to certain ways of formulating them, we must recognize that they have always been subject to a wide variety of interpretations. No one interpretation can claim for itself exclusive rights. No one is the sole, authentic, and official interpretation. Intellectual integrity makes such a monolithic Judaism impossible. Historical accuracy makes it clear that such a Judaism never existed. We would do well, especially in this age of pluralistic cultures and styles of thought, to recapture the openness of mind which has been so deeply characteristic of Jewish tradition. We must reject attempts to turn Judaism into an overly simple set of creedal formulas which ignores the richness of the history of Jewish thought and of the texture of Jewish experience. In one of his letters Rav Kook wrote, "Much as I love to study and to teach the fundamental principles of our faith, I am very far indeed from seeking to impose my views on any other person. This is something which is unthinkable, especially in our time." We would do well, indeed, to learn our lesson from this great teacher of our age. He understood both Judaism and the contemporary world more profoundly than many of his opponents.

"...AND I HAVE SAID IT ALREADY MORE THAN ONCE, THAT IF THERE IS DISAGREEMENT BETWEEN SCHOLARS CONCERNING VIEWS OR OPINIONS WHICH DO NOT AIM AT ANY ACTION, IT IS NOT POSSIBLE TO SAY THAT THE HALACHAH IS IN ACCORDANCE WITH A CERTAIN OPINION [AND NOT WITH ANOTHER].

(*MAIMONIDES, MISHNAH COMMENTARY SOTAH* 3, 4)

"I HAD TO WRITE ALL THIS BECAUSE I HAVE SEEN INSIGNIFICANT MEN, WHO THINK THEY ARE WISE, OPEN THEIR MOUTHS WIDE IN LENGTHY AND UNINTELLIGENT DISCOURSES AGAINST GREAT MEN. IT IS CLEAR NOW THAT EVERY INTELLIGENT PERSON IS PERMITTED TO INTERPRET THE BIBLICAL TEXTS IN ACCORDANCE WITH THE TRUTH AS IT SEEMS TO HIM.

JOSEPH ALBO, SEFER HA-IKARIM, BOOK I, CHAPTER 2
(*TRANSLATED BY I. HUSIK, THE SCHIFF LIBRARY OF JEWISH CLASSICS,* 1929, 0.55)

NOTES

[1] *Hovot ha-Levavot*, (Moses Hyamson, tr.), Shaar Hayihud, ch. 3. A similar attitude is expressed by Maimonides in his commentary to *Mishnah Berachot*, 9:5. Cf. also, Albo, *Sefer ha-Ikkarim*, I, ch. 2.

[2] See L. Jacobs, *Principles of the Jewish Faith* (2964), p. 17.

[3] See G. Scholem, *Major Trends in Jewish Mysticism* (1954), p. 222.

[4] Maimonides, *Guide of the Perplexed*, (Shlomo Pines. tr.), II, 8.

[5] *Kovetz Teshuvot ha-Rambam*, (Leipzig, 1859), pt. 2, 26b.

32

THEODICY AND ANTI-THEODICY IN BIBLICAL AND RABBINIC LITERATURE

The Philosophical Problem

In ordinary human experience we find almost no connection between virtue and happiness. The apparently wildly random distribution of pain or prosperity, the seeming arbitrariness of human destiny, is thought by many to be one of the strongest of all challenges to religious faith. It is widely taught that, according to the doctrine of the biblically based religions, God is all-powerful and all-good. Presumably, then, He should be able to prevent unmerited human suffering. The standard philosophical formulation of the puzzle is familiar to everyone who deals with this problem. Given God's power and His benevolence, how is it possible that there is evil in the world. If He wants to prevent it, but is unable, then His power is limited. If He is able, but does not choose to prevent it, then He is not good. Either way, the argument goes, standard religious claims about God are refuted.

This approach of some philosophers to the problem is countered by other philosophical arguments that try to justify God by introducing a variety of qualifications into the argument. These range from the claim that evil is a form of non-being and is thus purely illusory, to highly complex efforts to show that God has morally sufficient reasons for permitting evil to exist in the world, to the argument that God is limited in power and cannot fully control events. Typically, the philosophic treatments of this subject are carried on from a position that is external to the community of religious faith. The philosophers, for the most part, seem to have no personal stake in the outcome of the investigation. They are merely dealing with one more interesting technical problem that presents them with an intellectual challenge.

Biblical Responses

The approach to the problem from within the life of religious faith is, in certain respects, radically different because it is characterized by passionate involvement. This is especially evident in the Bible and in rabbinic literature where we find uncompromising faith in divine justice balanced by anguished concern to understand God's mysterious ways. Sometimes the answers are easy to come by, in particular when there seems to be a direct correlation between sin and punishment. Adam knows why he is condemned to exile from paradise and to a life of toil, since God tells him explicitly that it is because he ate of the forbidden fruit.[1] Noah is told that God has "decided to put an end to all flesh, for the earth is filled with lawlessness because of them: I am about to destroy them with the earth"[2] Similarly, Abraham, despite his challenge to God, knows finally that God is acting justly in His destruction of Sodom and Gomorra. As God says, their "outrage is so great, and their sin so grave"[3] that they must be destroyed.

At other times there is no answer readily available and suffering generates bitter complaint, even challenge to God, but hardly ever at the expense of continuing faith and trust. Jeremiah openly challenges God to a trial, knowing in advance that He will prevail. "You will win, O Lord, if I make claim against You, yet I shall present charges against You: Why does the way of the wicked prosper? Why are the workers of treachery at ease?"[4] Even his bitter certainty that he will receive no answer does not weaken the prophet's faith in God and in His justice. The classical biblical case, of course, is that of Job who in his bitterness proclaims, "Though I were blameless, He would prove me crooked... It is all one; therefore I say, 'He destroys the blameless and the guilty.'"[5]

In these few passages, which are a small selection from many such, we see that in the Bible we already have both theodicy and anti-theodicy as widely present counter-elements. Human suffering is often explained as a direct consequence of sin. We violate God's commandments and He punishes us. This simple explanation is opposed by challenges, even attacks, on God because there appears to be so much unjust and unearned human suffering. Job's friends offer the easy answer; he must have sinned grievously to have received such punishment. Yet Job himself never yields on this point, insisting that he is not guilty and demanding a trial. In the end, as we know, he does not receive a specific justification of his suffering, but yet he responds in humble faith as he submits to the divine decree. What is most instructive is that God condemns Job's friends, saying to them, "you have not spoken the truth about Me as did My servant Job."[6] This suggests to us that God Himself does not approve of those attempts at theodicy which reduce very complex questions to unacceptably simple answers and try to dispel the mysterious darkness with an artificial light that obscures more than it illuminates. It seems that in God's eyes, faith and trust, however troubled, are preferable to false or tendentious apologetics. As is often said in traditional circles of talmudic learning, not every question must be answered, nor must every puzzle be resolved.

Responses in Earlier Rabbinic Literature

The same two tendencies are present in rabbinic literature. We frequently find easy justifications of God which are just as frequently countered by a recognition of our inability to justify His ways in the world. Moses, the greatest of the prophets, is represented in the Talmud as asking God to explain why the righteous suffer and the wicked prosper. He wants desperately to understand how God works in human history. According to one view, his question was answered, although in a way that is far from satisfying. Moses was taught that the righteous man who suffers is the son of a wicked man, while the wicked man who prospers is the son of a righteous man. The one is apparently paying for his father's sins, while the other is the beneficiary of his father's virtue. This explanation is then modified by the assertion that the righteous man who suffers is imperfect in his righteousness, while the wicked man who prospers is not absolutely wicked.[7] It is self-evident that this explanation fails to give us a justification for God's actions. It is not clear at all why one who is mostly, although not perfectly, righteous should have a lower standing than one who is mostly, but not absolutely, wicked.

According to a second view, Moses received no answer at all. Rabbi Meir teaches that God turned down Moses's request for enlightenment bysaying that He acts as He chooses. "For it is said: 'And I will show mercy on whom I will show mercy', although he may not deserve it.:[8] One should not misconstrue this statement to mean that R. Meir was asserting that God behaves in ways that are purely arbitrary or capricious. All he is saying is that *we* are not capable of giving a full and satisfactory account of God's ways in the world. God makes His own decisions on grounds that are known to Him, but we humans cannot and need not justify His ways.

Our stance should be the stance of faithful trust in His justice and benevolence. This same position is set forth in the well-known story of Moses being transported forward in time to the lecture hall of R. Akiba. Having discovered the latter's remarkable greatness and creativity in understanding the Torah, Moses asks God to show him the reward that awaits the sage. When Moses sees the martyrdom of R. Akiba and its aftermath, he cries out bitterly, "Lord of the Universe, such Torah and such a reward!" To which God replies, "Be silent, for such is My decree."[9] Here again Moses is left without insight into God's ways, while he is challenged at the same time not to question, not to doubt, but to maintain his faith in God's justice and benevolence.

It is characteristic of rabbinic literature that these antithetical approaches to the problem of evil are found side by side, often within a single text. We shall see that this is true of both the earlier and later levels of that literature. Let us consider first some tannaitic sources. In a well-known text R. Yannai teaches that "the tranquility of the wicked and the suffering of the righteous" are both "beyond our grasp".[10] The exact meaning of *ein bevadenu* is not absolutely clear. However, the classical commentators illustrate our point by offering two main lines of interpretation. One asserts that we simply do not understand God's ways, while the other justifies God by explaining this passage to mean that we do not see His Justice in this world only because all will be rectified in the world-to-come. Both are agreed in taking for granted that, whether we understand human destiny or not, God is just.

In Sifre Deuteronomy[12] we find a striking instance of this dual approach. The passage is a midrashic exposition of the verse, "The Rock!— "His deeds are perfect, yea, all His ways are just; a faithful God, never false, true and upright is He." (Deuteronomy 32:4) Clearly this verse presents a challenge to anyone concerned with theodicy, and the midrash responds to that challenge. The initial response consists simply of a strong assertion that God's work is, in fact, perfect and His ways are just, however it may appear to us, and it is improper for us to question, to complain, or to try to explain His ways. This anti-theodicy by affirmation without explanation is followed by a standard justification of the apparent failure to reward the righteous and punish the wicked in this world. We are assured that all the seeming injustice in apportioning rewards in this world will be set right in the future judgment to which we shall all be subjected in the next world. There God "will sit in judgment on each one and give him what is appropriate for him." The wicked are rewarded in this world for whatever minor righteous deeds they performed, so that they may then be punished in the next world for all their evil deeds. In turn, the righteous are punished in this world for their minor transgressions so that they may receive the full reward for their virtue in the world-to-come. God's justice is absolute, but we fail to see it here since it is carried out fully only in the hereafter. Anti-theodicy and conventional theodicy live in this passage side by side. So far does the conventional theodicy go in this passage that it concludes by describing for us the procedure which will be followed in the final judgment. Each person, we are told, will be presented with an exact accounting of all his deeds on earth. He will be required to verify the account and to sign it as evidence that he acknowledges the absolute justice of God's verdict.

In a last step the passage then teaches that here on earth we must accept without complaint whatever is meted out to us, because only in this way do we demonstrate our faith in divine justice and perfection. The model is that of the great sage R. Haninah ben Teradion, his wife and his daughter. The parents are condemned to a martyr's death, and the daughter is reduced from her exalted station and assigned to work in a brothel, Yet, no word of complaint is recorded. Instead, the sage and his wife justify God while reciting portions of the verse we are expounding. The daughter similarly justifies God while reciting another verse (Jeremiah 32:19). As the midrash text puts, "The three directed their hearts [toward God] and accepted the justice of God's judgment." Here we are presented with the recurring model of true faith. Men and women who have committed themselves to the truth of the Torah and have lived meticulously by its teachings accept even the most horrible fate with equanimity because they are confident that God acts righteously. What is especially instructive is that R. Haninah and his family accept their fate without attempting to offer any explanation of why it is just or how they will be compensated for their suffering. In contrast, the text introduces a philosopher (who is clearly a non-Jew) who admires and praises the faithful martyrs. When he too is condemned to death by the authorities he rejoices because, "tomorrow my portion will be with them in the world to come." Note that the philosopher is driven to provide a theodicy, namely, the assurance that his suffering will be amply compensated in the world-to-come. For him faith must somehow be supplemented by a reassuring argument.

A final tannaitic example will show us how far the ancient sages were prepared to go in pursuing theodicy and anti-theodicy side by side.

One of the great moments in biblical history in which God's power is openly exercised to save His people is the splitting of the Sea of Reeds. After the children of Israel have safely crossed over and their pursuers are drowned, Moses leads the people in a hymn of glorification, proclaiming God's might and His saving power. "I will sing to the Lord, for He has triumphed gloriously; horse and driver He has hurled into the sea."[12] Throughout the song God is exalted and praised. The climax seems to be reached when He is proclaimed to be above all other beings who claim some divine status. "Who is like You, O Lord among the celestials [*ba-elim*], who is like You, majestic in holiness, awesome in splendor, working wonders."[13] These words of pure praise seem clear and unambiguous. Yet there is at least one tannaitic exposition of this text which construes it to have a vastly different meaning.[14]

The first comments on this verse are conventional variations on the basic theme which stresses God's power as it manifested itself by saving the Israelites and destroying the idolaters. This thrust reaches its height when the term "*ba-elim*" is read as "*ba-alamim*" i.e., those with vast power. The midrash now construes the verse in the following way: "Who is like unto Thee among the strong and who is like unto Thee in the wonders and mighty deeds which Thou didst perform at the sea."[15]

Remarkably, the very next words reverse completely the mood of praise in favor of seeming doubt and bitterness, and they do so with a play on the same key term. Now "*ba-elim*" is read as "*ba-ilmim*" and the whole verse is turned on its head. The highest praise becomes the most bitter condemnation. Not who is like you, O Lord, in the whole pantheon of those who claim to be divine beings, who has your power and your devotion to those who serve you? Instead the verse is now read, "Who is like You among the silent [mute], O Lord. Who like You sees the degradation of your children and remains silent [doing nothing to save them]?" God is here accused of apparent indifference to the bitter fate of His chosen people. His one time power exercised against the oppressors of the Israelites, is now held back in restrained silence. This text reflects the reality of later Jewish history in which the people often suffered bitterly at the hands of powerful enemies, while God remained silent, refusing to intervene to save them. If the first interpretation of our verse is theodicy at its most impressive, this later interpretation is equally forceful anti-theodicy. No explanation or justification is given for God's silence, just the almost laconic statement of the fact. This is no denial of faith, only a denial that we can give an account of God's action or inaction which is fully consistent with our understanding of His nature and of the biblical promises.[16]

Responses in Later Rabbinic Literature

This same combination of theodicy and anti-theodicy is present as well in the later rabbinic materials, in the Gemara and in the post-tannaitic midrashim. Our space permits us to examine only a few examples. R. Ammi teaches that there is no death without sin and no suffering without iniquity.[17] He offers a simple and familiar explanation of the painful aspects of human experience. Our suffering is punishment for our transgression of God's commandments, and our very mortality is the consequence of our sinfulness. However, instead of accepting this easy theodicy, the text goes on to refute it by considering a variety of cases which do not fit this model. The discussion concludes with anti-theodicy, stating that we have proof that "there is death without sin and suffering without iniquity. Thus the refutation of R. Ammi is [indeed] a refutation."[18] As in the other cases we have studied, we see here a rejection of easy answers to hard questions. The Sages had no problem about admitting that they could not give a fully satisfactory account of the phenomenon of human suffering.

An even more striking instance occurs in an extended discussion which introduces the concept of *yissurin shel ahavah*, suffering which is a mark of God's special love. As Rava puts it, "If the Holy One, blessed be He, is pleased with a man, he crushes him with painful sufferings."[19] Rashi explains the concept of *yissurin shel ahavah* in the following way: "The Holy One, blessed be He, causes suffering to a person in this world, even though that person is without sin, in order to increase his reward in the world-to-come beyond that which he strictly merits."[20] In the discussion which follows this justification of the suffering of the righteous is defended and explicated with various prooftexts and is refined in a number of ways. One view is that not only are these sufferings the prologue to great reward in the hereafter, but they also assure one that his children will have long life and that his Torah learning will never leave him. To guard against this explanation not working out, another view is introduced. "If a man busies himself in the study of Torah and in acts of charity and [nonetheless] buries his children, all his sins are forgiven him."[21] It seems that it is always possible, with sufficient determination and ingenuity, to find a satisfactory explanation of even the most painful human experiences. If one explanation goes contrary to actual events, another can be produced to cover the new situation.

It is against this form of theodicy that Antony Flew argued so vigorously in the famous "Theology and Falsification" debate. Flew makes the point that "if there is nothing which a putative assertion denies then there is nothing which it asserts either: and so it is not really an assertion."[22] Flew concludes his discussion with a challenge to religious believers. "What would have to occur or to have occurred to constitute for you a disproof of the love of, or of the existence of, God?" The answer seems to be that nothing can shake the faithful in their conviction that God is just, no set of events is sufficient to falsity the theodicy of the faithful. As we have seen, one can always provide an explanation or justification of human suffering, even that of the most virtuous. Moreover, if one explanation does not work, there is always another readily available. Once we claim to know God's ways in the world, we can always provide an account which defends Him against charges of injustice or lack of power or benevolence.

Yet, even in the talmudic passage concerning chastisements of love which we have been examining, there is also an anti-theodicy element. Sages of unquestioned standing and unquestioned piety reject for themselves the seeming attractions of suffering in this world so as to merit great reward in the world-to-come. The passage concludes by recounting several episodes involving some of the greatest figures of the age. In each case the sage has fallen ill and is suffering. A colleague visits him, and in the course of the visit asks, "Are your sufferings pleasing [*havivin*] to you?" One would expect a positive answer, since such suffering is thought to be evidence of God's special love and the great reward which it guarantees in the next world. Yet, in each case the sage replies, "Neither they nor their reward." At this point the visitor takes his hand and cures him of his illness.[23] We see here forceful anti-theodicy expressed not as theological theory, but as actually practiced in the lives of great scholars who are models of piety and learning. They reject outright the theodicy of "sufferings of love" and find no comfort in the idea that their pain in this world will be compensated by great rewards in the hereafter. The Talmud has no problem about setting antithetical views side by side, recognizing that there is a legitimate place both for theodicy and the denial of theodicy within the Jewish tradition. What matters is that in Job-like fashion those who reject the various efforts at theodicy remain fully within the community of faith, no less than those who accept conventional theodicy as their doctrine.

This tension between theodicy and anti-theodicy shows up again in the interpretation of a mishna by a later sage. The mishna teaches that whoever fulfills a single divine commandment is assured of reward. "Good is done to him, he is assured of long life, and he inherits an assured place in the world-to-come."[24] This seemingly extravagant claim is tempered by the discussion in the gemara that follows. It is qualified to mean that when a man's record is evenly balanced between good deeds and evil deeds, the addition of one more good deed tips the scale in his favor and assures him of divine reward. However, even this hypothesis is questioned on the ground that there is a teaching (which we discussed above) that the virtuous suffer in this world so that they may collect their full reward in the next world, and the reverse with regard to the wicked. This finally leads to the theodicy of R. Jacob that, "We receive no reward in this world for the commandments which we fulfill." Only in the world-to-come are we finally rewarded for our virtuous behavior.[25]

What moved R. Jacob to assign all reward to the next world was his experience of the seeming arbitrariness of human destiny in this world. He provides us with a classic model. There are two commandments in the Torah for whose observance long life is promised. One is honoring parents, and the other is sending away the mother bird before taking eggs or chicks from her nest.[26] Yet R. Jacob reports a case in which a father asks his son to climb up to the loft and bring down some young birds. Obeying his father, the son climbs up, sends away the mother bird, and takes the young birds. On his way down, he falls to his death, despite his explicit fulfillment of the two commandments that promise the reward of long life. This reinforces R. Jacob's view that there are no rewards in this life, only in the world-to-come. Clearly this is a paradigm of all simple theodicy. Whatever happens to a man in this world, we can be certain that it will all be set right in the next. If this is true even for those commandments which seem to promise long life in this world, how much more so for those that have no such promise attached to them. It is an act of faith to affirm, with whatever prooftexts one can muster, that God is just and benevolent, but that we do not see his justice or compassion in this-worldly life. R. Jacob, it is noted was the grandson of the great apostate sage, Elisha ben Abuyah (known as Aher, "the other"), whose apostasy was caused by witnessing apparent divine injustice and being unable to account for it. If he had understood the biblical promises of long life as his grandson did, Aher, we are assured, "would not have sinned."[27]

Yet all this strenuous effort at theodicy is rejected by a single prosaic comment in this same passage. An anonymous participant in the discussion evades all the theological puzzles by noting that the obedient son was imprudent and climbed up to the loft on a rickety ladder. No wonder that it collapsed and he fell to his death. The whole event is construed in purely natural terms, The text adds the observation that in dangerous circumstances where injury is to be expected we don't rely on miracles to save us. The young man was responsible for his own death because of his carelessness, and it is utterly inappropriate to expect God to intervene miraculously to save him. Even with divine promises of long life to assure us, we should never tempt fate. Again theodicy is balanced by anti-theodicy.

We cannot conclude this brief study without considering what is perhaps the most instructive anti-theodicy text in the whole rabbinic corpus. I refer to Leviticus Rabbah, Chapter 20,[28] where there is a long meditation on the implications of the death of Nadav and Avihu, the two sons of Aaron the High Priest. In the scriptural account we are simply told that at the consecration of the sanctuary in the desert they offered up a strange fire which God had not commanded. As a consequence, they were immediately consumed by fire. The midrash addresses the puzzling question as to why these two young men should have met such a violent death. What kind of divine justice was it that punished them so severely for a seemingly minor infraction?

Some sections of this long midrashic exegesis deal with the problem through conventional theodicy. In these discussions the death of Nadav and Avihu is understood as the inevitable consequence of their sinfulness. The range of their supposed improprieties is represented as broad and severe. They are supposed to have been deeply disrespectful to their father and to Moses, their uncle. They presumed to teach and to decide questions of law in the presence of Moses their teacher.[29] Walking behind Moses and Aaron, they said to each other, "When will these two old men finally die so that we can assume the leadership of the community?"[30] So great was their arrogance that they dwelt constantly on their aristocratic family connections and considered that there were no women worthy to be their wives.[31] They were guilty of a variety of ritual violations for which the death penalty is ordained.[32] Although there is almost nothing in the biblical text to support these charges, they serve one important purpose, namely, to show us that God does not punish arbitrarily. Here we have conventional theodicy operating in its usual way.

The other side of this same midrash, however, rejects out of hand these efforts to explain and justify God. Instead they depict Nadav and

Avihu as men of exemplary virtue, and they show God lamenting the tragedy of their death. They were guilty, according to this version of only one sin, namely the improper fire which they brought to the altar. It is difficult for the midrashic authors to understand why this one sin should have weighed so heavily against all their virtues, and they make it a special point to underscore those virtues. "R. Elazar ha-Moda'i taught: Come and see how difficult the death of the sons of Aaron was for God. Whenever He mentions their death, He mentions their [one] sin. He goes to such trouble in order to deny any ground on which to claim that they died because of evil deeds that they committed secretly."[33] In fact, we are told, so virtuous and beloved were they that God grieved over their death twice as much as their father did.[34]

The theme of anti-theodicy is forcefully introduced at the very beginning of this midrashic passage. Referring to the death of the two sons of Aaron, the text cites Ecclesiastes, 9:2 which sets the tone for much of what follows. "For the same fate is in store for all: for the righteous, and for the wicked; for the good and pure, and for the impure... This skeptical rejection of conventional theodicy is then amplified by a series of examples. They show that, according to the scriptural account, exactly the same fate awaited paragons of virtue and models of vice. Moses, the virtuous, spoke only in praise of the land of Israel, while the faithless spies denigrated the land. Yet both were equally denied entry into the land. Nebuchadnezzar, who destroyed the Temple, reigned as long as David, who planned and laid the foundations for the Temple. Wicked Korah and his band were burned to death, and the righteous sons of Aaron were also burned to death.[35] Perhaps the most devastating parallel is drawn between Titus the oppressor and Nadav and Avihu, priests in the service of God. "Wicked Titus entered the Holy of Holies [where only the High Priest was permitted to enter] with his unsheathed sword in hand. He cut the hanging over the Holy Ark and his sword was covered with blood. Yet he entered in peace and came out in peace [i.e., he was unscathed]. In contrast, the sons of Aaron entered the sanctuary to present offerings to God, and they were carried out having been burned to death."[36] Where then is divine justice?

Ecclesiastes seems to be correct when he argues that the same fate awaits the righteous and the wicked, In fact, the wicked seem sometime to be rewarded, while the righteous are condemned to suffering.

So far does this anti-theodicy go that it argues that it is utterly mistaken for us to expect joy and pleasure in our lives. God is represented as depicting the fate of great figures in early biblical history. Of each of them He says that they had no joy in God's world, why then should any of the rest of us expect lives of joy? The text lists Adam, Abraham, the people of Israel, all of whom experienced sorrow rather than joy. In a stunning climax the text concludes, "The Holy One, blessed, be He, had no joy in His world, why then do you expect to live in happiness?"[37] The straightforward theodicy which explains the death of Aaron's sons as a consequence of their very grave sins is here rejected out of hand. They were righteous men, but like other righteous men there is no connection between their virtue and their destiny. Perhaps we shall one day be able to get beyond the skeptical bitterness of Ecclesiastes and come to understand God's ways in the world, but for now we can only note the dark mystery. Even Ecclesiastes ends on a note of pious submission to the Almighty, and a confident assertion that we shall all be called to account for our deeds.

This reluctance to explain God's ways when we have no satisfactory explanations, this anti-theodicy, is validated in a talmudic discussion which is luminous in its clarity. The Sages noted that Moses instituted a standard way of speaking in praise of God. He described Him as "great, mighty, and awesome,"[38] a formula which is used to this day in the statutory liturgy. Yet, despite the authority of Moses, the Talmud notes, Jeremiah and Daniel each dropped one adjective from this formula. Jeremiah spoke of God only as "great and mighty" and Daniel spoke of Him only as "great and awesome."[39] These omissions are explained as protests against God's failure to protect His sanctuary and His people. "Jeremiah came and said, 'Aliens are dancing wildly in His temple. Where are His awesome deeds?' Daniel came and said, 'Aliens are enslaving His children. Where are His mighty deeds?'"[40] The prophets refused to praise God in ways which did not comport with the reality that they experienced. They did not abandon their faith, or even their confidence in His justice and compassion. Nevertheless, if the Temple was destroyed and the people forced to serve a foreign potentate in exile from their land, Jeremiah and Daniel were unwilling to praise God as awesome or mighty. These are protests of anti-theodicy now attributed to the most elevated leaders of the people of Israel. If God seems to have withdrawn from history, they are saying, we will not justify Him with empty praise. Most illuminating is the conclusion of the discussion. The question is raised, how could even these great prophets reject a formula instituted by Moses. The answer given by the Talmud is that. "Since they knew that the Holy One, blessed be He, is Himself committed to truth, they refused to speak falsely of Him."[41] 'This is a majestic anti-theodicy, one which is motivated by faith and trust in God, and by the conviction that we are not called on, nor are we qualified to defend Him.

A Halakhic Conclusion

I believe that this is the point underlying a halakha universally accepted in traditional circles. A mishna rules that we are obligated to praise God for the bad things that happen to us. just as we must praise him for the good.[42] This teaches us that Judaism reject Gnostic or metaphysical dualism. With Isaiah, the tradition affirms that there is only one God who must be understood as responsible for all existence, for the good and the bad.[43] Or as it is put in Lamentations, "Is it not at the word of the Most High, that weal and woe befall?"[44] This affirmation that God is the source of both "weal and woe" does not entail simple or conventional theodicy, although that is certainly one legitimate option. The requirement to praise God for the bad just as we do for the good puts upon the community of faith the responsibility to acknowledge that all that happens comes from God. Whether it is pleasant or painful, it is understood as carrying a divine imprimatur, and thus imposes on us the duty to accept whatever God determines as our lot. We may protest. We may rebel. We may question. We need not, however, seek easy answers. Anti-theodicy, when accompanied by a blessing for *dayyan emet,* the true judge, is a stance of faith which Judaism affirms as no less authentic than that of theodicy.

NOTES

[1] Genesis 3:17-19. Unless otherwise noted, all biblical quotations are from the NJPS translation.
[2] Genesis 6: 11-13.
[3] Genesis 18:20-22.
[4] Jeremiah 12: 1.
[5] Job 9:20 22.
[6] Job 42:7.
[7] b. Berakhot 7a.
[8] *Ibid.* In translating passages from the Babylonian Talmud, I follow the Soncino version with occasional minor adjustments.
[9] b. Menahot 29b.
[10] M. Avot 4:15.
[11] Sifre Deuteronomy, Piska 307, ed. Finkelstein, pp. 344-346; translated by Reuven Hammer, (Yale University Press, 1986), pp. 310-313.
[12] Exodus 15: 1.
[13] *Ibid.* 15: 11.
[14] The discussion which follows is taken from Mekhilta de-Rabbi Yishmael, Treatise Shirata, Chapter 8: Horovitz-Rabin edition, p. 142; Lauterbach edition, Vol. 2, p. 60.
[15] Lauterbach translation.
[16] It is important to note that the Mekhilta text follows the passage we quoted with a prooftext from Isaiah 42:14-15. If these verses are read in the context of the entire chapter, they may be construed as a kind of justification. God's silence is a consequence of the sins of the people of Israel.
[17] b. Shabbat 55a.
[18] *Ibid.*, 55b.
[19] b. Berakhot 5a.
[20] *Ibid.*, s.v. *yissurin shel ahavah.*
[21] *Ibid.* 5ab.
[22] Antony Flew, "Theology and Falsification," *New Essays in Philosophical Theology*, Anthony Flew and Alisdair Macintyre, eds., (SCM Press Ltd., London, 1963), pp. 96-99.
[23] b. Berakhot Sb.
[24] M. Kiddushin 1:10.
[25] For this discussion see b. Kiddushin 39b.
[26] See Exodus 19:12 Deuteronomy 5:16 for honoring parents, and Deuteronomy 22:7 for sending away the mother bird.
[27] b. Kiddushin 39b.
[28] See Vayyikra Rabbah ed. Mordecai Margulies, (Jerusalem, 1972), Parashah 20, Vol. 1, pp. 441-472. For a listing of parallel texts see the first footnote of each section in this edition. Our summaries sometimes follow the text of a variant reading listed by Margulies as preferable.
[29] *Ibid.*, Sec. 6.
[30] *Ibid.*, Sec. 1 0.
[31] *Ibid.*
[32] *Ibid.*, Secs. 8,9.
[33] *Ibid.*, Sec. 8.

[34] *Ibid.*, Sec. 10.

[35] *Ibid.*, Sec. 1.

[36] *Ibid.*, Sec. 5.

[37] *Ibid.*, Sec. 2. The statement quoted about God begins with the qualification, *keveyakhol*, that is to say, if we may be allowed to speak of God in human terms.

[38] Deuteronomy 10: 17.

[39] Jeremiah 33:18; Daniel 9:4.

[40] b. Yoma 69b.

[41] *Ibid.* On the statement that God is "*amiti*", Rashi comments, "He affirms the truth and hates falsehood."

[42] M. Berakhot 9:5. For a more extended discussion of this theme see M. Fox, "The Unity and Structure of Rabbi Joseph B. Soloveitchik's Thought," *Tradition* 24 (2), 1989, pp. 49-55.

[43] Isaiah 45:6,7.

[44] Lamentations 3:38.

33

JEWISH POWER AND JEWISH RESPONSIBILITY

With the fulfillment of the Zionist dream in the establishment of the State of Israel, Jews were transformed from a people without physical power to a military power of formidable proportions.[1] We had a long history of powerlessness, of personal and national destiny determined by the will of others, of being not makers of history, but victims of historical forces and processes which were not in our control. Symbolic of our historical condition is the revealing commentary of Nahmanides to Genesis 32:4, where Jacob is preparing for confrontation with the hostile military force of his brother Esau. Nahmanides, reflecting a well-established tradition, notes that in confronting such a threat we learn from Jacob that we have three strategic options. We may seek to win over the enemy through bribery. We may turn to God in prayer for help. Finally, we may go to war. So far, Nahmanides is simply repeating a traditional formula. But he then adds, that by "war" he means "*livro'ah u'lehinatzel,*" to save ourselves by running away. There could hardly be a more striking statement of self-perceived powerlessness. For this medieval Jewish sage, living under the control of alien powers in thirteenth century Spain, the only realistic conception of war was to save ourselves from danger by running away. The distance from that attitude to the stance, the sentiment, and the reality of modern Israel requires no comment.

Internal Jewish attitudes toward this new condition of great Jewish power have by no means been uniform. On the one hand, much of the official Zionist leadership saw the transformation from powerlessness to power as an essential condition of the redemption of the Jewish people from the bonds of galut. David Ben-Gurion observed in 1944 that, "The meaning of the Jewish revolution is contained in one word—independence!

Independence for the Jewish people in its homeland."[2] Earlier, Dr. Azriel Carlebach, reacting to oppressive measures of the British mandatory authority in Palestine, observed that the whole of Zionist doctrine could be stated in a single phrase: not to react, but to act, *lo lehagiv ela lif'ol.* He goes on to say that, "The teaching of Zionism is—to take the initiative in our own hands."[3] A contradictory view was expressed earlier by Dr. Judah L. Magnes in 1930, when he gave voice to his fear that having and using power was unseemly for Jews, because such use of power would compromise our moral purity. He felt that the Jewish ideal would be best fulfilled if the Yishuv would be "poor and small and faithful to Judaism [i.e. to prophetic morality], rather than large and powerful like all the nations."[4] He seems to have reflected approvingly the historical judgment of Shylock who says, "For sufferance is the badge of all our tribe."[5] "Sufferance" in this usage means "passivity." For Shylock the Jew can only be the victim of history, not the maker of history.

These ambivalences continued, and in some cases grew more intense as the newly formed State of Israel began to live its life as a normal political power equipped with a high level of military and strategic capability. Many felt and expressed deep embarrassment at what they perceived as the passive submissiveness of the victims of the Holocaust who went to their death without resistance, "like sheep to the slaughter." They felt some restoration of Jewish pride in the heroic battle of the Warsaw ghetto fighters and in other similar instances of Jewish resistance. The great victory of the Six Day War was an inspiration to these people in Israel and in the Diaspora. As the trite phrase was repeatedly heard, "we felt ten feet tall." The cringing self-effacing submissive galut Jew was replaced by the aggressive and independent fighter who had overnight become expert in the use of all the modern tools of war. Yet, even at that heady time, there were many who felt great discomfort and even shame at this Jewish abandonment of the version of prophetic morality that Dr. Magnes had preached much earlier. To have become great warriors was, in their eyes, a betrayal of the classical Jewish commitment to the ways of peace; to have become an occupying power ruling over other peoples meant total abandonment of our great moral tradition.

The issue was sharpened during the war in Lebanon, a war initiated by a government which was, in any case, bitterly resisted and resented by liberals and peace activists. They based their resistance on claims to a superior morality, one which rejected the use of power, at least in this instance. As one writer expressed it, the issue was drawn between those whose greatest fear was that we would abuse Jewish power, and those whose greatest fear was that we would again be reduced to a state of powerlessness.[6] That division continues to the present and accounts for the deep rifts in contemporary Israeli society and among supporters of Israel throughout the world.

In what follows I shall not attempt to resolve this dilemma, but rather to examine it from the perspective of the teachings of the classical Jewish tradition as reflected in selected Biblical, rabbinic, and medieval materials. From the practices and personal examples of patriarchs, prophets, kings, sages, and messianic models, we can learn much about what Judaism teaches on this subject.

The Bible provides us with many examples where the use of power is represented as both sound policy and morally justified. We are told that Abraham's nephew, Lot, was taken captive in a war not of his making. When the news reached Abraham, he immediately assembled a small military force to go the rescue of his kinsman. "He brought back all the possessions; he also brought back his kinsman Lot and his possessions, and the women and the rest of the people." On his return, Abraham is blessed by Melchizedek, a holy man, for his heroic action. Melchizedek praises Abraham for having carried out God's will.[7] When Moses leaves the palace of Pharaoh to observe the condition of his Israelite kin, he finds "an Egyptian beating a Hebrew." His response is to smite the Egyptian and hide his corpse in the sand.[8] Nowhere in the text is there any indication of divine disapproval of this act. It seems to have been recorded in order to inform us of Moses' caring concern for his brethren and his readiness to protect them even by violent action, if necessary. In both these cases an individual who is held up in the tradition as a model of piety and spirituality resolves a crisis by the unabashed use of physical power, and in both cases the text appears to approve fully.

These instances of the use of power by individuals are paralleled by cases in which the entire people of Israel is not only authorized, but even commanded to make use of military power. This is the response to an attack by the Amalekites where Moses commands Joshua, "Pick some men for us, and go out and do battle with Amalek."[9] That this battle has full divine sanction is evident in the assurance of the text that God will be permanently at war with Amalek. That attitude is re-enforced in a later passage which evokes the memory of Amalek's wickedness and commands the people to "blot out the memory of Amalek from under the heavens."[10] When the Midianites are perceived as constituting a serious threat to the Israelites, God commands Moses, "Assail the Midianites and defeat them, for they assailed you by the trickery they practiced against you."[11] Later this commandment is renewed and is followed by a fierce battle in which the Midianites are soundly defeated. Finally, we need only refer to the numerous biblical commands to the Israelites concerning the conquest of the promised land. In all these cases, and they are by no means exceptional, strong military force is viewed as a legitimate exercise of power for the achievement of noble ends.

This line of thought in the Bible rests on the premise that divine assistance is predicated on aggressive human effort. We are expected to do something to help ourselves, not simply to sit back and wait for God to save us. There is a striking exceptional case that requires some attention. When the Israelites have their backs to the sea as the troops of Pharaoh are bearing down on them, they are in total despair. Moses reassures them that all will be well and that the Lord will come to their aid. "Have no fear!... The Lord will battle for you; you hold your peace!"[12] Even in this case of seeming passivity, the rabbis taught that God did not act until Nahshon ben Aminadav jumped into the waters. Only then did the Lord split the sea so that the children of Israel could cross over in safety. It was apparently difficult for them to conceive a setting in which no human effort was required to achieve salvation from a threatening enemy.

There are, on the other hand, cases in which physical power is treated as futile and self-deceptive. Man is not saved by his own strength, nor by any amount of physical force. His salvation depends on God, who comes to the aid of those who are in the right. When David confronts Goliath, he threatens him not with his prowess as a warrior, but with the power of God whose cause he represents. He calls out to Goliath, "You come against me with sword and spear and javelin; but I come against you in the name of the Lord of Hosts, the God of the ranks of Israel, whom you have defied .... And this whole assembly shall know that the Lord can give victory without sword or spear. For the battle is the Lord's, and He will deliver you into our hands."[13] As the prophet teaches us in the oft-quoted passage, the success of Zerubbabel will not result from military power, but from the power of God. "Not by might, nor by power, but by My spirit said the Lord of Hosts."[14] One should note, however, that when we are certain that God's power is on our side, we are, in fact, resting on the greatest power of all. No human power, however massive, is of any account in the face of the infinite divine power. Totally confident reliance on God is not a denial or rejection of the legitimacy of the use of power, but the strongest assurance that we are protected by the one power that is never subject to defeat.

In many instances the biblical text, nevertheless, associates reliance on divine power with successful human use of physical force. David slays Goliath with his slingshot. He does not simply sit back and wait for an unassisted miracle to take place. The Psalmist expresses his trust in "the Lord, my rock, who trains my hands for battle, my fingers for warfare." In this regard there is no turning away from the use of physical force. What is instructive is that such use of force for right purpose is perceived as itself bringing divine power into the arena of human history. The Jew who has just blessed God for training his hands to do battle immediately construes this as itself a form of divine protection. The Psalm goes on to address the Lord as, "my faithful one, my fortress, my haven and my deliverer, my shield in whom I take shelter, who makes peoples subject to me."[15]

Study of these materials leads to the conclusion that there is no glorification in the Bible of power for power's sake, certainly no praise of sheer unrestrained power used without moral purpose or serving no virtuous ends. Power belongs not to man, but to God. When He allows man to exercise power in the world, it is only for the purpose of advancing a divinely sanctioned cause. The criterion for the legitimate use of human power is whether it is directed toward an end which God approves. In that case man serves as God's instrument in the world of human history, and his exercise of power is an act of obedience to God. We can readily see the restrictions on the use of power when we examine cases in which the ends served are inappropriate, or the extent of force is far greater then the circumstances require.

The case of the rape of Dinah, daughter of Leah and Jacob illuminates this point. Shechem the son of a neighboring tribe attacks and defiles the young woman. Jacob is distressed, but since his sons are out in the fields when he learns of the incident. he considers it prudent not to react. When his sons return and hear the news, they are very angry, because Shechem "had committed an outrage in Israel by lying with Jacob's daughter—a thing not to be done." Their anger is justified, as is their determination to exact retribution. As they themselves say in justification of their demand for retribution, "Should our sister be treated like a whore?"

However, things go seriously wrong. What they end up with is not retribution, not simple justice, but overkill of the worst kind. An agreement is made to form an alliance with the tribe of the offender, provided all the men will circumcise themselves. They agree, and while they are incapacitated by the surgery, Simeon and Levi attack the ailing tribe, killing all the males, seizing their wealth as booty, and taking the women and children as captives. This horribly brutal response to their legitimate grievance is condemned by their father as both imprudent and immoral. It is imprudent because it will blacken the name of Jacob and his family in the eyes of all their neighbors. A Jew who uses physical force, even in what he believes is a divinely sanctioned just cause, must pay full attention to the propriety of his actions. He must be concerned with what it does to the reputation of God's people, and thereby to the holy name of the God whom they worship.[16] The immorality of their action is self-evident, since it is this very immorality which will destroy Jacob's reputation.

To the very end of his life, Jacob refuses to forgive them for their violence and brutality. In his final testament to each of his sons, Jacob condemns Simeon and Levi in language which is unequivocal. "Simeon and Levi are a pair; their weapons are tools of lawlessness. Let not my person be included in their council, let not my being be counted in their assembly. For when angry they slay men, and when pleased they maim oxen. Cursed be their anger so fierce, and their wrath so relentless."[17] The use of power lawlessly and in unrestrained anger is categorically condemned. Such action disgraces the people and dishonors God. These men did not behave as instruments for the achievement of divine justice. Their use of power for revenge; their murder of innocent men; their seizure of booty and their capture of helpless women and children; all these are repulsive to their patriarchal father and to the God who becomes known as the God of Israel.

Even when force is divinely sanctioned, the tradition teaches that we should perceive its success as God's action, not the independent success of men. In the case of the war against Amalek, which God Himself has commanded, the Mishnah teaches us how to understand the military success of the Israelites. The Torah records that when Moses raised up his hands the battle went favorably for the Israelites, and when he lowered his hands the tide turned against them. On this the Mishnah makes the following observation. "But could the hands of Moses promote the battle or hinder the battle? It is, rather, to teach thee that such time as the Israelites directed their thoughts on high, and kept their hearts in subjection to their Father in heaven, they prevailed; otherwise they suffered defeat."[18] What stronger statement could there be expressing the idea that even in a legitimate cause the exercise of power is approved and effective only when it results from pious submission to God who is the source of all power. Moses warned the people that when they entered the land of Israel, conquered it, and prospered they might readily become filled with self-pride and a feeling of great independent power. They would then mistakenly attribute their success to "my own power and the might of my own hand."[19] This misperception would undermine and destroy them if they forgot that power and success are ultimately from God.

Even when the use of power is judged to be thoroughly legitimate by the most rigorous religious and moral standards, it is still not celebrated. It is seen as an unfortunate necessity, particularly when it is for self-defense, but not an occasion for pride or pleasure. There are familiar cases in which the tradition deplores the suffering of our victims which is entailed by our victory. We celebrate our liberation from Egyptian slavery and praise God's saving hand, but we also feel sorrow and distress at the fact that our oppressors were forced to suffer. They may have deserved their fate, but they were still human beings whose suffering was the necessary result of Israelite liberation. Our Sages teach that God takes no pleasure in the downfall of the wicked. That is why He is represented as rejecting the angelic chorus of praise when Pharaoh and his minions are being swallowed up by the sea. He says to them, how can you sing songs of praise when my creatures are drowning in the sea.[20] The late Professor Yeshayahu Leibowitz once made the penetrating observation that we have no holiday in the Jewish calendar to celebrate Joshua's conquest of the land of Canaan or David's conquest of Jerusalem. He points out that the only official celebration we have for a military victory is Hanukkah, and that celebrates a victory for the restoration of the Torah to centrality in Jewish life, not the conquest of territory or the taking of spoils.[21]

Jewish teaching has always understood well that an ordered society requires some governing authority and that authority must necessarily exercise power. Nevertheless, from the earliest times the power of government is viewed as legitimate only when it is used with very considerable restraint. Let us consider two instructive models, that of the king and that of the ultimate king, the Messiah. Early on the Torah teaches us that we may have a king, but that he must not be concerned with military power or with the accumulation of wealth. "Moreover, he shall not keep many horses or send people back to Egypt to add to his horses . . . nor shall he amass gold and silver to excess." The proper activity of a Jewish king is to spend his time studying the Torah so that he may rule the people in accordance with the word of God. Scripture teaches that the Torah shall remain with him and let him read in it all his life, so that he may learn to revere the Lord his God, to observe faithfully every word of this Teaching as well as these laws. Thus he will not act haughtily toward his fellows or deviate from the Instruction to the right or to the left..."[22]

The record teaches us that the people themselves did not always learn this lesson. When, at a later time, they demanded that the prophet Samuel appoint a king over them, he was unable to persuade them of the folly of such a move. He noted that kings naturally seek power and that they conscript their subjects for military service or forced labor in order to achieve and extend their power. What the people want, despite all of the prophet's warnings is to be "like all the other nations: Let our king rule over us and go out at our head and fight our battles."[23] There is, of course, a long history of kings of Israel and Judah engaged in military activities. The question of the religious and moral legitimacy of these activities is always present.

We can best get insight into the Jewish position on these matters if we review a classic medieval source. The last section of Maimonides' Code is entitled, "The Laws of Kings and Their Wars." As in all of his Code, Maimonides sets forth the law here based on his reading and systematic restructuring of the entire rabbinic literature. We can view his codification as the most authentic summary of Jewish legal and theological teachings on the subject of kings, their powers and responsibilities.

The title of the section is itself instructive. Although in popular parlance it is almost always identified as *Hilkhot Melakhim*, the Laws of Kings, the full title, as we already noted, is "Kings and their Wars." It is clear from the title itself that kings must have the power to engage in war when circumstances demand it. A king who cannot protect his people and his land from attack and conquest has failed in one of his most basic responsibilities. The very first law that Maimonides codifies under this rubric rules that when the Israelites enter their own land they are required to appoint a king, and, under his leadership, to destroy the Amalekites. To survive as a nation they must have a king, i.e., orderly government. This entails the legitimate power to enforce the law and to provide for the public welfare. The king must also have the power to protect his people from external enemies, as symbolized by the Amalekites. That is, he must be able to save the people from enemies who seek to destroy them and drive them from their land. For this he must have power, and he is authorized to use that power for the legitimate ends which we have already noted.

All this is, however, instrumental to a purely spiritual goal. In that same first paragraph Maimonides adds a third requirement for the king, namely, to build the holy Temple. A national home and a secure environment are not ends in themselves for the Jewish people. They are rather necessary means for the achievement of a life of divine service. For the people to be able to worship God, as He has commanded, requires a setting in which they are free of the external pressures which threaten their very survival. To conduct national and personal life in accordance with the teachings of the Torah, to aspire to the highest moral and spiritual perfection, presupposes that basic human needs have been satisfied. That is why a king must have the power to provide a safe and tranquil environment for his people. Building the Temple symbolizes having arrived at a settled state in which attention can be given to transcendent values rather than to the struggle for survival.

The qualities that are essential for a king who is to have and use this power are wisdom and piety. Of these piety, *yir'at shamayim*, is absolutely essential. With respect to any candidate for succession to kingship (or, for that matter, to any public office), Maimonides teaches us that, "the successor should equal his predecessors in wisdom and in fear of heaven. If his fear of heaven is sufficient, even if there is some deficiency in his wisdom, he is to be appointed to succeed his father, and he shall then be taught what he needs to know. One the other hand, one who has much wisdom, but is lacking in fear of heaven may not be appointed."[24] The only guarantee that the king will use his power legitimately is that he be a man of true piety. Such a person will not be deluded into imagining that he is the source of his own power. He will not be like the arrogant Pharaoh, puffed up with self-pride, who proclaimed, "My Nile is my own; I made it for myself."[25] Instead he will know that God is the source of his power and that his mandate is to use the Torah as his guide in fulfilling God's commandments.

Maimonides codifies in some detail the restrictions on royal power and wealth that we noted above from Deuteronomy. He stresses the rule that a Jewish king must live a sober and restrained life. He may not get drunk, but should instead "be preoccupied day and night with the study of

Torah and with the welfare of the people of Israel." He adds that the Torah is much concerned that the king's heart shall not be turned away from God and His teachings. He then adds the remarkable observation that "the king's heart is the heart of the whole congregation of Israel. It is for that reason that Scripture commanded that he cleave to the Torah even more than the rest of the people..."[26] It is the king who bears a special responsibility for all of the people. His heart beats for all of them, and the purity of his heart, reflected in his policies and leadership, is the strongest encouragement for similar purity in every member of the polity. What qualifies him to be king, then, is not primarily his power or his military prowess, but his mastery of God's Torah and his conscientious submission to its commandments.

The king's power is limited by the power of God. That is to say that the royal prerogative does not include rejecting God's commandments, nor does a royal edict have any standing against the first obligation of every Jew which is to serve God, not the king. "If one ignores an edict of the king because he is at that time occupied with the fulfillment of a mitzvah, even if it is a minor commandment, he is without any legal liability. Our rule is that the demand of the master [i.e., God] takes precedence over the demand of the disciple [i.e., the king]. It hardly need be added that if the king issues an edict which nullifies any commandment of the Torah, that we ignore him [i.e., his edict has no standing]."[27] Since the only legitimate ground of royal power and authority is the king's mandate to be above all a servant of God, any rejection of that mandate is *ipso facto* a nullification of the authority and power of the king. A Jewish government, in this view, has no legitimacy except as an instrument for service of God and loyalty to His law.

These are not mere inferences of what Maimonides might have meant. He states the point in explicit and unambiguous language. Having set forth rules about royal power such as instituting a military draft, drafting people for other forms of public service, taking of property under a rule of eminent domain, going to war, etc., Maimonides then notes: "In all these activities his purpose shall be for the sake of heaven; his goal shall be to elevate the true faith; to fill the world with justice; to break the power of the wicked and to fight the wars of the Lord. For the primary purpose of appointing a king is so that he will do justice and fight just wars."[28] Here we see a definitive and unambiguous summary of the Torah teaching concerning the nature and function of royal power in the Jewish polity. The legitimate use of government power is to provide for the public welfare and security so as to create a society in which the people are devoted above all else to the service of God through the study of Torah and the fulfillment of His commandments. In such a society, power will necessarily be directed toward the institution of justice and the practice of good works.

This is underscored when we shift from the temporal royal model to the messianic model. The Messiah will be the king of Israel in the truest and most complete sense. Maimonides, in his discussion of this topic, treats the Messiah as the ideal king and the messianic age as the ideal realization of the aspirations of non-eschatological Jewish kingship. The Messiah is a ruler who will succeed in freeing the people of Israel from their exile and restoring them to their own land. He will rebuild the Temple and make it possible for the Jewish people to live fully in accordance with God's law. To qualify as truly the Messiah, he must be himself a model of piety who inspires the people to follow in his way.

The Messiah is not to be conceived as a miracle worker, nor is the messianic age a time when the laws of nature will be suspended. A critical external mark of the messianic age is that the Jews will be freed from subjection to alien peoples.[29] Of the diverse views concerning the messianic age, Maimonides focuses on this one which eliminates all miraculous and supernatural elements from the picture. He assures us that the order of nature will remain stable and that '*olam keminhago noheg*, the world will continue in its normal course. The just power of the Messiah will be evident in his freeing of the Jewish people from subjugation, his restoring them to their land, and his rebuilding the holy Temple. What is the purpose of this exercise of power? Only to realize the highest possible level of Jewish religious achievement. Here again the precision and explicitness of Maimonides' formulation is important. "The sages and prophets did not yearn for the days of the Messiah so that they should rule over the entire world, or subjugate non-Jews, or that they should be elevated by the other nations. Neither did they seek to live a life of eating, drinking, and making merry. Their only desire was that they should be free to devote themselves to the Torah and her wisdom, without being under the heel of an oppressor who would deny them this life of Torah. Their aspiration was [to be able so to live this life] that they would merit life in the world to come."[30] The proper goals of the historical kings and those of the messianic king are identical. In both cases, power is to be used as needed only in order to achieve the very highest moral and spiritual ends.

In the classical Jewish religious tradition the lines are clearly drawn. Power as such carries no moral valence, only the uses to which power is put. Used in a just cause power is a virtuous instrument for the realization of God's purposes in the world. Used for selfish ends or for self-aggrandizement, power is an evil instrument which rejects the divine mandate in favor of man's corrupt goals. When the purpose is morally sound, even the power of a wicked person may be used by God to achieve the good. King Jeroboam son of Joash is described as deeply flawed. "He did what was displeasing to the Lord; he did not depart from all the sins that Jeroboam the son of Nebat had caused Israel to commit."[31] Nevertheless, it is he who restores the territory of Israel that God had promised to them. As the text notes, the Lord saw the "bitter plight" of his people and was determined to save them. Since there was no other appropriate instrument of this salvation, "He delivered them through Jeroboam son of Joash." Power may be put into the hands of a king who is spiritually corrupt, so long as it is used to achieve God's purpose.

While Scripture seems to prefer to leave vengeance toward enemies in the hands of God, it has no embarrassment about using inordinately strong language in open expression of resentment, even hatred, toward those who oppress the Jewish people. We tend to be familiar with the numerous biblical passages which leave acts of vengeance to God, but we often forget the passages which, though not a call to action, give expression to fierce anger toward the destroyers of Israel. In these cases, the active power is left to God, but man is seen as fully justified in taking pleasure at the downfall of the wicked. "The righteous man will rejoice when he sees revenge, he will bathe his feet in the blood of the wicked. Men will say, 'there is, then, a reward for the righteous; there is, indeed, divine justice on earth."[32] And who can forget the bitter invocation of recompense against Babylon for its unspeakable crimes. "Fair Babylon, you predator, a blessing on him who repays you in kind what you have inflicted on us; a blessing on him who seizes your babies and dashes them against the rocks."[33] There is here no shame or embarrassment at the use of power. There is rather the prayer that if Israel is itself powerless, then God should use His power to avenge their sufferings.

In fact, we have texts which are openly critical of even great leaders of the people when they behave submissively toward their enemies. The classic case is that of Jacob who is frightened by the threat of Esau's power, and gives expression to that fear. According to the established count, eight times over Jacob addressed Esau as "adoni", my master. As a result, according to the Midrash, eight kings ruled over Edom, the land of Esau, before there was a king in Israel. "When Jacob addressed Esau as 'my master,' God said to him, 'You have degraded yourself and addressed Esau as 'my master' eight times, I shall, in turn, raise up from among Esau's descendants eight kings before your descendants have even one.'"[34] It would appear that this strain of the tradition values and encourages defiance to an enemy, even when it seems certain that he has superior military power.

This tradition is carried forward when it praises Mordecai who refused to bow down to Haman. The text is clear enough in its stress on the stiff-necked resistance of Mordecai who will not pay homage to the oppressor. The setting is elaborated and given a historical context in the Targum Sheni to Esther. There Mordecai explains his refusal to bow down to Haman by virtue of the fact that he is a member of the tribe of Benjamin. When Jacob and his sons paid such abject homage to Esau, Benjamin was not yet born. Thus, he alone among Jacob's sons never bowed down to Esau. Mordecai notes that as a descendant of Benjamin he is heir to that proud tradition which he continues to carry out fearlessly.[35] He may not have had the military power to oppose Haman successfully, but this did not free him from the duty to make full use of his moral power. Moral power is indeed a most significant form of power, never to be underestimated.

If we return now to recent Jewish history, we can see that it is permeated by all the ambivalences which the tradition itself associates with having and using power. The instances which we introduced at the beginning of this essay from the history of the pre-State Yishuv, are re-enacted at a later time. On the one hand, we still have those who believe that Jewish morality requires us to be above the temptations and potential corruptions of having power. Since the establishment of the State, and especially since 1967, we have seen, at one extreme, a significant segment of Israeli society torn by moral anguish over Israel's having become a successful military force, to say nothing of a force of occupation. At the other extreme, there are those who not only justify the use of power, but believe that the duty of the State is to increase its power and to use it for the welfare of the people of Israel, with little concern as to who else may be affected in the process. It would be much too simple and unperceptive to reduce this to a debate between virtuous advocates of moral purity and power hungry advocates of pure national self-interest. Two models may help illuminate the issues and show us their complexity.

One might have thought that any Jew who suffered the horrors of the Nazi concentration camps would have thirsted for absolute and unrestrained power with which to avenge the evil, punishing and destroying the oppressors. Surely, there were many such, but there were others as well. In his magnificent work, "My Quarrel with Hersh Rasseyner." Chaim Grade presents us with a striking and instructive case. Rasseyner, a survivor of the worst concentration camps, is engaged in a long intense conversation with his old friend Chaim Vilner. They had been fellow Yeshiva students for many years. Hersh remained in that world, while Chaim abandoned it for the world of poets and writers. They meet by chance after the war, and engage in a long debate about the relative values of the religious tradition against artistic enlightenment, a debate which we cannot reproduce here. At a crucial moment in the discussion, Hersh speaks of his experience in the camps. He is, remember, a bearded, long-coated, observant Jew who experienced, in his own person, the full range of the catastrophe. Hersh describes a scene in which a German officer is trampling him with his hobnailed boots. He tells Chaim that at that moment he imagined that an angel came down from heaven and offered to let him trade places with the German officer. Here was the opportunity for supreme revenge. Yet, in a deeply moving statement, Hersh reports:

> If the angel had asked me... I would not have agreed at all. Not for one minute would I have consented to be the other, the German, my torturer. I want the justice of law! I want vengeance, not robbery! But I want it as a Jew. With the Almighty's help I could stand the German's boots on my throat, but if I had to put on his mask, his murderous face, I would have been smothered as though I had been gassed.[36]

Neither power, nor the opportunity for revenge are sufficient temptations for Hersh Rasseyner to exchange Jewish morality for pagan power. For him it is the true service of God that matters most, To become like the enemy, to assume his visage, to behave like him, would be the ultimate defeat.

Over against this response we see the reaction of one of the prominent members of the Israeli left when faced with the deeply disappointing reality that the Six-Day War was not followed by a comprehensive peace. Amos Kenan, writing in 1968, addressed "A Letter to All Good People – To Fidel Castro, Sartre, Russell and All the Rest."[37] Speaking to these well known "liberals" who are advocates of the Arab cause, he pleads for peace. He expresses his readiness as an Israeli to see all subjects open to discussion, including the return of occupied territories, but he will not compromise on the one absolute objective—peace.

> Until you agree to have peace, I shall give back nothing. And if you force me to become a conqueror, I shall become a conqueror. And if you force me to become an oppressor, I shall become an oppressor. And if you force me into the same camp with all the forces of darkness in the world, there I shall be.

Here we have a case of putting peace above all other values so that Kenan stands ready to assume, as he says, the role of conqueror or oppressor rather than yield on the objective of peace. If peace is not offered or not possible, then there is no limit on the power he would be ready to use to protect his people from danger or the threat of destruction. As he expresses it earlier in the same discussion, "After the death camps, we are left only one supreme value: existence." Where Rasseyner, only imagining the possibility of power over his enemy, feels tied, above all, to his concept of Jewish morality, Kenan, faced with the reality of military victory, will only give up power in exchange for peace, nothing less. Both are understandable and illuminating responses to the Jewish condition in the post-Holocaust, post-State reality.[38]

It is relatively easy to set forth in purely theoretical terms an account of power and responsibility in the Jewish tradition. From the sources it is clear, as we have already noted, that power by itself is neither moral nor immoral. Moral judgment comes only with an examination of the uses to which power is put in any given situation. We must, of course, note that the ideals of the prophets, the Israeli ideal of "purity of arms", become increasingly difficult to maintain in a world where no one else is bound by such values. Moreover, there is more than ample justification in the Jewish tradition for the use of power to protect the people and the land from vicious enemies bent on destruction. The point was made with admirable clarity by Thomas Jefferson, when he wrote:

> A strict observance of the written law is doubtless one of the highest duties of a good citizen, but it is not *the highest.* The laws of necessity, of self-preservation, of saving our country when in danger, are of higher obligation... To lose our country by scrupulous adherence to written law would be to lose the law itself, with life, liberty, property, and all those who are enjoying them with us, thus absurdly sacrificing the end to the means.[39]

Jefferson's lesson may well help to clarity the dilemmas concerning the moral value of power in the Jewish tradition.

The lines are clear enough, although most difficult to formulate and to put into practice when we are dealing with all the ragged edges of concrete historical circumstances. Power is legitimized when it is a necessary instrument of national independence and security. Such national independence is not simply a modern Zionist ideal, nor simply, in the dismissive language of contemporary Israel, "*tzionut.*" In the course of Jewish history, rooted in the biblical tradition, national independence was perceived as a condition for Jewish self-fulfillment. When we have the power to achieve this independence, we are heavily burdened with the responsibility of using it justly, wisely, and well. We also need to give weight to the rabbinic teaching that there are times when self-restraint is also a use of power, in some cases even the highest use. Their praise of *hakovesh et yitzro*, one who imposes restraint on himself, as the true hero, the person of true power,[40] underscores an important dimension of Jewish teaching. There may well be circumstances in which the highest morality and the most prudent self-interest require us to renounce even legitimate claims. This may even be the finest and the most noble use of power.

We have tried to set forth here a summary account of some of the main teachings of the Jewish tradition concerning the religious and moral issues surrounding the responsible use of power. It is beyond the competence of the scholar to give practical guidance in these matters. Here we are all equally responsible as thinking and committed Jews to arrive at our own decisions. Even in relatively simple cases, to say nothing of very complex cases, *halakha* does not provide us with fixed and ready-made answers to our questions. It provides only the range of general principles which must be applied to particular circumstances. This is the activity which Aristotle identified as prudence, or practical wisdom.

NOTES

[1] This paper is based on a lecture first given at the Institute for Jewish Affairs in London, in 1984.
[2] As quoted in Arthur Hertzberg, *The Zionist* Idea, (New York, 1960), p. 609.
[3] As quoted in *Maariv*, February 3, 1984.
[4] As quoted in Hertzberg, *op. cit.*, p. 446.
[5] Shakespeare, *The Merchant of Venice*, I, iii.
[6] Y. Klein in Moment, Vol. 9, No.2 (1984).
[7] Genesis, 14:13-20.
[8] Exodus, 2:11,12.
[9] Exodus, 17:9.
[10] Deuteronomy, 25:19.
[11] Numbers, 25:17,18.
[12] Exodus, 14:13,14.
[13] I Samuel, 17:45-47.
[14] Zechariah, 4:6.
[15] Psalms, 144:1,2.
[16] For the entire episode see Genesis, ch. 34.
[17] Genesis, 49:5-7.
[18] M. Rosh ha-Shanah, 3:8.
[19] Deuteronomy, 8:17.
[20] b. Sanhedrin, 39b; b. Megillah, 10b.
[21] Y. Leibowitz, *Yahadut, Am Yehudi, u-Medinat Yisrael*, (Jerusalem & Tel-Aviv, 1975), p.407.
[22] Deuteronomy, 17:14-20.
[23] I Samuel, 8:10-20.
[24] H. Melakhim, 1:7.
[25] Ezekiel, 29:3.
[26] H. Melakhim, 3:6.
[27] *Ibid.*, 3:9.
[28] *Ibid.*, 4: 10.
[29] *Ibid.*, 12:2; based on b. Sanhedrin, 91b.
[30] *Ibid.*, 12:4.
[31] II Kings, 14:24.
[32] Psalms, 58:11, 12.
[33] Psalms, 137: 8,9.
[34] Genesis Rabba, ed. Theodor-Albeck, 75:11, referring to Genesis, 36:31.
[35] See Targum Sheni to Esther, 3:2. There is no scholarly consensus about the date of this work, but it seems most likely that it is late seventh or early eighth century.
[36] Chaim Grade, "My Quarrel with Hersh Rasseyner," in *A Treasury of Yiddish Stories*, eds. Irving Howe & Eliezer Greenberg, (New York, 1954), p. 598.
[37] *Midstream*, October, 1968; quoted in Emil Fackenheim, *God's Presence in History*, (New York, 1970), pp.91-92.
[38] This is being written only one day after the most recent terrorist atrocity in Israel in which nineteen Israeli soldiers were killed while waiting for transportation to their base. It is hard,

at such a time, not to sympathize with the uncompromising line that Kenan took more than twenty-five years ago.

[39] Thomas Jefferson in a letter to J.B. Colvin, December 1810; cited in a review of *Freedom* by William Safire, by James W. Tuttleson, *Commentary*, 85(2), Feb., 1988, p. 92.

[40] M. Avot, 4: 1.

34

HOLOCAUST CHALLENGES TO RELIGIOUS FAITH

Serious literature that deals with the human condition necessarily has some philosophical and religious dimensions. This is especially true of the literature of the Holocaust. Even purely historical or documentary treatments of the Holocaust are permeated with philosophical and religious questions. These accounts of human behavior in extreme situations force us to confront questions about what it means to be human. Sober historical descriptions of heroism or degradation, of suffering or redemption, engage us in the effort to understand more than the facts. They force us to consider as well the ultimate significance of these manifestations of what is possible in human behavior.

When poets, short story writers, or novelists use their literary imaginations to reflect on human catastrophe, the religious and philosophical questions are more vivid and more demanding. The imaginative writer dealing with Holocaust themes forces his readers to confront directly the hard and agonizing questions about the role of God and the response of man in the grotesque world in which European Jewry was destroyed. Whether the confrontations with these themes are explicit or not, they are present, at the very least, as an undercurrent which informs the literary work and gives it a certain philosophical and religious character. There is no serious Holocaust literature in which these philosophical and religious concerns are completely absent.

In this essay we shall consider two short literary works which emerge from the Holocaust experience, works in which the religious and philosophical concerns are quite explicit. Zvi Kolitz, in his short story "Yossel Rakover Speaks to God," and Chaim Grade, in his story/essay "My Quarrel with Hersh Rasseyner" provide us with superb instances of how literary artists deal with some of the religious and philosophical dimensions of the Holocaust.[1] Both works were written in the early postwar years, reflecting the immediacy and urgency of the unhealed wounds of the great and terrible experience of destruction. The Rakover story is written in the form of a documentary account of the last hours of one of the last survivors of the Warsaw ghetto. It is set on April 28, 1943, the day of the final liquidation of the ghetto. It consists of a first-person narration of Rakover's thoughts as he contemplates the experience of the last years and confronts the inevitable fact that his life will very soon end.

Grade's work is longer and more complex. It is a kind of hybrid story/essay which has unmistakable autobiographical elements, as Grade himself has confirmed. The story is not literally true in the sense that the conversation which it reports took place in the exact form in which it is rendered here. Nor is Rasseyner the actual name of the central figure. However, there was such a type among Grade's friends. He did meet with him on various occasions in Bialystok and Vilna, and did have conversations with him in Paris. We cannot know whether any of those conversations are preserved literally in the story. Even if some of it reflects an actual conversation, it is, of course, embellished and transformed by the literary art of the writer. It reflects reality in the deepest sense, not as a simple stenographic report of a meeting, but as the intense confrontation of the artist/thinker with the profound problems of Jewish existence after the Holocaust. That Grade intended it to be taken as deep history, barely veiled as fiction, is evident from the fact that he himself is unmistakably identified as the person who carries on the long and arduous debate with Hersh Rasseyner. The story begins with two brief prewar episodes in which Chaim (i.e., Grade) confronts Hersh Rasseyner, his former yeshiva colleague. It continues with a meeting in Paris in 1948, where the two old friends come together by chance. Both the Kolitz story and the one by Grade confront critical questions posed by the Holocaust. For Rakover the urgent concern is how to die as a Jew in the face of the horrors he has witnessed and endured. For Grade and Rasseyner the issue is how to continue to live as Jews in a world which has suffered and survived the agonies of the Holocaust.

Three distinct Jewish types are portrayed in these two stories. Rakover identifies himself in his opening words as "a Hasid of the Rabbi of Ger," with all that that implies. Rasseyner is a product of the Novaredok musar yeshivot. It is in this setting that his spiritual and intellectual life was formed, and he has remained firm and fixed in the style of life and thought which he learned there. Grade is partially a product of the same musar education. In addition, he lived and studied privately for seven years with the great talmudic sage, Rabbi Avraham Yeshayahu Karelitz, known as the Hazon-Ish. Despite his deep attachment to the world of the yeshiva, and even more to his saintly teacher, Grade abandoned traditional faith and observance to become a secular Yiddish writer. The stories are studies in conflict. Rakover confronts the corrupt world around him and, at the same time, the God whom he serves faithfully even with his last breath. Grade and Rasseyner are in conflict with each other, with opposing ideologies, and with the evil which they have experienced in the years of the destruction.

Yossel Rakover's Inner Struggle

As we have already noted, Yossel Rakover identifies himself in the opening line of the story as a Hasid of the Rabbi of Ger. This is intended to convey to the informed reader a deep awareness of just what kind of man is being portrayed here. Ger Hasidism is characterized by its unremitting devotion to learning and the intellectual life. In this tradition, Rakover proves himself to be an intensely thoughtful man who, even in the last hours of his life, engages in reflection on ultimate questions in a way that is neither maudlin nor sentimental. It is, rather, the way of the disciplined mind, informed by learning, that grapples with the problem posed by the meaning of his life and of his impending death. Ger, faithful to its inheritance from the Hasidism of Kotzk, is also uncompromising in its devotion to truth. No quarter is given, not even to God, when truth is at stake.[2] In addition, as might be expected, Ger is based on profound faith and intense piety. Yossel Rakover, the Gerer Hasid, shows himself in this account of his last hours to be a paradigmatic representative of the Hasidic group that formed him. He is learned and reflective; he is totally committed to truth; and he is firm in his faith to the very end.

Rakover begins his reflections with a brief account of how in the previous period he lost his wife and six children. The world in which he lives is a place of unmitigated cruelty. He resents the commonplace comparison of the human oppressors to beasts, because he considers it an insult to the beasts. "It is," he says, "untrue that the tyrant who rules Europe now has something of the beast in him. He is a typical child of modern man; mankind as a whole spawned him and reared him. He is merely the best expression of its innermost, most deeply buried instincts." The Gerer Hasid looks at the contemporary world through his Hasidic Jewish eyes and sees in it the ultimate self-degradation of man. Modernity, with its lack of fixed morality, its relativism, its search for self-satisfaction, this modernity is the culprit. It has generated the depraved man who now rules Europe and the depraved society which serves as his instrument for causing the suffering and death of the innocent.

In a bitter confrontation with reality Yossel Rakover tells of a night in the forest when he met a pathetic dog that was hungry and ill. The two sad creatures huddle together and cry bitterly as they seek to bring some small comfort to each other.

> If I say that I envied the animals at that moment, it would not be remarkable. But what I felt was more than envy. It was shame. I felt ashamed before the dog to be, not a dog, but a man. That is how matters stand. That is the spiritual level to which we have sunk. Life is a tragedy, death a savior; man a calamity, the beast an ideal, the day a horror, the night relief.

This is the state of mind in which Yossel Rakover faces his death. He sees the corruption of the world which he is leaving. He is bereft of all that was dear to him, his wife, his children, his hope and his trust in man's humanity.

Remarkably, his last hours are not a time of bitter recrimination. He finds himself, rather, in a kind of ambivalent conflict with God and in open conflict with the human enemy. As he explores his relationship with God, he is clear about the complaints that he can legitimately raise, but he is unwilling to give up his faith under any circumstances. In his last words he addresses God and says to Him that all His efforts to drive Yossel away are unsuccessful.

> And these are my last words to you, my wrathful God: nothing will avail You in the least. You have done everything to make me renounce you, to make me lose my faith in you, but I die exactly as I have lived. Eternally praised be the God of the dead, the God of vengeance, of truth and of law, Who will soon show His face to the world again and shake its foundations with His almighty voice. Hear, O Israel, the Lord our God, the Lord is One. Into your hands I consign my soul.

In Job-like fashion, Rakover denies that the suffering of the Jews is punishment for their sins, anymore than his personal suffering is to be justified as a consequence of his sinfulness. On the contrary, he knows that he has lived a good, decent, and pious life of devotion to the service of God. He denies that there are any readily available explanations of the terrible catastrophe. One can only say that God has withdrawn from the world, has hidden His face, thereby leaving man free to behave in all his unrestrained cruelty. The effect of God's withdrawal is that mankind has been sacrificed "to its wild instincts." We have no choice but to accept the results of God's removal of Himself from the world, but we may not justify Him at the expense of His people. "For saying that we deserve the blows we have received is to malign ourselves, to desecrate the Holy Name of God's children." In so doing we also malign and desecrate our God.

With these declarations Yossel Rakover has prevailed in his conflict with God. No suffering, no injustice in the world, no level of human corruption will drive him from his faith in God. The Lord of the world with all His omnipotence cannot force this pious Jewish soul to deny Him. This is not to say that Rakover is passive or submissive. He is defiant and demanding. Even while affirming his faith, he also challenges God's action or inaction. He faces the divine majesty with remarkable self-assurance, refusing to bow his head or fold his arms in submission or withdrawal. His affirmation of faith, despite God's efforts to drive him away, is followed by an uncompromising self-assertion.

> I believe in Your laws even if I cannot excuse your actions. My relationship to you is not the relationship of a slave to a master but rather that of a pupil to his teacher. I bow my head before Your greatness, but will not kiss the lash with which you strike me. I love God, but I love His Torah even more. If I were to discover that I was deluding myself about Him, I would continue to observe his Torah.

Having thus affirmed himself, he goes on to make a striking argument that God must truly be the God of the Jewish people. How could He possibly be the God of the oppressors? 'Now I know that you are my Lord, because after all You are not, You cannot, after all, be the God of those whose deeds are the most horrible expressions of ungodliness. If You are not my Lord, then whose Lord are You? The Lord of the murderers?" In this way Yossel Rakover emerges strong and victorious from his conflict with God. With a clear eye and a totally realistic perception of what has happened to European Jewry, he fearlessly confronts the God of Israel, while remaining absolutely firm in his own religious faith.

Rakover also is victorious in his conflict with the oppressor. True, the oppressor can and will take Yossel's life, but all of his power cannot serve to destroy his spirit or to compromise his values. He looks at his persecutors with contempt and repugnance. All of their effort to degrade the Jews only generates in Rakover pride and confidence. As he puts it, "I am proud that I am a Jew not in spite of the world's treatment of us, but precisely because of that treatment. I should be ashamed to belong to the people who spawned and raised the criminals who are responsible for the deeds that have been perpetrated against us." His Jewish pride and his loftiness of spirit remain unbroken despite all the efforts of the enemy to induce in their victims a feeling of worthlessness.

He wins his conflict with the enemy not only through the preservation of self-pride and Jewish pride. He wins also at a practical level. In the end he will, of course, lose his life, as have millions of others. However, he is determined to fight actively and to bring down as many of the enemy as possible up to the very last moment. Rakover carries on this battle with an affirmative spirit and with singleness of purpose. Each German that he destroys is one more occasion for satisfaction, one more assertion of his own worth against the corrupt and cruel murderers of the Jewish people. Yossel relates that over the period of the battle in the Warsaw ghetto he exploded scores of bottles of gasoline over the heads of the enemy attackers. And now he has three bottles left, for which he has made careful plans. One will be emptied on himself to facilitate the burning fire in which he knows he is about to die. In this empty bottle he will place this document, his last testament and his message to those who survive. He hopes that it will be found after the struggle has ended and that it will serve to teach the world about "the emotions of a Jew, one of millions, who died forsaken by the God in whom he believed unshakably." The remaining two bottles of gasoline will be used to attack the enemy as they break into the room where he is hiding. In his last moment he still wants the satisfaction of going down fighting and taking with him to death some of his persecutors.

Rakover is in no way apologetic or defensive about his attacks on the enemy. Quite the contrary! He sees this as part of his sacred duty and he carries it out with deep satisfaction. There is for him no morality of turning the other cheek, of seeking to justify or placate the perpetrator. He recognizes unmitigated evil for just what it is, and he is convinced, as a pious Jew, that to fight against that evil is a most honorable and virtuous act. Moreover, he affirms that such attacks on the enemy are and should be accompanied by delight in his downfall. Western culture has often been embarrassed by the desire for vengeance, but not so Yossel Rakover. In discussing the earlier occasions when he blew up bottles of gasoline over the heads of his oppressors, he says:

> It was one of the finest moments in my life when I did this, and I was shaken with laughter by it. I never dreamed that the death of people—even of such enemies—could cause me such great pleasure. Foolish humanists may say what they choose. Vengeance was and always will be the last means of waging battle and the greatest spiritual release of the oppressed... I know now why my heart is so overjoyed at remembering that for thousands of years we have been calling our Lord a God of vengeance: A God of Vengeance is our Lord... We have had only a few opportunities to witness true vengeance. When we did, however, it was so good, so worthwhile, I felt such profound happiness, so terribly fortunate that it seemed an entire new life was springing up in me.

Here the victory over the oppressor comes to Rakover both by his success in killing some of the enemy and by the vindication he feels in doing so. Here too he, the Gerer Hasid, stands against what he sees as the corruption of modernity. It is a world which preaches love but practices hate; a world which openly deplores vengeance but takes secret satisfaction in the downfall of enemies. Rakover has the strength and honesty to be open about his feelings. He wants his enemies to be destroyed, and he delights in their deaths. In the religious traditions of the Western world it is often held that vengeance belongs to God alone, but Yossel sees himself as doing God's work when he destroys the Nazi persecutors. If God has chosen to be absent, then man must do His work. When man does that work, he is entitled to delight in it and to find satisfaction in his success. Whatever the "foolish humanists" may say about it, for the downtrodden vengeance is "the last means of waging battle." Again, even while death is only minutes away Yossel triumphs over his enemy.

This is Yossel Rakover. A Gerer Hasid who faces God lovingly, faithfully, but fearlessly. A Jew who, even in the most extreme circumstances, continues to use his learning and his intellect to think through and come to terms with the mystery of Jewish suffering. He remains true to the God of Israel, even when He tries to drive him away. He uses his intelligence to formulate his own account of the absent God. He values truth and will not compromise it by cheap or easy justifications of God. His untainted Jewish pride elevates him above the degraded enemy and thereby grants him the one victory which no power can take from him. His courage helps him to battle against the enemy and to exult in his small successes. He has answered the question of how to die as a Jew in a magnificent and moving way. The inner resources of faith and learning are the instruments which fashion his answer. The courage of true faith gives substance to that answer. Yossel Rakover dies as he lived. He is, to the very end, the man whom he describes in the opening sentence of his testament, "a Hasid of the Rabbi of Ger and a descendant of the great, pious, and righteous families of Rakover and Meisel."

Chaim Vilner and Hersh Rasseyner: A Battle of Searching Spirits

Chaim Grade's "My Quarrel with Hersh Rasseyner" is one of the great achievements of postwar Yiddish literature. Such a work could only have been produced by a literary master deeply rooted in the intellectual, artistic, and religious life of East European Jewry before and after the terrible years of destruction. The author could only be a Jew with profound classical talmudic learning, great philosophical and theological sophistication, and an intense personal experience of the allures and dangers of modern European society. Chaim Grade is one of the very few Yiddish writers with this combination of qualifications. This special background is evident in all of his writing, and particularly in "My Quarrel with Hersh Rasseyner." As we suggested earlier, this story, with all of its autobiographical elements, must be seen as a work of literature which, like all true literature, opens us up to a deeper and more sensitive grasp of reality than that which is possible in straightforward historical prose. Grade reflects on the spiritual struggles of Jews who, having survived the Holocaust, are challenged to work out an answer to the question how one should live as a Jew after the unspeakable suffering of the years of the destruction.

He and his antagonist, Hersh Rasseyner, share a common heritage. They both come from backgrounds of traditional Jewish piety and learning. They were both deeply affected by the life and teaching of the musar yeshivot in which they were educated. Those yeshivot were concerned primarily with building virtuous character. Greater emphasis was placed on virtue than on intellectual achievement. True, learning was not neglected, but it came second to constant self-examination, to discovering and exposing one's own moral flaws. This process of self-discovery and self-transformation tended to become a permanent and inescapable feature of the character of those who had been exposed to it. It was rooted in an attitude of contempt for the secular world, a conviction that what matters most is for man to turn inward so that he may perfect himself. Rasseyner never left the world of the musarists, and he emerged after the war more strongly rooted in it than ever. His years in concentration camps had the effect of deepening his piety and intensifying his contempt for the larger society, including the non-musarist Jewish world.

Chaim,[3] on the other hand, left the musar yeshiva in stages. First he became the private pupil and the personal companion of the great Hazon Ish. From him he learned both a more sophisticated method of talmudic study and a more balanced approach to the demands of musar. His seven years of continuous association with this unique teacher left permanent marks on his soul. One need only read the various elegies that he wrote after the death of the Hazon Ish to see the event to which even the "emancipated and secularized" Chaim Grade carried in the depths of his being the image and the teachings of his great master. He mourns his teacher without stop and confronts with great pain his personal failure to live up to the hopes and expectations of the saintly sage. In a moment of anguished confession, as he mourns his departed teacher, he says, "I know that I caused pain to my teacher, because I did not want to remain in the house of God." He concludes this elegy giving expression to the permanence of the influence of the Hazon Ish on his life and thought: "I shine in the reflection of his great love, although he did not want to give his blessing to my way of life."[4] Grade abandoned the house of study to become a Yiddish writer, a member of a literary society characterized largely by its secular humanism. Despite the pathos of his unbroken and unbreakable attachment to the Hazon Ish, he chose to follow an alien path. The Chaim whom we meet in the confrontation with Hersh Rasseyner is a product of more diverse and more complex forces than those which affected his old friend. He too wants to be able to live affirmatively as a Jew even after the horror of the Holocaust, but for him the path is not nearly so straight or so easily formed. The effect of the Hazon Ish on him is permanent. No less permanent is the effect of the years in the musar yeshivot. As Rasseyner says to him in their first meeting, "You surely know what we [musarniks] are accustomed to say: One who has studied musar will never again be capable of enjoying his life."[5] As we study their conflict and confrontation, we will see the effects of the richly textured worlds from which Chaim has emerged, and the tensions which are generated between him and Hersh Rasseyner.

The ambivalences with which Grade lived his later life are evident, as we have already seen, in his elegy on the Hazon Ish. We should note that to the very end of his life he was conscious of these ambivalences and the tensions they generated. In an interview late in his life he was asked about this point and replied openly and candidly.

> I know that despite the fact that for two-thirds of my life I have been away from the *bes-midrash* [talmudic study house], and despite the fact that, except for Australia, there is no corner of the earth where I have not been, I am still in the *bes-medrash* and in my hometown, Vilna. Whenever I go out, I go out for only a short time, and I am very angry that I am driven to return at once. I would like to leave Vilna and leave the *bes-medrash,* because I know the world as well as others, perhaps even better. But psychologically, spiritually, whenever I go out, I go a short distance, but invariably I return.[6]

This unbreakable tie to a past with which he seems to have broken is evident throughout Chaim's confrontation with Hersh Rasseyner.

There are two preliminary meetings before the long debate which is the main focus of the story. The first takes place in 1937 when the world of East European Jewry, although threatened, is still intact. Chaim Vilner (like Grade), the published poet, visits Bialystok, where he had earlier been a student in the local musar yeshiva. He returns now as a member of a very different society, a celebrated writer who will lecture and read from his works to an audience far removed from the world of the yeshiva. He meets some of his former fellow students, but feels alienated from them. The center of this first episode, however, is his meeting with Hersh Rasseyner. Here the conflict which will be repeated in other forms is first impressed on the consciousness of the reader.

Chaim meets Rasseyner on the street by chance, although he has been looking for him since arriving in Bialystok. The fact that we are told of his search for Rasseyner makes us aware of the event to which the connection to the musar world still lives somewhere in the recesses of Chaim's soul. The meeting becomes a bitter exchange. Hersh attacks Chaim for having gone over to the secular humanists, and Chaim counterattacks, taunting Hersh with the charge that he is afraid to look at the world because he might find it irresistible. Hersh accuses Chaim of having left musar society because he is seeking this-worldly pleasures. Chaim replies that he is only seeking truth. Grade's first book of poems was entitled *Yo,* i.e., "Yes." Rasseyner sneers at him, saying that he has heard that Chaim has written a *bichl* (a term that contemptuously dismisses the book as a trivial work of no importance) entitled "'Yes." "But," he retorts with fiery anger, "I say to you, no!"

Chaim's response gives expression to the abyss which divides him from his former colleague. It also shows us the ambivalence with which he is struggling even at this early stage of his career. He lashes out at Hersh Rasseyner in self-defense.

> And who told you that I left in order to seek worldly pleasures? I left to search for a truth which you don't have. In fact, I never really went away at all, I just returned to my street—to the street of the butcher shops in Vilna... I have written a book entitled "Yes" and you keep shouting in my face, "No"! You can't understand that I myself say to the world order as it is—No! Yet, at the same time, I force myself also to say—Yes! Because I believe in my street.

Hersh Rasseyner is capable of an absolute and unambiguous yes or no because he has chosen to live in a circumscribed world which leaves him untroubled by doubts or dilemmas. At least so it seems. Chaim, in contrast, has to struggle with the inescapable tensions between the Jewish world that he has chosen to leave and the literary secular-humanist world in which he is trying to find his place. His is a troubled soul, agitated and constantly searching. Rasseyner is only in conflict with the world. Chaim is in constant conflict with himself. In his search for truth he can no longer accept the easy certainties of the musarniks. He is condemned to work on himself as the musarniks do, but in a setting in which intensely opposed forces pull at him. If these problems were so demanding in a European Jewish society which was relatively stable, how much more urgent must they have become in the postwar world in which the pathetic broken remnants of European Jewry were trying to rebuild their lives.

The friends have a second chance meeting in 1939 after the war has already begun. Here too the conflict is joined, however briefly. The major confrontation takes place in 1948, when Hersh and Chaim meet by chance on the Paris Metro. Neither knew that the other had survived, and they are deeply moved to discover that they are both still alive. What follows is a long conversation that begins on the Metro and is continued throughout the day in a famous Paris square. As warm and emotional as is the first moment of meeting, it almost immediately turns into an intense and soul-searching debate. After an exchange of information about where they spent the war years, Hersh turns to Chaim with a soft-spoken but very sharp challenge. It is time, he says to him, for you to start thinking about repentance. Looking with contemptuous amusement at the young couples on the train who are hugging and kissing, he asks Chaim whether he still belongs with them. "Do you still believe in the cruel world?" To which Chaim replies in bitter anger, "And you, Reb Hersh, do you still believe that God's providential care is extended to every individual?... Miraculously, Reb Hersh, you were saved, but where is our entire people? And you believe?"

Hersh spent years in a concentration camp, where, we are told, he showed extraordinary heroism and total unconcern for his own safety. He is now the head of a yeshiva in Germany where he teaches youngsters who survived the concentration camps. Like Yossel Rakover his faith has remained firm, even much strengthened. Unlike Rakover, there is in him no spirit of defiance against God, no challenge to Him for being absent when He was most needed. Hersh affirms his unwavering conviction that God's providence is always and everywhere with us. For him life would be impossible without this certainty. The years of suffering and sorrow commit him even more firmly than ever to trust in God and to a life in His service. "How could I bear to live without Him in this murderous world?" he asks. The lines of battle are drawn in these first minutes. For Rasseyner, although the world has changed, he himself refuses to change. He clings with ever greater intensity to the convictions and practices which give his life meaning and hope. Chaim, meanwhile, is still beset by the old conflicts, now intensified by the experience of the loss of family and friends in the years of the Holocaust.

The two old friends leave the Metro at the rue de Rivoli in the Jewish quarter and carry on their conversation near the old Parisian city hall, the Hôtel de Ville. This very setting provides the occasion for the clash of their different worlds. The building is decorated with rows of statues commemorating some of the greatest figures of French culture and history. Hersh looks up at the statues which Chaim is admiring and asks sneeringly who these idols are. He sees no great human achievement here, just stone figures which he classifies with open contempt as *avoide zores,* forbidden idols. Chaim explains who they are and pleads with Hersh to pay attention to the magnificence of the sculpture.

In this phase of the conversation the battle lines are clearly drawn. Although the subject seems peripheral to the main issues which concern them, the debate is symptomatic of their conflicting attitudes and ideologies.

Their opposed responses to the statues are a small-scale version of their overall responses to their experiences of the years of the Holocaust. While Rasseyner only sees in the statues graphic evidence of the misplaced values of Western society, Grade sees in them permanent testimony to the greatness of the human spirit which expresses itself in art. He tries without success to open his friend's eyes to the goodness which is reflected in the faces of these great cultural heroes of France, to the special light which shines from their eyes. "You call it idolatry, but I say to you literally, without rhetorical flourishes, that I am moved to tears when I see these sculptures in the parks and squares and galleries of Paris. It is nothing short of a miracle. How could a human being breathe the breath of life into stone?" In an outburst of extraordinary love for the literary artist, Chaim goes on to affirm the unique value of great literature. It deepens and broadens our perceptions and awakens our compassion for man in all his weakness. The writer, says Chaim, helps us to understand the struggle of man to overcome his inner drives. He teaches us to judge "even the most wicked of men, not according to his bare deeds, but rather in accordance with the pain that he suffers in the war he wages with himself and with the whole world because of his passions. You do not justify the wicked man, but you now understand [with sympathy] that he cannot act differently."

Here we see Grade, the writer, speaking in praise of the special worth of art and the artist. The statues give him the opportunity to explain and defend his world, the world that he has chosen over the musar yeshiva, over the tuition of the Hazon Ish, over the *bes-medrash* which formed his own character as well as the character of so many earlier Jewish generations. Rasseyner sees in this choice the corruption of Chaim's soul, a corruption all the more painful because it continues to live in him even after the Holocaust. He finds deeply repulsive the idea that any Jew could still put his trust in the literary and artistic culture of the West. "Shame on you, Chaim, for babbling such idiocy." Our whole Jewish world lies in ruins and you are moved to tears by the so-called beauty of the statues. You say that you learn from the great writer to be sympathetic to the evildoer because he cannot overcome his passions. What kind of art is it that makes you sympathetic to the perpetrator rather than to his victim? "If you choose to make excuses for the absolutely wicked wrongdoer, then to me all your scribbling is a disgusting abomination. Condemn the evildoer! Condemn the glutton and drunkard! You say he simply can't do otherwise? He must do otherwise! What a fine hymn of praise you have sung to these decadent idols, Chaim Vilner."

Here Western culture itself is put on trial and the issues are sharply drawn. Is there place left for religious faith after the Holocaust? Can a Jew of our generation find hope outside the realm of God's Torah? Is it possible in our age to be a devoted Jew and, at the same time, a devotee of Western art and literature? Is there any ground for morality outside the teachings of the Torah? These are the issues, explicit and implicit, that generate the great debate between Hersh Rasseyner and Chaim Vilner.

Chaim's counterattack is weak and short-lived. He accuses Hersh of turning away from the world because he fears that he cannot resist its temptations. Hersh readily admits to the charge that when he was in the yeshiva he did everything to hide himself from what he perceived as the dangers of the world. He also recognizes that by itself this would not have been enough to build the virtuous character that he sought. Chaim counters that it was childish unreality to think that the methods of the musarists would be effective against human drives, lusts, passions, and desires. As he notes, even the terrible experience of the concentration camps did not transform human character. How much less could this have been achieved by the musar methods of self-examination and self-confrontation. Here Chaim reaffirms his confidence that only the light of art and science has the power to elevate and ennoble the human spirit.

To all of this Hersh Rasseyner responds in a tone more of sorrow than anger. The very idea that any Jew could still put faith in the power of Western culture to transform and purify human character strikes him as painfully blind to reality. True, he says, I made great efforts during my younger years to hide myself from the world so as not to be corrupted by it, but the Germans forced me to face reality with a new perspective and a deeper insight. In a declaration reminiscent of Yossel Rakover, Hersh tells Chaim:

> Yes, it is true! All of my youthful years I used to walk with my eyes cast down to the earth so as not to see the world. Along came the German and grabbed hold of me by my Jewish beard, yanked my head up, and ordered me to look him straight in the eye. I was forced to look into his wicked eyes and the eyes of the whole world. And I saw, Chaim, I saw—you know yourself what I saw: everything that we lived through. Now I can look at all the *avoide-zores* [idols], I can read all their writings which are abominations, and contemplate all the pleasures of this-worldly life, and none of it will ever tempt me again, because I have come to know the true face of the world. And you still say that I don't know the world and that I have unjustly slandered it. Oy, Reb Chaim, repent! It still is not too late.

Chaim is sobered some by this declaration, but is far from ready to yield. Instead he poses what he considers a key question. Since we admit that all men have free will, why is it that, according to Hersh, the philosophers and artists of the world were not able to become morally good? Indeed, why couldn't all the world make itself good? Here Hersh responds with an insight which was earlier expressed explicitly and eloquently by David Hume, a philosopher whose work could hardly have been known to the musarnik. "Reason," says Hume, "is, and ought to be the slave of the passions, and can never pretend to any other office than to serve and obey them."[7] Hersh makes Hume's point in his own way. He denies that good will alone can ever be sufficient for the acquisition of true virtue, nor can the intellect by itself form man's character. Reason gives us, at best, prudential grounds for seeking to be virtuous, but these grounds are always shifting. Today's prudence may seem like needless self-denial tomorrow. The only sound foundation on which to build a truly good life is God's commandments as taught to us in the Torah. This alone can be a stable ongoing force for human self-improvement and self-elevation.

> The person who lives with reason alone often inches his way, by his own devices, directly into temptation. He wants to become even more clever. He crawls directly into the fire and is burned up. Aside from the fact that reason cannot help him, it seems to me that it is wildly unreasonable to demand of a person that he should live according to his reason. Reason may tell him that it pays to be good... But if he must be good only because it pays for him, then today it may pay and tomorrow not... If a man has no God, then for what possible reason should he obey the philosopher who tells him to be good?... There is only one way out: a person should choose between good and evil only as the Torah chooses for him. The Torah is concerned only with human felicity and knows better what is truly good for man. The Torah is life's only true reality... Even when a man believes that he understands also with his reason how he should behave, he must not at that very moment forget that essentially he behaves so because the Torah commands him.

Rasseyner adds that even the Torah is insufficient if one supposes that he can casually choose to behave according to its precepts. It requires constant working on oneself, constant self-examination, an ongoing effort to form and habituate the will so as to produce a character which embodies and gives continuous expression to the values and the style of life which the Torah demands of us. Chaim's great mistake is to imagine that culture and enlightenment are substitutes for the Torah. Western culture, in reaching its lowest level of degradation during the Holocaust, has shown us the bankruptcy of its supposed attachment to the life of reason. If anyone was unclear about this before the great catastrophe, there is no longer any excuse to continue in this irredeemable error.

For Hersh, as for Yossel Rakover, the opposition between the moral foundations of Judaism and Western culture comes to its sharpest, most unambiguous expression in the Holocaust experience. There one experienced in a way that was almost palpable the meaning of Jewish chosenness over against the moral decay of the West. Secularist Jews are uncomfortable with the idea that God has chosen the Jewish people to be His representative in the world. Yet, Hersh taunts Chaim, you cannot escape your status and your destiny. However much you may want to cast it off, you cannot remove from your very being your Jewishness in all its force and meaning. Deny your chosenness as much as you like, "you must be chosen, because this is what God wants—notwithstanding you."

In what is perhaps the most moving scene in the entire story, Reb Hersh draws the contrast between himself, the faithful Jew, and his German oppressor. He pictures himself lying on the ground while the German kicks him with his hobnailed boots.

> If at that moment an angel of God would have bent over to me and said into my ear: "Hersh, in an instant I can turn you into the German. I will clothe you in his garments, and give you his murderous face. And he will become—you. Just say the word and the miracle will take place. He will lie in the mud and you will kick him in your—in his bloody face." If the angel asked this of me—do you hear, Chaim? —I would under no circumstance agree. Not even for a one minute would I agree to become him, the German, my torturer. I want the justice of law! I want to take revenge on the criminal! But I want it as a Jew. With God's gracious help I could somehow endure the German's boot on my throat. If, however, I had to pull over my face his mask, his murderous visage, I would have immediately suffocated as from gas. And when the German shouted at me, "You are a slave of slaves!", through my paralyzed lips I said to myself: "You have chosen me."

We need to take careful note of what is being expressed in this moving affirmation. Hersh Rasseyner, the archetypical Jew, will never agree to change places with his oppressor, even in the most extreme circumstances. He seeks justice, even revenge, but only as a Jew. To change places with such a representative of Western culture would be the ultimate act of self-destruction. The depth and grandeur of his Jewish commitment is clearest in the last lines. While the German abuses him as a slave of slaves, the lowest of the low, Hersh mutters to himself, "You have chosen me." Note that he speaks to himself, not to the German. What the German thinks is totally irrelevant to him. He has no need to impress his persecutor. It would, in any case, be a pointless exercise. He needs only to remind himself who he is, and he does so by affirming that he is one of God's chosen.

Grade makes the point with remarkable sensitivity and elegance when he has Hersh say *baharta bi,* "You have chosen me." The usual formula is "You have chosen us," an expression of a collective special relationship between the Jewish people and God. But Hersh goes further in affirming that this relationship is a reality for every individual Jew qua individual, not just as a member of a nation. You have chosen me. In my hour of agony, I, Hersh Rasseyner, survive and gain strength from my complete faith that I have been chosen by God to serve Him in a special way That confidence makes it possible for me to endure every torment, because I know who my tormentor is and who I am.

There is here a remarkable similarity to Yossel Rakover, who also wants justice and revenge, but rejects any suggestion that he would be willing to change places with the enemy. We cited earlier his statement, "I am proud that I am a Jew not in spite of the world's treatment of us, but precisely because of this treatment. I should be ashamed to belong to the people who spawned and raised the criminals who are responsible for the deeds that have been perpetrated against us." For those who live within the community of Jewish faith, it is crystal-clear that the worst possible consequence of the Holocaust would be to become like the oppressor, or to become the oppressor.

Hersh has thus challenged Chaim with his own rejection of the world. We must no longer allow ourselves to live in this corrupt world and to be contaminated by it, he argues. We must never forgive and never forget the crimes that were committed and the wickedness which we saw and suffered. To forgive the murderers is to commit the murders all over again. To the question what has changed for him as a result of the Holocaust, Hersh replies that he has become an even greater believer, he feels even more deeply than before trust in the God of Israel, and lives with the conviction that ultimately justice will be done. Without that faith he could not live at all, since it is within the wall of that faith that he has been able to build for himself his separate world. This is what separates and protects him from the moral bankruptcy of Western society. What he wants to know from Chaim is what has changed for him. How can he, after all that they have experienced, still choose to live in this world.

> But you, Chaim, how can you eat and sleep and laugh and dress so elegantly? Don't you first have to come to terms with yourself? How can you push yourself into the world when you know that it lives in companionship with the murderers of your family? You used to think that the world was getting better! But your world has collapsed! Have you learned from this, or not?... Where are you? Have you gone forward or backward? What has changed for you? What is your answer?

This is the critical question. Can a Jew, after the Holocaust, still affirm the value and validity of Western culture? Is the way of Hersh Rasseyner the only answer?

In Chaim's response, with all its ambivalences, we see clearly the chasm that separates him from Hersh Rasseyner. His faith in the redeeming power of artistic creativity is as unshaken as Hersh's faith in God. He affirms his Jewishness, but not at the expense of his participation in Western culture. He perceives Hersh's way as the easy way. It disengages itself from all the problems and all the ambiguities of living as a Jew in the contemporary world. For Rasseyner the choice is either/or; he admits no middle ground. But this is only achieved by closing one's eyes to reality. Chaim sees the solution as inclusive rather than exclusive. He wants to bring together in a single cultural framework Jewishness and secularism, *Yidishkeyt and Veltishkeyt.* What he seeks is "to find that essence of *Yidishkeyt and Veltishkeyt* which can live together!"

That essence consists, on both sides, of a genuine concern and respect for the individual, an effort to free the individual to be who and what he truly is. Chaim accuses Hersh of relating to his fellow Jews not as individuals to be prized and loved, but rather as types to be accepted or rejected. He claims that Hersh has no appreciation of the virtues and the moral achievements of non-religious Jews. He does not see their self-sacrifice, their heroism, their martyrdom. Hersh prejudges them all because of their secularism and rejects them as unworthy to bear the name Jew. In his bitterness Chaim goes on to charge that Hersh and his like are responsible for driving these Jews away from the Torah. They closed all the doors to those who were unable or unwilling to meet their own exacting standards. They substituted hate for love and left no place for secular Jews in their framework of true Jewish society. Hersh and those like him are totally blind to the wonderful character of these Jews. They suffer from the blindness of their own ugly prejudice. In fact, they really would prefer to deny that they are Jews at all.

> According to your view, it would appear that the German made an error in taking us [secularists] for Jews. But the truly ugly error is the one that you make. "The anti-Semites know very well that we are all the same, and they say so openly. And not only for the anti-Semites are we all the same, but also for the *Ribbono shel Olam* [God]... In the next world your soul will not be covered with a *yarmulke*; you won't be wearing a beard and *peyos*. Your soul will come there completely naked—just like mine.

Clearly it is this conception of the ideology and orientation of the religious community that has driven Chaim away, and it is a conception that continues to live in him and to embitter him. One cannot help but notice the passion with which he has turned on Hersh. In a sense all the ghosts of his youth seem to have been revived.

He sharpens the charges even more when he adds that if Hersh has no capacity to appreciate and to love Jews who are different from him, he is surely incapable of loving and appreciating gentiles, even the most truly virtuous among them. Hersh can only relate to the non-Jewish world by turning away from it with disgust and contempt. But in doing so he is closing his eyes to those saintly gentiles who risked their lives in order to save Jews. In his world there can be no place for such people, no way to account for them, integrate them, or relate to them, much less admire and reward them. Chaim relates briefly the story of two such elderly gentiles who with complete purity of heart, and for no possible gain, exposed themselves to life-threatening dangers in order to save Jews. Says he to Hersh, "I ask you: where in your world is there a corner for this gray-headed couple? You drive them out into the dark night... The old man and the old woman thought that all of us belong now to one better world, but you spit on that world."

After all these *ad hominem* attacks, Chaim now introduces a serious religious problem. How, after the terrible destruction in which millions of innocent people were tortured and murdered, is it still possible to have faith in God? Chaim considers it an inexcusable deficiency in Hersh that he does not even feel driven to raise the question. The ancients were already concerned about the problem of why the wicked prosper and the righteous suffer. That problem is multiplied a million times over by the million children who were murdered. To say that your faith is even stronger than before while you do not even raise the question of God's justice is monstrous. Although you know in advance that you will receive no answers from heaven, that in no way justifies your not asking. Job and the prophets were no less pious than Hersh Rasseyner, yet they asked the question in sharp and uncompromising ways. A faith which is strengthened by the Holocaust without even confronting the moral and religious problems that the catastrophe poses is a faith to which Chaim is unable to return. He wants to live as a Jew, but his model cannot be that of Hersh Rasseyner.

What is it then that Chaim wants to realize? How does he hope to resolve the conflict? His initial effort is in the final statement of his position as a secular Jew who cherishes both worlds. In baring his soul in these last moments of the conversation, Chaim tries to explain clearly what has changed for him. It is striking that nothing seems to have changed in his dedication to the secular world of art and literature. The only change in his relation to the non-Jewish world is that he will not forgive the monstrous evil which was done. At the same time, he will not permit even that evil to cause him to reject the world. He still sees high value in Western culture, and still hopes for a better world in which we can all live.

What has changed strikingly, by his own admission, is his feeling toward the Jewish religious world which he had abandoned. Despite his harsh language toward his old colleague, Hersh Rasseyner, he now turns to him with a declaration of his love. Chaim assures Hersh that he has never hated him, but does admit that there were tensions and resentments.

> When you became angry with me before I went away from the yeshiva, I also became angry with you. But now I push myself to you with my love... This is what has changed with me and, in general, with all the Yiddish writers. Our love for Jews has become more tender and deeper. That is to say, I do not renounce the world, but—in fact, I should say—we want to dig up within ourselves the inherited hidden potentialities of the Jewish people, so that we can continue to live. I beg of you: do not deny us our heritage.

Even while affirming this great change which has resulted from the Holocaust experience, this newfound love for his old yeshiva associates, Chaim reaffirms his commitment to the value of the Western world and its culture. No matter how much evil he has seen, he is not prepared to write off or to reject that world to which he is still deeply committed.

Is there then any resolution of the conflicts? Has the long debate led Chaim to any clearer program for how to live as a Jew in the post-Holocaust world? Apparently not. Yossel Rakover, rooted in the tradition, knew how to die as a Jew. Hersh Rasseyner, intensifying his unequivocal commitment of faith, was confident that he now knew even better how to live as a Jew. But Chaim Vilner, who is, of course, Chaim Grade, embraces all the ambivalences of a Jew who loves his people and its traditions, but loves no less the world of art, literature, and culture, which he sees as the core of Western society at its best. As he himself told us, he has never really left the *bes-medrash,* even when he has tried. He goes out into the world, but he is always pulled back. His struggle is to keep both worlds in balance, to remain faithful to apparently conflicting moral, intellectual, and cultural demands. In his final words to Hersh, Chaim reaffirms his love for the Jewish people.

> Don't think, Reb Hersh, that it is easy for us Yiddish writers. It is hard, very hard. The catastrophe befell us all equally. But you have a ready answer for everything, and we have not yet been able to resolve our doubts. Who knows if we ever will. But we serve the Jewish people, even when they turn their back on us. I want you to know that the only happiness which is left to us in our lives is our creative work, and in all the pain of creation we draw closer to our people.

We see here Chaim's unambiguous love for the Jewish people together with all the unresolved ambivalence of what that means for the formation of a life style and a value system. This is reflected in Chaim's final words to Hersh. "I pray that we will both have the good fortune to meet again and see then where we stand [on all these questions]. I pray that I shall be no less committed then to *Yidishkeyt* as I am today. Reb Hersh let us embrace and kiss."

This is the answer to Chaim's dilemma. How shall we live as Jews after the great destruction? Not by a theoretical resolution of theological and moral questions, but simply by one Jew kissing his fellow Jew. For Grade, we can live as Jews in this post-Holocaust world only by embracing and loving our fellow Jews, whoever they may be. Those who reject the culture of the West and those who affirm it, all merit our love and our regard. To the very end, Chaim is determined to live as a Jew by making his world as broad and inclusive as possible, rather than narrow and exclusive. His victory over the Holocaust is just this stance. He will never permit Hitler to drive him away from his fellow Jews, nor will he permit him to drive him out of the world. Whatever the tensions, *Yidishkeyt and Veltishkeyt* must be able to live together. Hersh Rasseyner does not respond to the invitation to embrace and kiss. We are left only to conjecture what his attitude is to this passionate invitation to openly love all fellow-Jews, whatever their relationship to traditional Jewish faith and whatever style of life they may have chosen.

NOTES

[1] Grade's work was first published in Yiddish under the tide "Mein Krieg mit Hersh Rasseyner," in *Yidisher Kemfer*, 32, no. 923 (September 28, 195 1). An abridged English translation by Milton Himmelfarb appeared in E. Greenberg and I. Howe, eds., *A Treasury of Yiddish Stories* (New York 1958). Kolitz's work was first published in Yiddish in 1946 and was translated into English in his *The Tiger Beneath the Skin* (New York, 1947). For the full details of its strange publication history, see the contributions by P. Badde and F. J. van Beeck in this volume.

[2] For a study of the Kotzker commitment to truth as a supreme value, see Abraham Joshua Heschel, *A Passion for Torah* (Philadelphia: Jewish Publication Society, 1973), and his two-volume Yiddish work, *Kotzk: in Gerangl far Emesdikeyt* (Tel Aviv, 1973).

[3] I leave deliberately unresolved the ambiguity of the name "Chaim" as referring both to Chaim Grade, the author, and Chaim Vilner, the character in the story. The overlap between the lives of the author and the fictional character is so great that one can hardly distinguish them. The ambiguity is made stronger when, as we shall soon see, Hersh Rasseyner identifies the Chaim of his conversations as the author of a book of poems carrying the actual title of Grade's first published volume.

[4] Chaim Grade, 'Elegie oyfn Hazon-Ish," *Die Goldene Keyt* 18 (1954): 5-7.

[5] The English translations from "Mein Krieg mit Hersh Rasseyner" are largely my own. I have made free use of the translation of Milton Himmelfarb and have also had the benefit of an unpublished translation of the entire work by Professor Herbert H. Paper of Hebrew Union College—Jewish Institute of religion. I am grateful to Professor Paper for making this excellent translation available to me, end am equally grateful to Milton Himmelfarb for his pioneering effort Where I have not followed them entirely, it is because I wanted to emphasize certain details of the text with even greater precision than they brought to it.

[6] Interview with Rabbi William Berkowitz, *Algemeiner Journal,* September 28, 1990. Although published on this date, the interview took place years earlier, since Grade died in 1983.

[7] David Hume, *A Treasure of Human Nature,* ed. L. A. Selby-Bigge (Oxford, 1888), Book II, "Of the Passions," part III, sec. III, p. 415.